KING ALFRED'S COLLEGE
WINCHESTER

To be returned on or before the day marked
below :—

PLEASE ENTER ON ISSUE SLIP:

AUTHOR SAMPSON

TITLE The form of language

ACCESSION No. 52613

The Form of Language

The Form of Language

Geoffrey Sampson

Weidenfeld and Nicolson
London

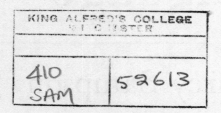
Weidenfeld and Nicolson
11 St John's Hill London SW11

ISBN 0 297 76890 5 cased
ISBN 0 297 76900 6 paperback

Printed in Great Britain by
Willmer Brothers Limited, Birkenhead

For Winifred and George
who programmed me

Contents

Acknowledgements

My first debt of gratitude must surely be to Noam Chomsky, for creating the subject on which I have written (as well as for being kind enough to discuss a number of points I raised with him in correspondence). His are giant's shoulders indeed for the linguist to stand on; if I have in a number of cases disagreed with his opinions, I know he will be the last to resent this (though I hope he will be the first to refute me).

Next, I would like to thank those from whom I have learned; in particular, John Lyons and L. Jonathan Cohen, under whose guidance I was introduced to linguistics and to philosophy, respectively. Among a wealth of other names I would mention Alvin Liberman, whose teaching has influenced a number of points in this book.

I am further indebted to John Lyons and Jonathan Cohen, and to Dick Hudson and Neil Smith, for the comments, in some cases extremely detailed, which they have made on my manuscript. Others who have made useful suggestions on portions of the book include Jean Aitchison, F. W. Householder, and Geoffrey Pullum. I have not always been wise enough to accept their advice, and the scholars mentioned are in no sense responsible for the shortcomings of the finished work.

My debt to my students is considerable. They have demonstrated to one who was initially sceptical the truth of the notion that one learns by teaching. I thank Susan Chuang for the calligraphy which appears opposite.

Finally, my greatest debt in connection with this book is undoubtedly to Margaret Gilbert. But for her, not only would the book lack many of such virtues as it may possess; for various reasons, it would not exist.

Strand on the Green, Chiswick, Middlesex
April 1974

Ich möchte sagen: du siehst es für viel zu selbstverständlich an,
daß man Einem etwas mitteilen kann.

Wittgenstein

述而不作　信而好古

Confucius

I

Introduction

Linguistics is a subject which has changed in the last decade from a specialized and little-known occupation, pursued by a small coterie of scholars, into one of the more rapidly growing and (for better or worse) highly fashionable denizens of the academic scene. Modern linguistics claims to shed important new light on matters traditionally regarded as falling under the purview of psychology, philosophy, and related disciplines; and some, though by no means all, of these claims are justified. Since the novel findings of linguistics concern the nature of Man as a rational being, these findings should be of interest not only to the academic psychologist or philosopher but to all thinking men.

At the same time, contemporary linguistics is a highly technical field. Although linguistics like other subjects has its mediocre practitioners who use barrages of mathematical symbols as shelters to conceal the shallowness of their thinking, much of the formalism of linguistics is genuinely integral to the subject, and can be dispensed with only at risk of trivializing the ideas being expounded. As a result, modern developments in linguistics have often been inaccessible even to those professional academics in neighbouring disciplines to whom linguistics might seem most relevant, let alone to the general reader.

The present book is written in the belief that the path between obscurity on the one hand, and trivialization on the other, though narrow, does exist. The essentials of modern linguistics, including everything in the subject having important implications outside linguistics, can be stated in terms which do not presuppose any prior acquaintance with the subject on the reader's part. Indeed, if this were not possible, it would suggest some conceptual confusion within linguistics itself. It is easy to be seduced into unquestioning acceptance of in-group jargon, and excellent discipline to force oneself to do without it.

I believe it is correct to say that linguistics gives us insight into human nature. In the following pages I hope to provide the reader lacking experience of linguistics with all the evidence he needs to evaluate this claim for himself.

Let us begin with basics. Linguistics is briefly defined as 'the scientific study of language'. It is usual to divide the field of linguistics into two parts, called *diachronic* (or 'historical') and *synchronic* linguistics respectively. Diachronic linguistics examines the development of languages or families of languages through time; synchronic linguistics investigates languages as systems of communication used by groups of people at some particular point of time, for instance the present.

Of the two, diachronic linguistics was the first to emerge in the modern world. At the end of the eighteenth century, it was discovered that a classical language of India, Sanskrit, showed affinities with Greek, Latin and other European languages which could not be explained on the basis of cultural contact; there must have been some previously unguessed-at 'Proto-Indo-European' language from which both Sanskrit and the European languages descended. The discovery of Sanskrit sparked off a programme of research into the history and interrelationships of the Indo-European family of languages; centred on Germany, this research programme dominated linguistic scholarship throughout the nineteenth century.

(A main reason for qualifying the statement that diachronic linguistics came first with the phrase 'in the modern world' is that, ironically, the body of Sanskrit writings which provided the impetus for diachronic linguistics in Europe contained, among other things, a large quantity of *synchronic* linguistics of a very high order. It is only in recent years, as we have rediscovered the problems that they dealt with two millennia and more ago, that we have begun to appreciate the genius of the Indian grammarians.)

There were many reasons for the nineteenth-century enthusiasm for historical linguistics. One was the rise of the Romantic movement, with its interest in racial and cultural origins. Another influence, later in the century, was Darwin's shocking (in its day) but ultimately successful evolutionary explanation of biological species; scholars are always attracted by successful paradigms of intellectual inquiry, so it became very natural to think of languages as organisms quite parallel to plants and animals, and to feel that the appropriate account of language was an evolutionary account.

Although diachronic linguistics came first chronologically, synchronic linguistics has a certain logical priority: how can one discuss the changes of a system over time, if one has no techniques for describing the system as it is at any given time? Accordingly, at about the turn of the century synchronic linguistics began to develop as a subject in its own right; by now, synchronic linguistics is felt to be the core of linguistic science, and historical linguistics to be one particular specialization among many.

Synchronic linguistics started more or less independently in Europe and in the USA. The man who coined the terms 'synchronic' and 'diachronic' was the Swiss, Ferdinand de Saussure. De Saussure was eminent in the field of Indo-European historical linguistics; towards the end of his life he pointed out (in lectures in the year 1911) the possibility and desirability of synchronic analysis, and discussed a number of the concepts which were to play a central role in the new subject. The first synchronic linguist* in America was Franz Boas, an immigrant from Germany. Boas, too, had been trained in Indo-European historical linguistics, but he turned to anthropology, being interested in the relationships (or lack of them) between race, language and culture. Boas was commissioned by the Smithsonian Institution to organize a survey (published, coincidentally, also in 1911) of the American Indian languages; this work provided the initial impetus for synchronic linguistics in America.

While de Saussure drew conceptual distinctions and illustrated them from the familiar European languages, Boas spent most of his time grappling with the very concrete problems of describing languages lacking a philological tradition, and which

---

* For want of a better word, those who study linguistics call themselves 'linguists'; in this book the word will be used exclusively in this sense, rather than in its more everyday sense as 'one who speaks several languages'.

3

are as different from English, and from each other, as it is possible for human languages to be. After Boas, the leading figure in American linguistics was Leonard Bloomfield, who worked both on the Algonquian languages of North America and on languages of the Philippines. Bloomfield's book *Language*, published in 1933, was regarded until recently as the classical account of the nature of linguistic science. From Boas and Bloomfield onwards, a pattern was set whereby the great majority of practical linguistic research took place in America. Subsequently the balance has evened itself to a limited extent, but the pattern still largely holds true today.

Although synchronic linguistics is about as old as our century, the present work will be concerned almost exclusively with the kind of linguistics invented by Noam Chomsky of the Massachusetts Institute of Technology, whose first book, *Syntactic Structures*, appeared in 1957.

The main reason for this is not that Chomsky's views are right and those of his predecessors wrong. True, there are a few instances of this kind (and also some examples of the converse). But there are really very few points on which Chomskyan and pre-Chomskyan linguistics directly contradict each other. Much more important is a difference in goals.

Any version of linguistics deals with two sorts of object of study. On the one hand, linguists treat individual *languages*: English, French, Chinese, and so on. On the other hand, they consider the general phenomenon of human *language*, of which particular languages are examples. Although all linguists discuss both language in general and one or more particular languages, linguists differ in which of these activities they regard as end and which as means. One may see the job of general linguistics as that of providing analytical tools to help him describe some particular language or group of languages in which he is interested; another may have no interest in the structure of any individual language except in so far as it provides evidence for or against theories about the nature of human language as a general phenomenon. Let us call these attitudes to linguistic study the *particularist* and the *generalist* approaches respectively. The particularist will tend to think of linguistics either as one of the humanities ('philology', as it used to be called in Britain), alongside history and literary studies, or as a branch of anthro-

4

pology. (Whether the particularist thinks of linguistics as philology or as a kind of anthropology may depend on whether the language which interests him is that of a civilized or of a primitive society.) The generalist, on the other hand, will be inclined to see linguistics as more closely related to psychology and philosophy.

Linguists of both categories have existed both before and after Chomsky; but there was a marked tendency for the pre-Chomskyans (the *descriptivists*, as they are often called) to take the first line, whilst Chomsky himself, and most contemporary linguists, explicitly take the second.* Chomsky in fact regards his linguistics as a branch of psychology. Although the modish term 'psycholinguistics' will not appear in these pages, this is not because we ignore psychological matters, but rather because, having announced that we are adopting Chomsky's approach to linguistics, the prefix 'psycho-' seems otiose. (The distinction drawn in practice between psycho- and plain linguistics has to do more with styles of research than with the substantive nature of the problems dealt with.)

Each of these contrasting approaches to linguistics is entirely legitimate. The choice between them, like the decision whether to study history or mathematics, is a matter purely of personal taste: it happens that the present author's tastes coincide with Chomsky's in this respect. Unfortunately, great heat has been generated on the question of the status of linguistics as an academic subject, because of failure by people taking one of the two lines to appreciate the possibility of the alternative. Members of university departments of linguistics often encounter hostility from their colleagues in modern-language

---

* The school of American linguists which began with Boas and Bloomfield, and against which Chomsky reacted, is often called the 'structuralist' rather than the 'descriptivist' school. However, the term 'structuralism' is ambiguous. 'Structuralism' is used, particularly in France, to denote a general intellectual movement (if it merits such a title) concerned with a wide range of social sciences, together with literary criticism. The 'structuralists' in this sense frequently appeal to the findings of linguistics, but for the most part are not linguists themselves (one of the influential members of the movement is the anthropologist Claude Lévi-Strauss); and they discuss Chomskyan as much as pre-Chomskyan linguistics, if indeed they appreciate the difference between the two. It is not clear that 'structuralism' in the French sense is more than a fashionable slogan adopted by a group of writers with rather diverse interests; but, to avoid ambiguity, I prefer to call the pre-Chomskyan linguists 'descriptivists'.

departments, who have seen the rather forbidding, symbol-bespattered pages common in current linguistic treatises on, say, the English language, and who are sceptical about whether these really tell us anything about English that could not be put in the clearer, less technical language of traditional philology. Often the answer is 'no'; frequently the older descriptions of English are in fact better, if we judge them as descriptions of English. If our purpose, on the other hand, is to use the evidence of English to test hypotheses about the nature of human language, the abstract formalisms may be indispensable. (I hasten to add that misunderstandings of this kind occur in both directions.)

The generalist – the man who studies languages in order to study language – and the particularist – the man who studies linguistics in order to get to closer grips with some particular language or languages of interest – may happen both to investigate the same individual languages; but the features of those languages which preoccupy the particularist will typically differ from the features in which the generalist is most interested. The particularist focuses on the respects in which his favourite language differs from other languages; the generalist wants to eliminate from consideration the properties which differ from language to language in order to discover what all languages have in common.

The particularist, we have said, is typically an anthropologist or a philologer. The anthropologist studies culture: and a culture, by definition, is what distinguishes the way of life of one society from that of another. All societies have a system of producing and distributing food: since this characteristic of societies is universal, in itself it is of no anthropological interest. If, on the other hand, the food of one society is produced by a hereditary caste of slave labourers, while in another society all levels from lowest to highest participate in farming, then the anthropologist is in business. Again, the philologer will be interested in the fact that classical Greek subsumes the concepts of 'art' and 'craft' in a single word, *technē*, since this is not the case in other languages (English, for example), and under-standing this fact about Greek may help, perhaps, in inter-preting Plato. On the other hand, if every language has a word for 'I', then the philologer's only interest in first-person pronouns will be to remember how they are pronounced and declined in the languages with which he is concerned.

The generalist, however, might be able to use the universality of 'I' as a datum to support a psychological theory about innate awareness of a distinction between 'self' and 'other', or the like; but there is little to be made, psychologically, of the fact that one language distinguishes terms for 'art' and 'craft' while another language lumps them together. The philosopher works at an even greater remove than the psychologist from contingent, culturally-determined facts: he may perhaps treat the universality of the distinction between pronoun and adjective (assuming that we can speak of this as a universal distinction) as reflecting an ontological distinction between categories 'thing' and 'property', but from the *non*-universality of some linguistic distinction the philosopher can draw none but negative conclusions.

(It would be wrong to say that philosophical theories are never derived from facts specific to one language – some of the 'ordinary-language' philosophy fashionable in Britain in the decades since the Second World War has been based on the individual quirks of English usage in just this way. However, the statement that some linguistic construction is peculiar to English counts as a valid criticism of a philosophical theory which appeals to that construction. The ordinary-language philosophers are as generalist as others in intention, even if they are sometimes guilty of linguistic provincialism in practice.)

Since they are primarily interested in the differences between languages, it is understandable that the particularists have tended to overlook similarities and to exaggerate the extent to which human languages do in fact differ. (Conversely, the generalists often exaggerate the extent to which the languages of the world resemble one another; however, there is a self-correcting mechanism in the latter case which does not apply to the former. If the generalist claims that all languages resemble one another in such and such a respect, he can be refuted by citing one language which differs in that respect; on the other hand, if the particularist claims that languages can differ in some respect, one cannot refute him even if the limited number of languages one happens to know are alike in the given respect.) The anthropology-oriented linguists of America were especially inclined to believe in extreme diversity of languages. After all, the primary day-to-day concern of these scholars, in many cases, was to get down on paper accounts of languages which, in their pronunciation, in their grammar, and in the *Weltanschauung* implied by their vocabulary, were as exotic and as bewildering to the scholar of European descent as any subject of study well could be. It was difficult enough to avoid being blinkered by prejudices inherited unconsciously from one's European background, without deliberately donning an extra pair of blinkers in the shape of a hypothesis that linguistic diversity is limited. The view that resulted (the 'Boas tradition', as he calls it) was summed up by Martin Joos in 1957: 'languages [can] differ from each other without limit and in unpredictable ways'.*

Taken literally, this quotation is surely false: languages must have *some* properties in common, or why do we call them all 'languages'? But many of the pre-Chomskyan descriptivists did believe in unlimited diversity, in the sense that the only features which they envisaged as common to all languages were either features that applied to languages by definition – so that it was simply tautologous to say that all languages possessed them – or else features which, though not logically necessary, were trivial. For instance, it is probably true that all natural human languages – excluding sign 'languages' used primarily by deaf-mutes, or communication systems used only in special situations, e.g. racecourse tic-tac – have vocal sound as their medium, or as one of their media. Now it is logically possible that this is not so: there might be somewhere a tribe of humans whose primary means of communication is by gestures of the hands, or by a written language whose characters have no relation to spoken sound; but, although these possibilities might obtain, it would come as no great surprise to learn that they do not. There are solid, obvious advantages in sound as opposed to sight as a medium for language; for one thing it allows us to communicate in the dark. If the only features common to the languages of the world were features of this sort, we might well regard Joos's remark as essentially correct, even though not quite literally true.

* For the sources of this and subsequent quotations, see the Notes beginning on p. 197.

Published in the same year as Joos's book, Chomsky's *Syntactic Structures* for the first time suggested that it was worth trying to construct a theory about limitations on the diversity of human languages. In this and a number of subsequent works, Chomsky and his followers have claimed that there are specific bounds on linguistic diversity, and that the universal features of language – the respects in which human languages do not differ – are not limited to trivialities such as the fact that all languages use vocal sound, but include quite arbitrary properties which we could not predict *a priori*. Furthermore, Chomsky claims that his findings about 'universals of language' demonstrate the truth of some rather original and exciting assertions about the intellectual nature of Man: language, for Chomsky, is proving to be one of the best windows on to the workings of the mind.

In the following pages we shall examine these claims and assess their merits. At a number of points, we shall disagree with Chomsky and with what are currently accepted linguistic doctrines; but these points will in most cases not affect Chomsky's central arguments. Frequently, we shall find that Chomsky lays himself open to damaging criticism by the sceptic; but, often, revising Chomsky's ideas about language to meet these criticisms turns out to strengthen rather than weaken the wider implications of linguistics. While taking issue with Chomsky on many points of detail, in its over-all drift this book will strongly support Chomsky's novel way of looking at language.

Many readers will be people who approach language from the particularist standpoint – who are primarily interested in some individual language or group of languages – and for them especially I should like to stress the limitations on what is being claimed for the sort of linguistics under discussion. I hope this book will persuade such readers that linguistics of the Chomskyan kind is an alternative and equally valid approach to language, and that it comes up with results which are no less interesting than their own findings, though of a very different type. I shall not suggest that Chomskyan linguistics has contributions to make to the problems with which the particularists are centrally concerned. Philology is a subject with a long and honourable

9

tradition, and it would be foolish to claim that a theory born less than twenty years ago has much new to say about problems of a type familiar to philologers for a century and more. Many Chomskyans whose enthusiasm exceeds their wisdom have been heard vociferously claiming that Chomskyan linguistics holds the answers to all possible linguistic questions, and supersedes any previous approaches to language. Nothing has been more disastrous for our discipline: when people see through these grandiose claims, as sooner or later they must, the understandable reaction is often a contemptuous rejection of Chomskyan linguistics *in toto*. To the particularists I would say: 'We are doing one thing, and it seems to us interesting; you are doing rather different sorts of thing which are clearly interesting also. There is room for all of us; let us respect each other's domains and coexist peacefully.'

For readers who already approach linguistic behaviour from a generalist point of view, for the psychologist and the philosopher, this kind of comment is less relevant. For them, however, another kind of disclaimer is appropriate. Linguists who claim psychological or philosophical relevance for their subject often make statements on psychological or philosophical matters which reveal lamentable gaps in their knowledge of these disciplines. In the next chapter we shall see that this is true of some of Chomsky's arguments about the 'nativist' and 'rationalist' implications of linguistics, and later in the book it will apply even more strikingly to linguists' views on meaning. Again it is quite understandable that the psychologist or philosopher often reacts by saying, 'Here is an upstart subject which claims that it can solve my problems for me; if this is all the linguist knows of my discipline, I need take no further notice of the pretensions of linguistics.' One of the aims of this book is to argue that the assumptions about psychological and philosophical matters made by linguists do often ignore or grossly distort the current state of these subjects; but that, when these deficiencies are corrected, linguistics still turns out to have interesting things to say to its neighbour disciplines.

In the same year, 1957, in which Joos made his comment on linguistic diversity and Chomsky raised the question of limitations on that diversity, Chairman Mao quoted an ancient and excellent Chinese principle for the conduct of intellectual affairs: 'Let a hundred flowers blossom, let a hundred schools of thought contend!' The present book is concerned with the cultivation of one of the hundred blooms in the academic garden. If we give short shrift to various contemporary linguistic dogmas, the reader may reflect that a rose may be improved by pruning.

2

The Implications of Linguistics

The logical development of this book would be to begin with Chomsky's account of the constraints on the diversity of natural languages, and then to discuss the general inferences Chomsky draws from the existence of these constraints. Instead of doing this, we shall begin near the end by examining the psychological, biological, and philosophical consequences which Chomsky claims to follow from his linguistic theory. Once we have sorted out these ideas, it will be easier to grasp the point of the various particular observations Chomsky makes about language. In this chapter, then, we examine Chomsky's claims about the implications of linguistics for our understanding of human nature.

Chomsky's central claim is that a human's ability to use a language is, in an important sense, innate rather than learned. Now the first problem here is not whether or not this claim is true, but what it means. To make it clearer, let us consider some less controversial examples of innate v. learned abilities. We shall take on the one hand the ability to digest food, and on the other the ability to drive a car.

Beginning with the second case, it is certainly true that the ability to drive involves, among other things, a number of innate characteristics. One cannot drive unless one can see: the fact that we are aware of sense-inputs corresponding to the light-waves approaching our faces is because our genetic inheritance includes a pair of eyes. Again, the motions of the arm by which one changes gear involve co-ordinated activity by a number of complex mechanisms, e.g. muscles, and it was not by learning that we acquired muscles. However, it is obvious that many of the abilities a driver possesses are not inborn in the same way. When I react to the sight of an obstacle at some distance by pressing my left foot down to let out the clutch and moving my left arm to change gear, I do so not beause I am genetically programmed to do so (as I am genetically programmed, say, to react to the touch of a hot coal by flinching away), but rather because I earlier set out to learn to react in this way to this kind of stimulus. Even if we did not know how recent an invention cars were, we would know that my reactions are learned rather than inborn, for instance because others have quite different reactions – or no reactions – to the same stimuli. Many humans cannot drive, foreigners change gear with the right hand, some people drive cars with automatic transmission and react in the same situation by gentle pressure with the right foot, and so on.

Compare, now, my ability to consume and metabolize food. Again, a complete description of what is going on involves both learned and innate abilities. There is a certain skill, which a child has to be taught, in getting food off the plate, masticated, and down one's throat: the fact that the first part of this process is a learned skill become particularly obvious when the food is, say, spaghetti bolognese. It is also true in the author's case (again, particularly after spaghetti) that the process of digestion is more comfortable and, perhaps, more efficient if I go for a brisk walk rather than sit in an armchair after lunch: but it is a consciously learned habit rather than an inborn reaction which sends me out of the house. However, these techniques or learned habits are only a quite small part of what there is to say about human digestion. The complex mechanical and chemical processes by which food is moved into and out of the stomach and through the gut, by which it is broken down and its valuable products extracted and absorbed, by which the liver filters out the resulting impurities from the bloodstream: in no sense can we be said to have *learned* to perform these processes, rather we do them because we are built that way.

We might sum up the situation by saying that Man is destined by birth to eat, whereas he is not destined by birth to drive (even though he is born with abilities which permit him, among other things, to learn to drive if opportunity offers). Eating is an extreme case – not only does our genetic inheritance permit us to eat, we *must* eat if we are to survive. However, this is not essential to the distinction I have in mind:

a woman is destined by birth to bear children in the same sense that we are all born to eat, even though she may happen to lead a celibate life.

This notion of 'innate predestination' has a suspiciously teleological ring, as if the way a newborn infant is constructed now is determined by the fact that in the future he must eat – science does not like explanations that locate effects earlier than their causes. But Darwin has made this sort of teleology respectable, by showing that it is only a convenient abbreviation for longer-winded but non-teleological accounts. 'Species s has property p because it needs to perform action a' means simply that, among the various consequences of possessing p, it was the ability to perform a which caused the ancestors of s to win in the struggle for survival against rivals lacking p.

I have admitted that both eating and driving involve both innate and learned abilities, and I do not pretend to have drawn a clear distinction between the two kinds of ability I am discussing. Indeed, I feel about the distinction as St Augustine felt about time, that I understand it just so long as I am not asked to explain it. However, to me it seems intuitively clear that there is a genuine distinction here, if not necessarily a sharp one; I hope the reader will agree. It may be that we should think of the distinction between innate and learned human behaviour, not as an intrinsic difference in the behaviour itself, so much as a difference in which aspects of that behaviour are most in need of explanation. Someone who sets out to explain the ability to drive does not need to spend much time discussing the operation of the muscles – these matters are adequately discussed already by physiologists and may be taken as given. But he will need to go into detail about how one learns to correlate visual stimuli with arm and leg movements, since we feel quite ignorant here and cannot look to any existing body of knowledge for enlightenment. Conversely, an account of the metabolization of food will be most fruitful if it passes rapidly over knife-and-fork technique and concentrates on mysteries such as the effect of gastric juices on carbohydrate.

Human linguistic behaviour, too, involves both innate and learned aspects. Speech has the function, among others, of helping to cement a social group into an atmosphere of friendly cohesion; the need or desire for social bonds of this kind presumably is, and has always been admitted to be, a characteristic innate in our species. On the other hand, only through learning, clearly, can we know that the sentence **What do you reckon on Spurs for the Cup?** will do more – in many social circles – to promote the desired relationships than will **How high do you estimate the probability of Spassky winning the Championship?*** Chomsky is saying, first, that his predecessors judged it more fruitful to concentrate on learned aspects of language; and, secondly, that this view is unjustified – in our present state of knowledge it is appropriate to devote a great deal of effort to investigating the innate side of language. (Even if this is so, it may still be worth while to continue studying the learned side as well, of course; Chomsky is sometimes unduly dogmatic in condemning, as pointless, approaches to language which differ from his own.)

In one sense, admittedly, no linguistic behaviour is 'innate': the newborn child utters no sentences. But the fact that it takes some years before a child masters his mother tongue is irrelevant to the point at issue. A newborn child cannot digest beefsteak; and a woman takes much longer from birth to develop the ability to bear children than anyone does to speak, but one does not therefore talk of passing through the stage of puberty as 'learning' to bear children. Indeed, there is an important parallel here. Puberty occurs at a particular age which varies a little between individuals but is more or less independent of environment: girls in affluent cultures reach puberty a few years earlier than those living in poorer regions, but very few women reach puberty as early as ten or as late as twenty. Similarly, the acquisition of language occurs at roughly the same age for different individuals; and there is evidence that if a child misses the boat because he is for some reason not exposed to a speech-filled environment at the normal age of language-acquisition, then he can never subsequently join the voyage. On the other hand, except for some relatively marginal considerations (such as speed of reactions), one is equally capable of learning to drive at ten or sixty.

---

* We adopt the convention in this book of writing linguistic forms used as examples in bold type; this enables us to reserve italics and inverted commas to mark emphasis, quotations and the like.

The obvious evidence against linguistic ability being an innate endowment is the diversity of human languages. Certainly, any fact of our behaviour which varies between languages must be learned rather than inborn. I call water **water**; but a Chinese calls it **shui**, and, if my own son were brought up among Chinese, he would call it **shui** too. Therefore the fact that I say **water** must be because I have learned to do so. And human languages are very diverse, not just in their vocabulary but in many other respects. But Chomsky's point is that, although many features of language do vary, many other features which one might *a priori* expect to be equally variable in fact turn out not to be. (We shall consider what these features are in chapter 5.) The wealth of differences which do occur between languages should not blind us to the things which might differ but do not. As we have seen, even the human consumption of food involves learned abilities to some extent; and those aspects of the total process which are learned may vary between individuals, just as the learned aspects of language vary. The Chinese eat with chopsticks, while we use knife and fork. But we agreed that what needs to be explained in an account of the human food-consuming process is to a very large extent a matter of inheritance rather than learning; there is no reason to change our minds on this just because there exist superficial differences in the eating behaviour of the Chinese and the English.

Chomsky actually uses two separate arguments for the thesis that language is largely an inherited characteristic. The argument that only inheritance can explain the existence of universals of human language is one of these. The other argument has to do with the complexity of human languages. Much of linguistics consists in producing descriptions of individual human languages. Most people who for the first time come across a linguistic analysis of their native tongue react with amazement that what seems to them a straightforward enough part of their intellectual equipment should turn out to be so tremendously intricate, when set out explicitly on paper – particularly when the linguist tells them that the best current description is only a crude approximation, known to be defective in many respects. One may well argue, in fact, that much of the general educational value of the study of linguistics is that it teaches respect for humanity, by suggesting how endlessly subtle are the behaviour patterns which even the humblest of our fellow men master without conscious effort.

Now, one of Chomsky's arguments for the innateness of language runs along these lines: 'All human languages are enormously complex. It is unreasonable to suggest that humans manage within the first few years of their lives to master such complex systems, if they have to start completely from scratch. Therefore they don't: much of what is needed to use a human language must already be "built-in" at birth, and the task of learning whatever remains is a much smaller and more manageable one.' Chomsky illustrates this argument with a striking parable: were a Martian to land in England (Chomsky suggests), he would almost certainly conclude that the whole of the English language was part of the human genetic endowment – until an encounter with foreigners showed that it could not be.

The trouble with the argument from complexity is that it is a quantitative argument which deals with unquantifiable phenomena, namely, the rate at which humans can learn, and the amount to be learned about a language 'starting from scratch'. The argument sounds as if it could be paraphrased: 'Human learning proceeds at a maximum rate of n units per month; a child masters his mother tongue within, say, 50 months from birth, but a human language contains more than $50n$ units of complexity, therefore some of the facts about the language must be available to the child before he starts.' Put like this, it is obvious that one has no idea what these 'units' could be. Indeed, it is not just that we are ignorant here; rather, there seems to be a conceptual unclarity in the very notion that one might reduce the relative difficulty of learning to speak a language, to drive a car, to find the way from home to work, and so forth, to different points on a linear scale of complexity. Chomsky says (in effect): 'How complex languages are, and how surprising that children need only three or four years to learn them.' One might equally well take the line: 'What idle creatures children are; their time is all their own, yet it takes them three full years and more merely to learn their mother tongue.' We have no grounds for regarding this latter attitude as less appropriate than Chomsky's.

As for the Martian, the hypothesis he finds most plausible *a priori* will surely depend wholly on what Martians are like. If Martians have wheels instead of legs but lead solitary, unco-operative lives, then a Martian who visits Earth will no doubt start by assuming that humans are born with the ability to drive, but that languages are a product of advanced Earth technology, which individual humans have to learn from scratch.

Chomsky shores up his argument from complexity by claiming that the data available to the infant acquiring his first language are 'degenerate', as he puts it: that is, not only do children master their mother tongue surprisingly quickly, but the examples of it to which they are exposed are typically very poor, containing many false starts, grammatical slips, extraneous 'ums' and 'ers', and the like. This seems to make the child's achievement all the more remarkable. But it is an empirical question whether the data are as 'degenerate' as Chomsky claims. Chomsky himself quotes no evidence: the research that has been done tends to show that, while university lecturers discussing intellectually demanding subjects do indeed produce a fair proportion of substandard sentences, the overwhelming majority of utterances a child hears during the period of language acquisition are complete and well-formed by any criterion.

The argument from complexity, then, has no force and we shall not consider it further. The argument from linguistic universals, on the other hand, is a good argument. It is not quantitative: it says: 'Human languages all have the set P of properties, though it is not necessary for something to have P to be called a language; innateness provides an explanation for the universality of P, so we shall hypothesize innateness.' The argument is not watertight: if someone can offer a better explanation than innateness for the universality of P, then this explanation loses its force. We shall consider some such possibilities in chapter 6. But, until a superior explanation of P is offered, the mere fact that the innateness hypothesis is in principle vulnerable cannot be taken as a criticism of that hypothesis; for this is the general condition of science. Even the best and most certain-seeming of scientific theories may be overturned by a better theory which someone thinks up tomorrow. Until tomorrow comes, we must stick to the best theory that we have today.

Although the assertions of science are by nature vulnerable, some aspects of the innateness of language in our species can be demonstrated in a particularly clear and concrete way. Consider, for instance, our ability to produce the wide range of vocal sounds which our languages use. One might assume here that language simply exploits mechanisms which evolved for independent reasons: after all, other species make noises, and each individual organ that takes part in producing speech sounds has some independent function connected with eating or breathing. As recently as 1967, the phonetician David Abercrombie summed up this commonly-held opinion:

'. . . there is no part of a human being which is specifically designed for talking. The parts of the body which produce the sounds of language are incidentally useful for this purpose, but they all have other duties to perform which from the biological point of view are older and more important . . .'

Subsequent research has made this view untenable. Although each of the organs we use in vocalizing has its homologue in species related to Man, their relative size, shape, and arrangement is unique to us and can be explained only as a development designed to facilitate speech. Philip Lieberman has examined the vocal tracts of the chimpanzee (the closest extant relative to Man) and, via fossil reconstruction, of Neanderthal Man (an even closer relative who flourished about 100,000 years ago), as well as that of the newborn human. (The anatomy of the newborn child reflects that of species ancestral to Man – a principle known as 'ontogeny recapitulating phylogeny'.) Lieberman finds that the adult human vocal tract is very much the 'odd man out' when set beside these three cases, and it departs from them in a direction which enables us to produce a much wider range of sounds than the chimp, the Neanderthaler, or ourselves when very young. Lieberman cites R. A. Dart's claim that the growth of human culture accelerated greatly some 30,000 years ago, and he makes the fascinating suggestion that it may have been the mutation in our ancestors' vocal-tract anatomy which was responsible for the development of human language and thus for this flourishing of culture.

One might nevertheless imagine that the novel vocal tract which differentiates us from our close evolutionary relatives was selected because it conferred some independent benefit on us, and happened incidentally to be useful for linguistic purposes. But the opposite is true. Our vocal-tract anatomy has a great disadvantage in that it allows food to get caught in the windpipe and choke us to death: a risk which the chimp, the Neanderthaler, and the newborn human do (or did) not run. In Britain, some five hundred people die this way annually, making it one of the leading causes of accidental death. In other words, our species has found it worth making a considerable sacrifice in exchange for a repertoire of sounds which permit us to use efficient languages.

Parallel discoveries have recently been made in connection with hearing. The view that language merely exploits pre-existing capacities is prima facie even more compelling in the case of hearing than in the case of the production of sound. Species quite distantly related to Man have ears: even Fido answers to his name. But the fact that a species possesses some organ does not guarantee the ability to detect the same distinctions between stimuli that humans use that organ to detect. For instance, many species which have eyes are completely colour-blind. Recent work by Alvin Liberman and others shows that, although humans have just one pair of ears, with respect to the way in which heard sound is processed in the brain we may be said to have two quite different hearing systems. One system responds exclusively to certain of the phonetic distinctions occurring in speech, while the second responds to the remaining distinctions of speech, and also to music, traffic noise, the sound of waterfalls, and all the rest. Furthermore, the phonetic distinctions to which the first system responds are exactly the distinctions which do most of the work of keeping different words apart in natural languages; and the first system processes the sounds to which it is sensitive in a way which reflects the fact that their source is a human mouth.

Consider, for instance, the syllable **di**: if we examined the pattern of air-waves which make it up, we would see the first part of the pattern as having more in common with the first part of **bi** than with the first part of **du**. But the consonants of **di** and **du** are both pronounced with the tongue, as against that of **bi** which involves the lips; and, accordingly, we hear the consonants of **di** and **du** alike (and write them with the same letter). With the hearing system which processes non-speech sounds, on the other hand, our perceptions correlate directly with the sound-waves we are hearing, irrespective of their source.

In other words, the perception, as well as the production, of speech is mediated by mechanisms designed specifically for linguistic purposes. Fido answers to his name; but perhaps he would answer to any other trochee just as readily.

According to a widespread view of language (a view with which Chomsky disagrees), the use of language involves only traits which our species evolved for quite independent purposes. The reason why we have complex languages, while other species have at most rather crude, restricted signalling systems, is said to be simply one particular consequence of the fact that Man is more intelligent than other species, that we have a higher degree of the ability to think abstractly, a more complex nervous system, or the like. For Chomsky, on the other hand, the notion of 'intelligence' as a general scale of some kind on which Man occupies one rung, dolphins a lower rung and sparrows a lower rung still, is an unfruitful notion without clear sense. Chomsky and his collaborator Eric Lenneberg, who discusses language from the biological point of view, suggest that what we call 'intelligence' is merely a catch-all term covering a number of diverse traits possessed by Man, of which language is one. To say that Man is the most intelligent species is not really to make a substantive assertion: we *define* 'intelligence' to include exactly those abilities Man happens to possess, and we do not condemn ourselves as unintelligent because we cannot build a bird's nest. Looked at in this way, our disposition to use language is just as specific a trait as our possession of ten rather than twelve fingers, or a bee's disposition to build hexagonal honey-combs, or the blue base of a blue-based baboon.

Since Lieberman's work on speech production and Liberman's work on speech perception demonstrate that human linguistic behaviour involves biological traits which serve no other purpose, these discoveries do go some way to vindicate Chomsky's view. But Chomsky is making a much stronger claim about language than merely that humans have evolved speaking and hearing mechanisms which are particularly well adapted for efficient communication, as Lieberman and Liberman have shown.

In the first place, speech sound is only the medium in which linguistic messages are transmitted. (Since the invention of writing, in fact, sound has been just one of the media of language, and in the modern world it might appear the less important of the two. Biologically, however, the sound medium has a special relationship with language not enjoyed by the visual medium.) The universal properties of human languages to which Chomsky is pointing are properties of the *messages*, not of the medium.

Secondly, these properties are arbitrary in a way which the distinctive characteristics of our speaking and hearing mechanisms are not. Presumably it would be perfectly possible to use a language that was restricted to the few sounds which a chimpanzee can utter; but a language which exploits a wider range of sounds will clearly be more efficient, so, given that humans use languages at all, it is hardly surprising that they have evolved the ability to produce a large vocal repertoire. Similarly, our special speech-perception system has clear advantages: according to Liberman, it enables us to hear sounds uttered at a more rapid rate than would otherwise be possible, in other words it speeds up the communication process. In the case of Chomsky's linguistic universals, though, there is no clear sense in which a language possessing them is 'better' or more 'efficient' than languages lacking them. For one thing, one cannot talk about a trait as 'efficient' unless one can specify the function which that trait performs; and, as we shall see when we consider the matter in chapter 6, in the case of language it is quite mysterious what that function is. Intuitively it seems clear to us that the ability to speak to one another is very useful; but it is extraordinarily difficult to say *what* use this ability has without begging the question.

In other words, according to the view we shall be defending, the human disposition to use language is arbitrary in a quite deep sense. In the first place, it is more analogous to the property of possessing some particular organ, such as wings or eyes, than to the property of having some pre-existing organ developed to a particular state, for instance having strong wings or acute eyes. Secondly, unlike wings or eyes this 'organ' is one whose use is unclear: and, consequently, we have no way of explaining the form of language by reference to its function.

A good way of making more precise our statement of the implications which Chomsky draws from linguistics will be to contrast his position with various existing views in the disciplines to which he claims linguistics is relevant. There are at least three such disciplines: psychology, philosophy, and biology.

Both in psychology and philosophy, Chomsky uses the findings of linguistics to argue for one of the extremes on a recognized spectrum of possible views. The psychological spectrum and the philosophical spectrum each cover a number of questions which are related, in the sense that the answers people give to one of the questions tend to correlate highly with their choice of answer to the other questions; but the questions are logically distinct – it is quite reasonable to take one line on one of the questions and the 'opposite' line on another. Furthermore, the issues involved in the psychological spectrum of opinion overlap to a considerable extent with the issues involved in the philosophical spectrum. Various names are associated with the opposite extremes of the spectra: 'behaviourism' v. 'mentalism', 'empiricism' v. 'nativism' or 'rationalism'; but these words are used in different ways, and, like most 'isms', they are no substitute for statements in plain English of the points at issue.

The first strand in the psychological debate, which we shall call *nativism v. empiricism,* is the question we have already discussed: to what extent is a person's behaviour determined by inheritance as opposed to interaction with the outside world? – or, to use familiar shorthand, by nature rather than nurture?

Notice first of all that this question has nothing to do with the problem of determinism itself – 'Are future eventualities fully predictable from the present state of affairs?', 'Is our belief that we have free will an illusion?', and so on. It may well be that human actions, the physical world, or both, are non-deterministic. That simply means that not *everything* can be predicted. But the whole of science rests on the assumption that at least some things can be predicted, even if only in terms of probabilities. One can believe in free will without objecting to that assumption.

However, in so far as a person's behaviour is determined at all, one can distinguish two factors on which it depends: the initial state of that person (what sort of entity he is when he begins life, say at conception), and the various subsequent inputs to him from the environment. The empiricist claim is that, in discussing the determination of behaviour, one needs to say a lot about inputs from the environment but relatively little about initial state.

It is worth pointing out that, though this thesis may be correct, it contrasts sharply with what everyone (including empiricist psychologists) agrees to be the case with respect to characteristics of a person other than his behaviour. Consider the *anatomical* properties of an adult man, for instance. It is true that in some ways these will depend on his history of inputs from the environment: whether a man is fat or thin depends partly on how much he has eaten, not merely on his genes. But most of the extremely intricate and complex anatomy of a man – the structure of his eye, for instance – is a direct consequence of his initial state and is almost completely independent of his subsequent history. The empiricists, however, maintain that those facts about a person which one categorizes as 'behaviour' differ sharply in their causation from all the other facts about him.

Having said that Chomsky takes the nativist side in this debate, it is important to stress that the issue is not a sharp one dividing scholars into two camps. The debate is about the *relative* importance of nature and nurture in determining behaviour: everyone agrees that both genes and the environment play some part, and one may adopt any position on a scale of possible views about how the two are balanced. Whether one thinks of oneself as a 'nativist' or an 'empiricist' will depend as much on what ideas one is reacting against as on what one's own views are. Chomsky is reacting against the view that languages differ unpredictably (remember the Joos quotation), which implies that all our linguistic abilities are learned rather than innate; so he calls himself a nativist by contrast.

Chomsky attacks modern psychology for being too empiricist. One of his influential early writings was a hostile review of a book by B. F. Skinner. Skinner has carried out experiments in which one chooses some action to be performed by, say, a pigeon. Any chance movement by the pigeon which will serve as the beginning of the target action is rewarded by a pellet of food, and accordingly the pigeon starts to make that movement regularly. One then 'reinforces' just those movements which are somewhat closer to the target. Eventually one can make the pigeon perform quite complicated tasks. This is a classic case of behaviour determined by environment; and Skinner claims to explain all human behaviour also in terms of 'reinforcement', so he is clearly an extreme empiricist.

But Skinner is far from typical of current psychology. It is true that opposition to nativist explanations was once very strong in psychology, and this attitude was taken over from psychology into linguistics and lasted rather longer there. (Scholars tend to be at least ten years out of date in their ideas about the next-door subject!) However, psychology in recent decades has moved a considerable distance in the nativist direction for reasons quite unconnected with linguistics. One thing that has influenced psychology in this way has been the development of *ethology*, the science of animal instinct. Konrad Lorenz's findings about how newly-hatched ducklings are 'imprinted' with the image of the first large moving object they see and treat it thereafter as their mother, or Karl von Frisch's discovery of the dancing of bees, by which they tell the others in their hive where to find nectar, are clear cases of complex behaviour patterns which are inherited rather than learned. Another influence has been the advance of neurophysiology. The work of David Hubel and Torsten Wiesel of

MIT, in particular, who have identified individual neurons in the brains of cats which react only to quite specific visual stimuli – for instance, to diagonal lines oriented top-left to bottom-right – has brought it home forcibly to many people that the nervous systems of mammals are not simply very general association-forming devices, but quite intricate mechanisms with highly specific properties.

It may well be, then, that Chomsky is attacking a straw man when he criticizes empiricism in psychology. Donald Broadbent, for instance, recently published a book, *In Defence of Empirical Psychology*, in which he explicitly sets out to refute Chomsky's attacks on empiricism. But, when we look at the views about human psychology which Broadbent expresses in that book, as opposed to the label he gives his views, we find they are very close to Chomsky's own views. Broadbent points out that nativism is fashionable in contemporary psychology, and he calls himself an empiricist in reaction against this fashion. Chomsky, on the other hand, calls himself a nativist because he is reacting against an older, empiricist fashion.

There is perhaps a sense in which Chomsky's linguistic nativism is more startling than nativism applied to other aspects of psychology. Language is closely related to thought, and thought, we intuitively feel, is the area of human life where we are most completely free and untrammelled by physical limitations. To demonstrate some arbitrariness in the structure of human thinking is to do more than Lorenz has done by identifying the innate mechanisms by which ducklings attach themselves to their mothers. If, as our last chapter will suggest, we can infer a concrete model of human thinking machinery from Chomsky's linguistic universals, then linguistics does indeed lead to an understanding of the nature of human beings which goes beyond anything currently offered by non-linguistic psychology. But, having said this, to quarrel about who is a true empiricist seems to be as fruitless as to object to the statement that China is in the East on the grounds that it is west of Japan.

A psychological issue related to, but distinct from the empiricism/nativism issue is an issue we shall call *behaviourism v. mentalism*, although many writers (Broadbent for instance) extend the word 'empiricism' to cover what we call 'behaviourism'. This second issue is a sharp yes-or-no rather than spectrum-of-opinion question, concerning the *evidence* for psychological theories as opposed to the nature of the theories themselves. The question is: 'May psychological theories appeal to our introspections about what occurs in our minds (mentalism), or must they stand or fall solely by reference to physical facts which can be checked by independent observers (behaviourism)?' Here Chomsky takes the mentalist side, while linguists before Chomsky and psychologists both then and now agree in supporting behaviourism. In this case, however, I shall argue (in chapter 4) that Chomsky's view is simply mistaken, and that his own work in linguistics neither requires him to be a mentalist (as he thinks) nor provides any support for mentalism.

The issues of empiricism *v.* nativism and behaviourism *v.* mentalism might seem prima facie to have nothing to do with one another. The two are linked, however, because of a still further difference of opinion – this time relating to the nature of science in general rather than to psychology in particular. This third question is as follows: 'Should we think of scientific theories merely as elegant and convenient summaries of the evidence used to support them, or do the technical terms and principles of a scientific theory correspond to some reality lying behind the observable facts?' We may call the former of these alternatives *descriptivism*, and the latter *realism*.

For instance, the theory of gravity tells us that material objects exert forces of attraction on one another which vary in accordance with the masses of and distances between the objects. Nobody has seen or touched a gravitational force: these forces are posited purely in order to make sense of very varied observations which can be made directly, e.g. observations of the different positions of the planets at different times, observations of the ebb and flow of the tides, observations of the behaviour of stones thrown in the air and bullets shot from guns, and so forth. For the descriptivist, 'gravitational forces' are merely convenient myths: the superstitious scientist may believe in them, but the enlightened philosopher realizes that statements which appear to be about gravity are in fact concise summaries of quantities of statements about planets, tides, cannon-balls, and the like. For the realist, on the other hand, gravitational forces are as real as cannon-balls. One should not regard gravitational forces as less real than cannon-balls, or Tibet as less real than France (says the realist), just because one's knowledge of gravity or of Tibet is less direct than one's knowledge of cannon-balls or of France.

Pre-Chomskyan linguists such as Bloomfield were in many cases descriptivists, like many other scholars in the inter-war years.* Descriptivism has become much less popular since, for several reasons. (For one thing, the descriptivist view pre-supposes that there is a class of basic statements about observations, to which all theoretical statements can be reduced; yet it is not clear that such basic statements exist, or, if they do exist, that they are reliable enough to serve as the foundation of science.)

What is the connection between the three issues we have discussed? Logically, there is none: one can adopt any combination of positions on the different issues without contradiction. But, in practice, one who is a descriptivist and a behaviourist is very likely also to be an empiricist. Descriptivism says that a science is about its data: any theoretical terms not referring directly to observables are just convenient myths. Behaviourism says that the data of psychology are restricted to the outward movements of human bodies, and exclude mental phenomena such as sensations. Accept both these, and psychological theories are concise generalizations about physical behaviour. Now, it might be that the behavioural data could be elegantly treated by means of a complex theory containing many theoretical terms. If such a theory accounts for the facts well, a realist will accept it and assume that the theoretical terms will eventually turn out to be correlated in some way with characteristics of the nervous system

---

* In chapter 1 we *defined* the term 'descriptivists' as a name for the school of linguists who preceded Chomsky, and within linguistics this term is often used without any implications about linguists' philosophical opinions on the status of scientific theories. When linguists do wish to contrast the view that linguistic analysis uncovers true facts with the view that it merely summarizes data in a more or less elegant way, they commonly use the terms 'God's-truth' and 'hocus-pocus' rather than the philosopher's 'realism' and 'descriptivism'. However, since Bloomfield and his disciples tended to take the 'hocus pocus' view of linguistic analysis, i.e. they were 'descriptivists' in the philosophical sense, the double use of this term should not lead to confusion.

– even though our current knowledge of the nervous system is far too sketchy for us to be able to translate the psychological theory into statements about neurons, synapses, and the like. For the descriptivist, no such interpretation is available: he has to treat the many theoretical terms as so many myths. Now, of course, he may be willing to do this. The theories produced by physicists contain much more intricate systems of theoretical terms than any extant psychological theories, and the descriptivist has to view all these as necessary fictions. But no thinking man likes paying lip-service to myths. In the case of physics, the descriptivist has no option: physics has been a going concern far longer than the philosophy of science, and the physicists, quite rightly, are too busy developing physical theories to take any notice of philosophers urging them to cut down on their theoretical terms. Subjects like psychology and linguistics are in a rather different case. Here, the philosopher of science can claim some relative seniority; after being snubbed by the physicists, he will be all the more eager to offer aid and counsel to these new subjects which are anxiously trying to discover how to turn themselves into respectable sciences. Now it seems very likely that the version of psychology which will be most sparing with terms denoting unobservables, and therefore most appealing to the descriptivist's sensibilities, will be one that attributes very little inherent structure to the mind. So a psychologist influenced by descriptivism will automatically lean towards empiricism rather than nativism. The realist view of science, on the other hand, involves no bias either way on the empiricism/nativism issue.

Let us turn now to the philosophical issue to which Chomsky regards linguistics as relevant. This is closely related to the empiricism/nativism issue in psychology; indeed the philosophical controversy was at its height at a time long before psychology was regarded as a subject in its own right, distinct from philosophy. In philosophy, the view which Chomsky advocates is called *rationalism*: the alternative view is again called *empiricism*.

The question here concerns the genesis of human knowledge and belief: 'Does the nature of our knowledge reflect, at least

29

in part, our own nature (rationalism), or are our minds mere *tabulae rasae*, in Locke's phrase, passively registering whatever impress Nature happens to impose on them, and contributing nothing of their own to the construction of our belief-systems (empiricism)?' According to Chomsky, the existence of invariant aspects of human language supports rationalism, as against the empiricist philosophical tradition prevailing in the English-speaking world.

Specifically, Chomsky uses linguistics to argue in favour of Descartes's theory of *innate ideas*; one of Chomsky's books, *Cartesian Linguistics*, claims that Descartes and other seventeenth-century French scholars influenced by Descartes anticipate in their views on language much of Chomsky's own linguistic theorizing.

It is very unclear, though, how Chomsky's linguistics relates to Descartes's innate ideas. In ordinary usage, an 'idea' is a concept, e.g. the concept of *God*, or a proposition, e.g. the proposition *that God exists*. Descartes used the term in just these ways: the examples I cite were in fact among the 'ideas' he claimed to be innate. Descartes's theory was fairly generally rejected, not only by the Anglo-American empiricists but also by later Continental philosophers, and certainly it seems clearly false as it stands. If it is true that God exists, it is certainly not an innately-known truth – whole civilizations (such as the Chinese) have lacked any concept which can usefully be identified with the European notion of God, and *a fortiori* have not believed in the existence of such a Being. Chomsky's theory of linguistic universals deals with concepts and propositions which he claims to be valid for the description of all human languages, but he does not suggest that speakers of the various languages are conscious of these concepts and properties. Thus, an example of a Chomskyan linguistic universal would be the claim that the description of any natural language involves the concept *clause*; but there is no question of claiming that all speakers of English are familiar with the notion 'clause', or with the truth of the statements 'The sentences of English are composed of clauses' or 'The sentences of all languages are composed of clauses' – such claims would be patently false.

Since the publication of *Cartesian Linguistics*, in fact, a number of writers have claimed that Chomsky misunderstands both

Descartes and the other seventeenth-century scholars whom he discusses, and that he misrepresents the historical relationships between the work of these various figures. The present author is not qualified to take an independent position on the controversy; but much of this criticism has a ring of truth. Even if Chomsky's account of Descartes is more accurate than his critics allow, the connection between Chomsky's own theory of language and the theory Chomsky attributes to Descartes is so tenuous that it is hard to understand Chomsky's motive in writing *Cartesian Linguistics*, unless it was a misguided desire to equip himself with a respectable intellectual ancestry – misguided, since Chomsky's theory of language is important in its own right and needs no precedent.

Chomsky also seems to exaggerate when he treats his arguments for rationalism as constituting an attack on current philosophical fashions in the English-speaking world. It is true that empiricism dominated Anglo-American philosophy in the seventeenth and eighteenth centuries, and that this tradition has not subsequently been actively rejected. However, the question Chomsky takes up, namely the source of human beliefs, simply is not a live issue now as it was earlier. Modern epistemology (theory of knowledge) is much more concerned with how we decide whether our ideas are correct than with where we get them from in the first place. Although Chomsky may have something novel to contribute to the question about the sources of our beliefs, his contribution will be less controversial than he suggests.

It seems likely that Chomsky's quarrels with the American psychological and philosophical establishments may have as much to do with his personal feelings about his native country as with the recent history of the two subjects. Chomsky has a deep dislike and distrust of the contemporary social and political structure of the USA. These are matters which it would be impertinent for an outsider to discuss.

We have said that Chomsky has no need to appeal to intellectual precedents. However, it happens that there is a philosopher whose views are strikingly reminiscent of Chomsky's, namely Immanuel Kant. Kant held that the nature of human knowledge was determined by the knower as well as by the known, so he also may be called a rationalist. For Kant, though, unlike Descartes, human nature determined, not the substantive *content* of human knowledge, but the *form* of our beliefs and of the logical rules by which we infer new beliefs from established ones.

A common analogy is with a man wearing tinted spectacles. If his spectacles are red, for him red objects and white objects are the same colour. Unless he takes his spectacles off, the range of possible colours for him is different from what the rest of us perceive it to be, and different in a global way. It is not simply that the colour spectrum which he can perceive remains constant, but because of the glasses he never happens to see any white things: if one performs the experiment, one finds that post-office vans and wedding dresses look the same colour, but one is as inclined to say that the post-office van looks white as to say that the wedding dress looks red – **white** and **red** become synonyms.

For Kant, to be human is to perceive the outside world through a particular kind of spectacles, which we can never take off. Although the structure of reality 'in itself' may be quite different from the structure which we impose on reality, we cannot possibly come to know the former. Kant's spectacles determine, not the colours we see in the world, but the categories into which we organize experience. For instance, one common type of belief is that which attributes some property to an individual entity (which may be concrete, as when we believe that the *Post Office Tower* is *tall*, or abstract, as when we believe that the *Treaty of Rome* is *inequitable*). For Kant, the particular beliefs about the Post Office Tower or the Treaty of Rome are derived wholly from experience; but the fact that the world is organized into (among other things) *properties* and *individuals* is our own contribution. If someone questions whether the Post Office Tower is tall, or whether the Treaty of Rome is inequitable, we can examine appropriate aspects of the world to check whether our belief is well-founded; but one cannot imagine what it would mean to examine the world in order to check whether we are right to analyse it into properties and individuals.

Notice that this is very different from saying that the notions of 'property' and 'individual', or the fact that we categorize experience in terms of these notions, are innately familiar: that is certainly not so. Kant did claim that there is a rich structure of facts – including philosophical generalizations such as *All events have a cause*, together with mathematical propositions – which we can come to know independently of experience; but he does not suggest that we are born knowing them, rather they have to be painstakingly inferred by the philosopher from a contemplation of the structure of our everyday beliefs. Indeed, although Kant took his analysis of the *a priori* component of human knowledge quite a long way, the details of his analysis have survived criticism much less well than the general claim that there is such a component.

All this is much more Chomskyan than anything Chomsky finds in Descartes. For instance, the *a priori* nature of the categories 'property' and 'individual' correlates quite directly with the existence in all languages of the clause structure whereby adjectives are predicated of nominal phrases (if this is indeed a linguistic universal). Clearly humans are not innately familiar with the categories 'adjective' and 'nominal phrase'; these are terms of art, even though they comfortably antedate Chomsky's own linguistic theories. But, if all humans speak languages which are most adequately portrayed by descriptions involving 'adjective' and 'nominal phrase', or equivalent terms, while there are conceivable languages whose descriptions would make no use of such terms, then we may well take Chomsky's linguistics as evidence in favour of the Kantian view of human thought.

The third subject to which Chomsky sees his work as relevant is biology. In particular, Chomsky claims that a study of linguistics leads to dissatisfaction with Darwin's theory of evolution.

Chomsky's chief objection to Darwinism is that human language constitutes a case of what is called *emergence*, and as such is not the sort of phenomenon which the theory of evolution can predict. Chomsky condemns Darwin's theory as 'tautologous', because it merely asserts that species will develop new characteristics which make them better fitted for survival, without giving us any way of predicting what particular new developments will occur in the future; the theory just points at past developments which have as a matter of fact survived and says: 'Those changes occurred because they increased the chances of survival.'

The notion of 'emergence' involves the assertion that biological evolution is a 'creative' process, in the sense that the arts and sciences are creative: not only can we not predict which particular new development will occur, we cannot even enumerate the range of possibilities. Consider the process by which a science develops: hypotheses and theories are formulated, they are tested against the observable facts, flaws are discovered, new and better theories are invented to replace them. No one imagines that we could now define the set of all possible future theories of, say, physics. If we could do that, it should be possible to work through them systematically and find which fits the facts best; that done, physics would be complete. But few people seriously suppose that the sciences will ever come to an end: we go on evolving better and better theories, but the ultimate theory is like the pot of gold at the end of the rainbow. Only rarely in science does a theory which had been known about all along but judged inferior to the accepted theory end up replacing the latter. Commonly, when a theory is dethroned, the new theory combines ideas which had never before been thought to have any relationship with one another.

If we agree with this view of science, the invention of a theory is a genuinely original act which could not in principle be predicted. And, if we think of science this way, we may well feel that the parallel between the evolution of scientific theories and the evolution of biological species is compelling enough for us to regard the latter process also as unpredictable in principle. Certainly, if we contemplate a contemporary species and the environment it has to contend with, we may guess at possible future improvements in the traits it already possesses – if it is a bird of prey, perhaps its wings will become stronger, its eyes acuter – but we hardly know how to predict the appearance of whole new organs. If we lived at a time when birds had not yet appeared, would we formulate as a future possibility the notion of flappable planes of flesh, bone, and feathers which allow their possessor to move through the air?

Commonly, people have thought of human language as simply a particularly well developed example of the communication systems possessed by many species – the cries of various birds, the bee dances already mentioned, and so on. In that case, the development of human language would be analogous to the case of relatively weak wings in an early species evolving into stronger wings in descendant species: language would offer no special difficulties with respect to emergence. But it is a consequence of Chomsky's findings about linguistic universals that there no longer seems to be a useful sense in which we can assign human language to one point on a scale on which other communication systems occupy lower points: if we chose to do this, we would not know how to interpret the scale. Human languages are, admittedly, quite complex; but what is interesting about them is not their complexity – indeed, this often obscures the logically-arbitrary features which make them really interesting. So, for Chomsky, human language does seem to be a case of emergence, and thus to pose a problem for Darwinism.

Some scholars condemn the whole doctrine of 'emergentism' as conceptually confused, and suggest that if one tries to clarify it it falls to pieces. I am inclined to accord emergentism more respect; indeed, in later chapters I shall use it to construct arguments *against* Chomsky. However, if the doctrine does hold water, there is nothing original in Chomsky's use of it to demonstrate limitations in the theory of evolution: emergentism is a quite standard objection to Darwin. My analogy between the evolution of species and that of scientific theories is borrowed from Sir Karl Popper, who argues that what makes humans distinctively human is that, instead of evolving more or less successful biological innovations in response to environmental pressures, humans produce new scientific hypotheses to 'perish in our stead'. Popper lays great stress on the creativeness of scientific theorizing: he and other writers apply the same term, 'tautologous', to Darwin's theory which Chomsky uses in his turn. All Chomsky has done with respect to biology is to show that human language seems to be another example of a long-recognized class of problems.

Nor is it clear that any of this constitutes an objection to Darwinism. It has been standard to think of prediction as the essence of scientific explanation; but Michael Scriven suggests that the importance of Darwin for our understanding of science is precisely that he provides a model of explanation without prediction. There is much that Darwin never set out to explain (for instance, the reason why variations, which might or might not be advantageous, should ever occur in inheritance at all); the emergentism doctrine does not seem to show that Darwin failed to explain anything he aimed to explain. At most it serves as an antidote to the widespread notion that Darwin has dispelled all the mysteries connected with biological evolution, by suggesting that what Darwin left untouched is at least as mysterious as the problem he solved. Indeed, the emergentists claim that the problem of predicting future developments cannot be solved by any possible theory: so they can hardly criticize Darwin's theory for failing to solve it!

The existence of human language poses more specific problems for Darwinism than the philosophical problem of emergence. For instance, we have admitted that natural languages are quite complex systems; but Darwinian evolution proceeds by tiny changes, each of which must be useful to the species in itself, rather than merely as a step on the path to a fully developed complex trait. We have said that there is no obvious continuum leading from the communication systems of non-human species to human language as a higher stage of the same class of dispositions, so it is difficult to see by what path language-using men could have evolved from non-language-using ancestors. But, again, this is simply one more example of a well-known type of problem about Darwinism. Darwin himself devoted much of the *Origin of Species* to countering the objection that his theory cannot account for complex traits which are useful only when all their components are present simultaneously. Darwin's approach was to take a couple of difficult examples – he chose the human eye, and the disposition of bees to build honeycombs of a particular shape – and to suggest plausible paths by which they could have developed step by step. It is by no means clear that Darwin's treatment of the objection is satisfactory, but Chomsky's discussion of language does not appear to increase the difficulties that already exist. Even Chomsky's specific claim that Darwinism fails to explain Man's intellectual abilities (including language) is far from original: the point was argued at length by Darwin's contemporary A. R. Wallace.

This concludes our outline of Chomsky's claims about the implications of his theory of language. In the next chapter we begin to examine the structure of this theory.

By the end of the book the reader will, we hope, agree that Chomsky is quite justified in most of the positive claims he makes about language: in particular, that we use the kind of language we do because we are built that way, and that we may deduce a great deal about the kind of machine a human mind is from an examination of human language. As we have seen in this chapter, however, when Chomsky turns from his independent theorizing about language to criticism of the views of others, his touch becomes less sure. It seems a pity that Chomsky spends so much of his time tilting at psychological, philosophical, and biological windmills; but perhaps this is a necessary feature of his pattern of thinking, and it is certainly far better to have Chomsky's positive ideas mixed with the negative material than not to have them at all. One of the aims of this book is to persuade the reader not to let his objections to Chomsky's remarks on peripheral issues put him off Chomsky's views on the subject with which he is chiefly concerned, linguistics.

3

The Scope of Linguistic Descriptions

Chomsky's theory of language is essentially a theory about *syntax*, that is, about how words are put together to form sentences.

Any given sentence can be viewed as a sequence, or *string*, of elements drawn from some stock of basic units. For instance, we may treat the English sentence **She walked to the door** as a string of twenty-two elements drawn from the set of characters (including 'space') on a typewriter keyboard, as a string of twelve sounds, or as a string of five words drawn from the English vocabulary. Rather than letters, sounds, or words, it is convenient for our purposes to use as basic units what are called *formatives*, i.e. the stems and inflectional suffixes which in English are run together as single words. Thus the sentence cited will be treated as a string of six formatives: **she walk -ed to the door**; and, if the verb were the irregular **went**, this would be treated as a pair of formatives **go -ed** by analogy with regular verbs like **walked**. A full account of the English language will of course have to say not only how formatives can be arranged to form sentences, but also how sequences of formatives such as **go -ed** are realized as written or spoken words. But this latter problem is a fairly trivial one of little general interest, and we shall ignore it. (Where the word/ formative distinction is not crucial, we shall often speak of 'words'.)

There are problems in the assumption that we may treat sentences as strings of elements. For instance, presumably we shall want the contrasting intonation patterns of **She walked to the door?** *v.* **She walked to the door.** to count as elements of the respective sentences, but it is not clear that the intonation can be regarded as occurring at any particular point in the sequence of words. This kind of problem becomes more salient in languages such as the Semitic ones, where root and grammatical inflection are indicated by the consonants and vowels, respectively, of a single word. Thus, in Hebrew, **lomed** means 'studying' and **lamad** 'studied'; we can distinguish the root formative **l-m-d** 'study' from the '-ing' and '-ed' formatives **-o-e-** and **-a-a-** respectively, but we have no grounds for treating **l-m-d** as preceding **-o-e-** or vice versa.

However, in such cases we can simply make an arbitrary decision: e.g. in Hebrew we can choose to regard the root as preceding the inflectional formative, and in English we may choose to treat the intonation pattern as the last formative of the sentence (in line with the writing system, which puts the question mark or full stop at the end). Since sentences of human languages are overwhelmingly linear, it is much simpler to treat them as if they were completely linear (adding a clause or two to our descriptions of various languages to take care of the few cases in which linearity is violated) than to develop a whole new analytic system specifically designed to handle non-linear sentences. Nothing is going to hang on linearity (we shall not, for instance, be citing the linearity of sentences as a linguistic universal), so this procedure is harmless.

The next assumption made by the theory is far more open to objection, however, and we shall spend much of this chapter defending it. Having identified sentences with strings of formatives, Chomsky goes on to identify languages with sets of sentences. That is, Chomsky treats 'English' as simply a name for a certain set of strings of formatives: the set which count as grammatical English sentences, as opposed to strings such as **Of of the of** which do not constitute sentences of English. The set of strings called 'English' may have infinitely many members: but any given sequence of English formatives must be either in it or outside it.

Let us for the time being suspend our scepticism about this way of looking at languages. Accepting that one can choose to treat a human language as a set of strings of formatives (as a *stringset*, let us say for short), what does Chomsky's linguistics do with this notion?

In the first place, linguistics aims to provide a specification of any stringset that occurs as a human language – the stringset called 'English', the stringset called 'French', the stringset called 'Chinese', and so on. A specification e.g. of the stringset called 'English' is known as a *grammar* of English. A grammar of English will be a body of statements which, taken together, classify the set of all possible strings of English formatives into two subsets: a subset claimed to be grammatical in English, and a subset claimed to be ungrammatical. Any grammar actually produced by a linguist may turn out to imply an incorrect classification, of course; but the linguist constructing a grammar of English aims to produce a body of statements which classify the grammatical sentences of English as grammatical and the ungrammatical strings as ungrammatical.

There is an obvious question: how do we find out which strings are or are not grammatical, in order to test the accuracy of the grammar? Briefly, we discover that a string is grammatical in English by hearing an Englishman say it (or by coming across it in a piece of English writing); to say that a string is ungrammatical in English is to predict that no English speaker will ever utter it.* However, I return to this question in the next chapter, since Chomsky's answer is radically different from the one I have given. Let me just add here that, when we use the term 'grammatical', the distinction we have in mind is not between what we are taught at school to be correct and what some of us actually utter in our careless moments. The sense in which one might call **The play is hard to fully understand** 'ungrammatical' by contrast with **The play is hard to understand fully** is irrelevant here. Rather, we refer to the distinction between what we might utter, at any level of formality, and what we would simply not think of uttering – the difference e.g. between either of the sentences just quoted, and the string of **Of of the of.** Split infinitives are objectionable, perhaps, because they violate an accepted rule of good style; but it makes little difference to linguistic theory whether we choose to describe stylistically pure or stylistically slipshod English. What is wrong with **Of of the of** is not that it is stylistically faulty: it just is not English at all, even though composed of English words.

---

* I shall use the term *utter* as an abbreviation for 'say or write': the distinction between the two linguistic media has no importance in Chomsky's syntactic theory.

A grammar of a language defines that language by dividing the set of possible strings into a grammatical and an ungrammatical subset. In Chomskyan linguistics, the construction of grammars is a means towards the construction of a general *theory of language*, which is a body of statements that divide the *set of possible stringsets*, or the set of possible languages, into two classes: a class of 'natural' languages and a class of 'unnatural' languages.

As we have seen, Chomsky believes that there exist properties common to all the various human languages, and that this is because languages must have certain properties in order to fit our innate psychological apparatus. Let us call the languages which infant humans would be capable of learning to use as their mother tongue the *natural* languages; and let us call the languages which are actually used by groups of humans (e.g. English, Chinese) or which have been used in recorded history (e.g. Latin), the *attested* languages. Each attested language must by definition be a natural language, but it seems unlikely that every natural language is attested. New languages have developed from old ones throughout history, and no doubt this process will continue. Indeed, it may well be that there are infinitely many natural languages. We may reasonably assume, however, that the attested languages are a fair sample of the natural languages. To show what makes a language 'natural', we have to classify the set of possible languages – the set of all stringsets – into two classes, in such a way that all the attested languages fall into one of the classes. By adopting such a classification, we are predicting that no language from the second class – no language we classify as 'unnatural' – will ever be found to occur as an attested language. To claim that there exist 'universals of human language' is precisely to claim that there exists a classification which meets these conditions, and in which the 'natural' class of languages is small relative to the set of all possible languages.

The notion of a general theory of language, which defines 'naturalness' for stringsets as a grammar defines 'grammaticality' for strings, is a very abstract one. To make the problem more concrete, let me give an example of a language which the theory of language will predict to be unnatural. Take some vocabulary – say, the words of Chinese. Now consider the set of all strings of Chinese words whose length is a prime number. Thus, the string **Ni lai le** will be in the set, as will the string **Ni ni ni** (3 is prime); **Ta xi huan chi tang** and **Tang lai lai ta ta** will both be in the set (5 is prime); but **Ta ta ta ta**, or **Xiao ying guo qi che fei chang piao liang**, will be outside the set (4 and 9 are non-prime). Let us call this set the *prime-number language*.

Now, the prime-number language is a well-defined stringset and thus counts as a 'possible language' by Chomsky's definition. But I imagine most readers will feel, as I do, that the prime-number language is hopelessly 'unnatural' as a human language, and will happily predict that no group of humans will ever be found to speak the prime-number language as their mother tongue. And notice that this reaction to the prime-number language is not a consequence of the fact that sentences which are grammatical in it use words in a way which clashes with their use in the genuine, attested language from which they are borrowed. Presumably most of my readers come to the prime-number language with no prejudices about the correct usage of **ni** or **lai**; yet, just on the basis of the information I have given, they see that there is something very peculiar about this language. One may readily invent further examples: thus, we can use the name *odd-token language* for the set of strings meeting the condition that no word can be repeated an even number of times, so that **Ta chi fan** and **Ta chi fan chi cai chi tang** are grammatical but **Ta chi fan chi cai** is ungrammatical. Again, the odd-token language is a stringset but clearly not a natural human language. Length of sentences, or number of occurrences of individual words, are just not the sort of factors which determine grammaticality in human languages.

To recognize the weirdness of the prime-number language or the odd-token language is easy enough. What is not so easy is to make explicit just what characteristics of stringsets distinguish these languages, and other equally unnatural examples, from the natural languages. To put it another way, it is very far from obvious how to define a class of natural stringsets which rules out examples like the prime-number language, the odd-token language, and all the other unnatural stringsets which one could think up, without at the same time ruling out some of the quite diverse languages which are in fact attested around the world.

It is this task which Chomsky's general theory of language aims to carry out. A grammar defines a stringset; so, by defining a class of grammars, we indirectly define a class of stringsets. Chomsky's theory of language consists of a definition of a class of grammars: by putting his theory forward, Chomsky predicts that the best grammar linguists can construct for any attested language will turn out to be one of the grammars allowed by his definition. The natural languages, Chomsky claims, are just those stringsets for which his theory provides grammars; and these languages are rare among the set of all stringsets, in other words there exist strong universal constraints on natural languages.

Even if we accept the assumption that human languages can be treated as stringsets, there is a problem about the goal of the general theory of language: what counts as an individual attested language? For instance, there are strings which Englishmen utter but Americans do not, e.g. **Her skin had spots on**, and strings which Americans utter but Englishmen do not, e.g. **The pool is in back of the house**; should we treat American English and English English as two different languages, and provide them with similar but not identical grammars, or should we construct a single grammar which permits both of these examples? More generally, how are we to parcel up the utterances that can be observed all over the world into groups which count as one language each for purposes of testing the theory of language?

The language v. dialect issue is a thorny one, which I do not want to take up here. There are compensating advantages and disadvantages in alternative choices. If we are very severe in our criteria for what counts as one language, so that most individual people are treated as speaking slightly differing languages, then we shall have a very large number of languages against which to check the predictions of our theory of language; but our grammar of each individual language will be correspondingly unreliable, since it will have been constructed on the basis of relatively limited data. In practice, we will do better to identify a 'language' with, say, the speech of a nation, rather than with the 'idiolect' (i.e. one-man dialect) of an individual: then it will be easy to check the accuracy of our grammars, and there will still be plenty of different languages to test our theory of language against. In the American-English/ English-English case and the like, we can make an arbitrary decision: we expect the general theory of language to hold true for any reasonable decision about what counts as one language.

We must now return to the question to which we drew attention earlier in the chapter: is it reasonable to treat a human language as simply a set of strings of words?

There are two kinds of objection to this way of looking at language, each of which has considerable force, and neither of which has been adequately discussed within linguistics. Eventually, I believe, both can be answered; but this will be possible only if we recognize the strength of the objections. The first objection is that to identify a human language with the set of word-sequences which are grammatical in that language is to close one's eyes to a huge proportion of the facts of language: indeed, one may well feel that the material ignored by Chomskyan linguistics includes just the facts that make language worth studying. The second objection is that to treat a human language as a fixed set of sentences is positively to misrepresent the nature of language as a flexible, living medium of communication.

We shall consider these criticisms in turn, beginning with the charge that we are ignoring valid data. Whether it counts as an objection or not, this statement is certainly quite true. Consider some of the many aspects of language which will find no place in a theory dealing in specifications of stringsets. In the first place we would be ignoring the meanings of the sentences we describe, although in fact our definition of the scope of linguistics will be broadened later in the book to encompass meaning. But we shall continue to ignore completely all the social dimension of language: for instance, the fact that some sentences are more appropriate than others in given social settings for reasons having nothing to do with their meaning; that the structure of a conversation may serve the function of determining social relationships among the group who participate in it, independently of its function of communicating particular ideas; and many other sociological

44

properties of language. We shall, further, be blind to the aesthetic properties of language. For us there will be no interesting difference between the sentences of Ernest Hemingway and Henry James; these, together with the remarks of the barmaid in the public bar, and the stilted phrases of the regulations about Value Added Tax, will rank equally as examples of English sentences to be specified by our grammar of English. Even such elementary facts as statistics of frequency will be left out of account. I know the word **car** and the word **helicopter**, but I use the former much more frequently, and for obvious reasons; for the linguist, though, **car** and **helicopter** are simply two English words of the same syntactic class.

One could go on; but already the reader may feel that, if Chomsky's theory ignores all this, then it has nothing to offer him. I shall argue, however, that the narrowness of the linguist's field of vision turns out to be a positive advantage.

In the first place, the fact that Chomsky's theory ignores certain data cannot be a criticism of its validity as a scientific theory. One can never predict, before a new theory is created, what sorts of data will turn out to fall under its purview. Consider Newton's invention of the theory of gravity. Here was a theory that dealt with such data as the motions of the various planets, the ebb and flow of the tides, and the behaviour of cannon-balls and apples. One can imagine a sceptical contemporary of Newton objecting: 'I seek to understand the mysteries of the heavens, so when you claim to have a theory which tells me something new about astronomy I give it my attention. But I find that, while you talk about the *orbits* and *speeds* of the planets, you do not touch on some of their most interesting properties – for instance, you nowhere explain why Venus is so brilliantly white while Mars is red; and you never attempt to relate the different planets with the characters and fortunes of the people born under them. On the other hand, much of your treatise concerns trivial matters such as apples and cannon-balls, in which I have no interest. I ask for bread and you give me a stone: your theory is worthless!'

One would understand such a criticism, but at the same time one sees that it is misguided. *A priori* one might well suppose that the movements of the planets, their appearance, and the times of birth and subsequent character of individual people belonged together as a class of facts which should be explained by an integrated theory; while the behaviour of dull, sublunary objects such as apples might seem to have little to do with the majestic, unchanging cycles of the celestial bodies. Now that we look back after centuries of acceptance of Newton's theory, we see that this supposition is simply false: the movements of Mars and the movements of a decaying Worcester Pearmain do belong together in a class of naturally related phenomena, whereas the redness of Mars, or the choleric disposition of one's father, although requiring explanation, are not facts which connect in any way with this class of phenomena. Scientific theories are the things which *tell* us what facts belong together; one cannot criticize a theory for omitting to discuss particular phenomena, but only for saying things that are untrue about the phenomena it does deal with.

However, the sceptical reader may feel that this misses the point: his criticism of Chomsky's theory will be not that it is false, rather that it is perhaps true as far as it goes but uninteresting.

Here one must reply that what makes a scientific theory interesting is not the *data* on which the theory is based, but rather the theoretical *conclusions* which are drawn from those data. What could be more banal than the fact that a heavy cannon-ball and a light musket-ball, dropped simultaneously from a tower, reach the ground almost simultaneously? – yet it was on the basis of facts of this order that Galileo, Newton and others created a theory of physics which not only has taken men to the moon and back but is widely felt to be one of the most stimulating and satisfying achievements of the human intellect. In chapter 2 we discussed a number of implications for matters of general interest which Chomsky derives from his theory of language. I suggested that, although some of Chomsky's claims were unjustified, others are sound. If it is at all plausible that one can draw the conclusions Chomsky does from the syntactic facts with which he deals – even admitting that, conceivably, all of Chomsky's arguments may turn out to be invalid after all – then this seems to be quite adequate justification for studying syntax.

The success of linguistics in telling us something genuinely novel about ourselves is due in large part to exactly this restriction of scope, which enables linguistics to avoid a problem that has bedevilled many of the other social sciences. It is often objected that what are called 'social sciences' are not true sciences: that they merely classify, rather than making assertions. The assumption behind this comment is Popper's principle that the essence of science is *refutability*. A scientific theory must state that certain logically conceivable situations are scientifically impossible, so that the theory can be refuted if those situations are observed. We cannot refute a theory merely by failing to observe something which it treats as possible – perhaps we just have not looked far enough; but we refute it at once if we observe something which it treats as impossible. The best theory will be the *strongest*, i.e. the theory which rules out the largest number of possibilities and is thus most vulnerable to refutation. Refutability is desirable, because only by being refutable in principle (while not refuted in practice) does a theory tell us anything about the world. A theory which permitted all possibilities would be safe from refutation, but would tell us nothing.

We may illustrate this point by a simple example. The statement 'If one drops an apple it either moves or remains still' rules out no possibility and is thus worthless. 'If one drops an apple it moves downwards' is better, because it rules out the case of an apple moving in other directions or remaining motionless in mid-air. 'If one drops an apple it accelerates downwards at 32 feet per second per second' is better still, since it rules out everything forbidden by the previous statement together with cases of apples falling at other rates of acceleration.

It follows that a science which provides a vocabulary enabling us to describe or classify the situations which can be observed, if it does no more than that, does nothing. For a science we need a vocabulary enabling us to describe a range of *logically possible* situations which includes those that occur in practice, but also includes many situations that are never realized. Then the science can make a refutable assertion by drawing a boundary round some subset of the situations which can be described in its vocabulary, and saying, 'All the describable situations outside this boundary are impossible.' A chief requirement for a scientific theory is that it must provide a means of describing impossible states of affairs.

To invent a descriptive system of this kind is not a particularly natural activity. One difficulty is that our everyday languages embody many assumptions about reality. To continue with our example, one would like to say that the sentence 'John dropped an apple and it moved upwards' describes a logically possible state of affairs which is permitted by the first of the three cited mini-theories but forbidden by the other two; but it may seem that the statement is actually *contradictory*, i.e. fails to describe a logically possible state of affairs, since one may feel that it is part of the *meaning* of 'drop' that dropped things fall.

Experience has shown that the most successful strategy is to invent a system in which what counts as a description of a given 'state of affairs' is as simple as possible. Thus, in the theory of gravity, a 'state-description' (description of a given state of affairs) consists just of a statement of the mass, position, and direction and rate of acceleration of each of a set of bodies. For instance, each of the following statements constitutes an exhaustive state-description of a simple physical system:

(1) Two one-tonne bodies one kilometre apart in equilibrium.

(2) Two one-tonne bodies one kilometre apart accelerating towards each other at 0.000000067 metres per second per second.

(3) Two one-tonne bodies one kilometre apart accelerating away from each other at 0.0000035 metres per second per second.

Any physical system, even one comprising only two bodies, will have many more properties than these statements mention: the bodies will be of such and such sizes and colours, made of such and such materials, and so on. However, by resolutely ignoring everything but mass, position, and acceleration, it becomes easy to specify precisely a range of *logically*-possible state-descriptions, so that the theory can then demarcate a subset of these as privileged, and say '(2) (e.g.) is *physically* possible, but (1) and (3) (e.g.) are physically impossible'.

The social sciences, on the other hand, commonly proceed in a different way, and suffer as a result. Consider, for instance, sociology. I criticized Chomsky in chapter 2 for attacking scholars working in disciplines he is not fully conversant with, and I have no wish to commit the same mistake; certainly my criticisms of sociology do not apply to the work of scholars such as Durkheim, nor no doubt to the best modern sociologists. But it is perhaps not too controversial to say that a good proportion of the conclusions which emerge from contemporary sociological research, when shorn of their technical jargon, express nothing more than fairly obvious generalizations which an intelligent layman will have worked out for himself without benefit of sociological training. (One thinks, for instance, of a recent sociological research project which went to some trouble to discover that the main reason why we send our acquaintances Christmas cards is to remind each other of our continued existence, rather than to commemorate the Nativity.)

This becomes relatively understandable when we consider what motivates the typical sociologist. The young man who decides to study sociology is aware of the tremendous achievements of physics and the other 'hard' sciences. He contemplates the varied facets of human interaction – foreman/worker tensions on the production line, young people courting, relations between the races, cocktail-party behaviour, and, if you will, the exchange of Christmas cards; and, for very laudable reasons, he feels that there ought to be a science which does for these phenomena what physics does for inanimate matter. Often, the budding sociologist wants to develop pure sociology as a means to an end, because he cares about the shortcomings of contemporary societies and hopes sociology can show him the cure. Since he is emotionally committed to his chosen field of study, in a way that the physicist is not emotionally involved with his falling apples and beams of light, the sociologist will be unwilling to restrict his focus of attention. He wants a theory that ties up all the fascinating details into one comprehensible bundle.

But this is not how science works. One does not first choose a category of data and then look for a theory to explain those data; rather, first an original mind produces a new theory, and then the theory itself tells us what class of data is relevant to it. If one refuses to look away from the fascinating complexity of social reality, one will hardly be able to set up a descriptive system which specifies anything akin to the range of state-descriptions of physical theories; and thus one will not be able to demarcate a class of impossible social states of affairs. The sociologist will be limited to constructing a vocabulary which makes distinctions between different types of social states or affairs which do occur; and there is more to science than that.

Compare this with Chomsky's theory of language. A language, for Chomsky, is merely a stringset: the specification of a stringset plays the role of the state-descriptions of the physical example. Now it is very easy to suggest impossible state-descriptions: for instance, the prime-number language, the odd-token language. Notice that it is only by permitting us to describe linguistic impossibilities that Chomsky tells us anything new about human language. The positive properties which he attributes to the natural languages will not include anything very surprising: we live with these languages, and all linguistics does with them is to make explicit features with which we have been intuitively familiar all along. What is novel is the realization that these languages, whose properties seem so normal or even inevitable to us, are in fact only a handful among a much wider range of logically possible languages.

My picture of the methodological difference between linguistics and sociology has been deliberately exaggerated, in order to make my point clear. Undoubtedly sociology and other non-linguistic social sciences do produce refutable assertions, if often rather low-level ones. But the more austere the data of a science, the easier it will be for that science to make strong and therefore worthwhile statements. By contrast with most other social sciences, Chomsky's linguistics is extremely austere with respect to its data, and this austerity has paid off amply. Chomsky's conclusions, whether they eventually turn out to be right or wrong, far outweigh in novelty and significance anything implied by earlier, less austere theories of language.

There remains, however, the second objection: to treat languages as stringsets may be not merely to ignore many aspects of human language but to misrepresent the phenomena with which linguistics does aim to deal. This objection, clearly, is potentially the more damaging of the two. Chomsky takes it for granted from the outset that we may validly identify a human language with a set of sentences, and all his subsequent work is concerned with the problems of specifying such sets: if there is no sense in which a human language can be treated as a stringset, then the body of Chomsky's and his followers' work tells us nothing at all about human language – which is worse than telling us something true but uninteresting, as the first objection suggested.

There are two reasons why one might be unwilling to admit the possibility of identifying a human language with a stringset. Both reasons have been cited by the same linguist, Charles Hockett; however, Hockett's views have received quite inadequate consideration. The first reason is that grammaticality may be a gradient property; the second is that the stringset treatment ignores the creativity of language.

The point about gradience is the more widely appreciated, but the less worrying, of these two. The point is this: by defining 'English', say, as a particular set of strings of English words, Chomsky implies that any particular string either definitely is or definitely is not grammatical in English. This does not mean that the linguist will always *know* whether a given string is English or not; Chomsky suggests that there will be a number of clear cases, and the linguist should construct a grammar giving the correct answer for the clear cases and should allow the grammar itself to decide in the cases where the linguist is in doubt. If grammaticality is in fact a yes-or-no affair, this procedure is very reasonable. We need not assume *a priori*, though, that grammaticality must be a yes-or-no matter. The question 'Is such and such a string grammatical in English?' might be like the question 'Is such and such a body of water hot?' Some water we would unquestionably call hot – that in a saucepan which has just come off the boil, for instance – and some unquestionably cold – that in the stream leaving the foot of a glacier, for instance. But, if we are unwilling to say that some water is either hot or cold, it need not be because we do not know whether the water is hot or cold: it may be precisely because we know very well that it is lukewarm. What we look for from the scientist who sets out to discuss the hotness or coldness of liquids is not a method for dividing all bodies of liquid into two classes, but rather a linear *scale* of temperature which renders more precise the notion that liquids are *relatively* hotter or colder than one another.

There are sequences of English words which strike one as not quite right, but not definitely wrong either: **The child seems sleeping** is an often-quoted example. Should we not treat strings like this as genuinely intermediate between the poles of grammaticality and ungrammaticality, and think of the 'clear cases' as simply strings which happen to be relatively close to one of the two poles?

Perhaps we should. But Chomsky's claim is that this is not necessary: the facts of grammaticality can be handled quite adequately by grammars which simply divide strings into 'grammatical' and 'ungrammatical' subclasses, and any differences between the members of either one of these sub-classes will turn out to have independent explanations. For instance, according to Chomsky **The child seems sleeping** is simply ungrammatical: a native speaker of English will not utter it (unless that English speaker is a linguist citing an example of an unnatural utterance!). Certainly there is a clear difference between the mild oddity of **The child seems sleeping** and the stark incoherence of, e.g., **Of of the of**. But this can be explained by pointing out that **The child seems sleeping** is quite similar to various strings which are perfectly grammatical, e.g. **The child seems sleepy**, **The book seems interesting**, while **Of of the of** does not resemble any grammatical string. Since we can explain why **The child seems sleeping** is less peculiar than **Of of the of** from the fact that the former string is relatively similar to various strings which are grammatical, we do not need also to posit any difference in grammaticality between these two strings themselves.

Conceivably, this solution might not always work. There might be two strings, of which the less natural-sounding was actually the one which resembled more closely some fully grammatical sentence. Chomsky does not explicitly consider the possibility, but we may interpret him as implicitly predicting that such a situation will not in fact occur. We have seen that it is the scientist's job to make refutable assertions. Ideally, a scientist is aware of all the points at which his theory is vulnerable to refutation; but, in practice, all scientists take many of their empirical assumptions to be self-evident truisms. What matters is not whether the empirical status of a principle is appreciated by its author, but whether the principle can withstand the scrutiny of the scientific community. At present I would judge that the all-or-nothing view of grammaticality is one of the least problematical of Chomsky's assumptions.

The final objection to the 'language-as-stringset' doctrine is that it ignores the fact that the use of language is a 'creative' activity, in the sense that the arts, science and, I have suggested, biological evolution are creative.

It may seem odd to readers familiar with Chomsky's work to suggest that he ignores creativity, since Chomsky frequently emphasizes that his theory differs from those of his predecessors in placing great weight on the creative nature of linguistic behaviour. For instance, some psychologists have suggested that we learn our mother tongue by associating particular utterances as responses with particular stimuli in the shape of situations evoking those utterances. This model might account adequately for the communication systems of some species, which comprise a finite set of different calls each representing an atomic message – 'Danger!', 'Food!', and the like; but, Chomsky points out, sentences of human languages are constructed according to productive rules which in principle permit infinitely many different sentences. Most of the sentences we hear or read are being encountered by us for the first time, so our comprehension cannot depend on prior experience of those particular sentences: our linguistic ability enables us 'creatively' to extrapolate from sentences we have met to new sentences constructed in accordance with the same rules of grammar.

All this is true: but Chomsky's use of 'creative' in this connection differs sharply from the everyday use of the term. By a similar argument, I could call my ability to multiply pairs of numbers 'creative'. My ability to multiply, say, 2,897 by 374 is independent of my having met that particular problem before; rather, I do it by rules which in principle allow me to solve any of an infinitely large class of multiplication problems. Yet we would not in everyday speech call the solution of problems of simple arithmetic a 'creative' activity. Indeed, in the days when humans rather than machines were employed to do such tasks, this was regarded as a paradigm of 'uncreative' work, by contrast e.g. with the activities of the painter or the composer of music.

The dispute here is not about correct usage: Chomsky is entitled to use words as he sees fit. However, there is an important distinction which is in danger of being obscured. The relevant difference between multiplication problems and paintings has to do with definability. The rules for multiplication apply to each of infinitely many problems; nevertheless, the set of possible multiplication problems, with their correct working, is perfectly exactly defined in advance by the simple set of rules for solving them. There is no similar sense in which one can define a set of all possible paintings or a set of all possible symphonies (or, as we have seen, a set of all possible scientific theories or living organisms). When a painter produces a new picture, he does not simply choose a particular one out of a set of possibilities known in advance. If that were all that art consisted of, there would be little point in actually painting the picture: like the prisoners who were too debilitated to go to the trouble of telling each other their well-known stock of jokes, the painter would do better simply to announce 'Number 72!' to his admiring public. Art is not like this. Our notion of what counts as a painting is constantly redefined by the activity of painters. In each generation, reactionaries such as the present author regard the products of the avant-garde as simply not painting, or music, or whatever; obvious masters such as Beethoven or Cézanne encountered identical reactions in their day.

In a common sense of 'creative', then, a creative activity is one whose future products will typically fail to fall under a definition constructed to account for past instances. By treating human languages as well-defined sets of strings, Chomsky implies (again, without explicitly discussing the question) that the use of language is *not* in this sense a creative activity.

This is disturbing, because it conflicts with arguments by the linguists Edward Sapir and Benjamin Lee Whorf, and the philosopher Ludwig Wittgenstein, for the view that our linguistic behaviour is indeed creative in exactly the relevant sense. Sapir and Whorf made substantially the same point earlier and, in some ways, more clearly and concretely than Wittgenstein. However, Wittgenstein's version of the argument is the most directly relevant here, and the one which has had most influence on the subsequent development of the social sciences; so we shall discuss the issue in Wittgenstein's terms.

Wittgenstein considers the question of what determines whether a given word is applicable to a given phenomenon: his example is the word **game**. Any particular state of affairs that we are called on to express in speech will differ in some respects from states of affairs which we have previously experienced, while resembling them in other respects. One might imagine that there is some fixed set of criteria for calling something a **game**: we simply check the relevant properties of the new phenomenon and, if it resembles previously-encountered **games** in those respects, it is also a **game**; if not, not. But the obvious next questions would be: 'What are these fixed criteria, and how do speakers know what they are?' According to Wittgenstein (and I accept his argument), language is not like this: we call a new phenomenon a **game** if we can see it as analogous to **games** we have already encountered, but there is no limit on the ways we can analogize between phenomena. The properties possessed by any individual phenomenon are numberless; the construction of analogies between phenomena is a creative, 'open-ended' activity.*

Peter Winch has used this view of Wittgenstein's to argue that the very notion of 'social science' is a contradiction in terms. It is a consequence of Wittgenstein's view that human languages will not in general be intertranslatable. Rather than the vocabulary of each language referring to a stock of properties which can be defined independently of particular languages, for Wittgenstein a sentence of a given language acquires meaning only from the use to which it is creatively put in a particular human situation. If, say, English and French can be translated each into the other rather satisfactorily, this is only because the 'forms of life' of English and French speakers

---

* The reader may have noticed that, if Wittgenstein is right, then the statement quoted from Joos in chapter I about the unlimited diversity of languages is not self-contradictory after all; what Wittgenstein says about the word **game** might equally be applicable to the word **language**.

C

happen to be rather similar. Now a social *scientist* must describe the phenomena of a given society in a neutral language independent of the particular society under study, since it is essential for a science to abstract from particular instances; but a *social* scientist must describe just those aspects of what he observes which can be stated only in the language of the society observed. I can say that Mark placed a gold ring on Anne's finger in neutral observer's language, but I can say that Anne and Mark were married only in the language of the society to which Anne and Mark belong. The latter statement has no translation into the language of a society lacking the institution of marriage. Thus, according to Winch, it is impossible to describe one society in the language of a different society; hence no generalization between societies, and therefore no social science, is possible.

Winch's claim to have refuted the possibility of social science in general has been widely criticized as unsound. However, the assertion that Wittgenstein's views are incompatible with the existence of social sciences may seem to apply with particular force to linguistics. If a sequence of words acquires a use only by virtue of a 'creative' act, as Wittgenstein suggests, then the notion of a grammar with predictive consequences seems to be a mirage; and, if no grammars, then no Chomskyan theory of language.

Chomsky provides a partial answer to this question by drawing a sharp distinction between 'grammaticality' and 'sensicality'.* His famous example of a grammatical but nonsensical sentence is **Colourless green ideas sleep furiously.** Now, according to Chomsky, a grammar should distinguish grammatical from ungrammatical strings, but, among grammatical strings, should not attempt to distinguish sensical from nonsensical strings. A grammar of English must treat **Colourless green ideas sleep furiously** as being fully on a par with, e.g. **Brash young men argue vehemently**, while forbidding, e.g. **Of of the of** as, not simply nonsensical, but not even grammatical. (We return to the justification for this distinction in the next chapter.)

* I use *sensical* (rather than Chomsky's 'meaningful') as the opposite of 'non-sensical'.

The boundaries of *sensicality* may well be changing constantly through the creative use of language: Marvell gave a use to the phrase **green thought**, so why not **colourless green ideas**? This is irrelevant for Chomsky, who claims only that the boundaries of *grammaticality* remain fixed (except for quite infrequent changes), so that it does make sense to predict what will be grammatical in future on the basis of what has been grammatical up to now.

Wittgenstein discusses only sensicality rather than grammaticality, given that the distinction is a valid one.* But it is quite possible to suggest, as against Chomsky, that the boundaries of grammaticality are also determined creatively. Hockett has made just this point. He argues that speakers coin novel sentences by analogizing from sentences already encountered (an uncontroversial point), and he suggests that the range of possible *syntactic* analogies is intrinsically 'open-ended'. It is foolish to attempt to write a grammar to define what is and what is not English, since English-speakers change English in speaking English. There will no doubt be utterances which fit the pattern of previous utterances perfectly, without extending English syntax in any way; but there is no reason to treat these cases as the norm.

To illustrate the diversity of syntactic analogies available to speakers, Hockett quotes the example of a boy who was heard to say **It's three hot in here!** One sees what the boy meant: if **too hot** (**two hot**) is hot, **three hot** should be hotter still. But how could one hope to specify in advance all the analogies of this kind which speakers might seize on in order to construct new sentences?

The suggestion that human languages might be 'syntactically creative' in this way is a quite coherent one. However, Chomsky implies that the suggestion is incorrect. Isolated cases like the **three hot** example do not seem sufficient as grounds for rejecting Chomsky's view. After all, a mature English speaker would say **It's three hot** only as a joke; it is not clear that punning of this kind commonly leads to syntactic innovations being seriously accepted. Probably it is true to say that the

---

* Wittgenstein frequently writes about the 'grammar' of a given word, but what he means by this is 'how the word can be used in a *sensical* utterance'.

range of *conceivable* 'syntactic analogies' is unlimited. Chomsky, however, claims that human languages exploit only analogies of a very special type.

Consider the child who is learning how to form questions in English. Suppose the child has heard one example – he is aware, say, that **Is Mary coming?** is the question corresponding to **Mary is coming** – and he wants to extrapolate from this example to form a question from **John's mother must be asleep**. In other words, the child has to guess what string is to **John's mother must be asleep** as **Is Mary coming?** is to **Mary is coming**.

A priori there are many analogies he might hit on. **Is** is the second word of **Mary is coming**, so perhaps questions are formed by moving the second word of the statement to the front – in which case **John's mother must be asleep** would give the question **Mother John's must be asleep? Is** is also the shortest word of **Mary is coming**, so perhaps length is the relevant variable: but that hypothesis produces the question **Be John's mother must asleep?** Third, **is** is the main verb of **Mary is coming**, and this is in fact the relevant point: **must** is the main verb of the longer statement, so the question is **Must John's mother be asleep?**

According to Chomsky, of these three conceivable hypotheses (and it would not be difficult to think up further possibilities), the third is not only the one that happens to be correct for English, but the only one of the three which *could* be correct in any natural language (and accordingly the only one of the three which the child will try out). Human languages simply do not use rules involving properties such as 'second word' or 'shortest word', though they often use rules involving the much subtler concept 'main verb'. (This example is unnaturally simple; in practice a child will no doubt have heard more than one question, enabling him to eliminate many alternative hypotheses about the question-forming rule, before he tries uttering a question of his own. But the principle is unaffected; however many examples a child has heard, there will still be many alternative logically-possible hypotheses about the rules of his language, each of which is compatible with all his evidence.)

Chomsky is asserting, then, that despite the limitless diversity of *conceivable* syntactic analogies, natural languages use only analogies (or 'rules') of a particular well-defined type; much of linguistics consists of an attempt to specify precisely the range of analogies which occur in natural languages, and we shall return to this subject in chapter 5. Chomsky asserts, further, that at a given time an individual language uses only a specifiable, finite set of these analogies or rules: a grammar of a language consists largely of the specification of such a set. The rules of a language must change occasionally, or we would still be speaking Chaucerian English. But grammatical change is a quite infrequent occurrence, rather than being the normal state of affairs as Hockett suggests.

These assertions of Chomsky's are not necessarily correct. If linguists are consistently unsuccessful in producing either an adequate theory of language, or adequate grammars of individual languages, this will suggest that perhaps Chomsky is wrong and Hockett right. However, the present author judges that the success of linguistics so far has been great enough for Chomsky's view of syntactic behaviour as 'uncreative' to be a reasonable one. It is no criticism of Chomsky that his claims are not certain and may eventually prove to be mistaken. This vulnerability, as we have seen, is the penalty any scientific theory pays for being empirical, and hence worth holding.

4

The Evidence for Linguistic Theories

The evidence on which a linguistic theory is based, whether this is a theory about an individual language (what we are calling a *grammar*) or a general theory of language, consists of people's utterances. The data for a grammar of English are the utterances of English speakers; the data for a theory of language are the grammars of the various languages of the world, so that ultimately the general theory of language is again based on utterances.

This point might seem too obvious to be worth making. But in fact Chomsky, and linguists influenced by Chomsky, have taken a radically different line. According to Chomsky, grammars (and hence, eventually, the general theory of language) are based on people's 'intuitions' about, or 'knowledge' of, their native language. 'The empirical data that I want to explain [Chomsky says] are the native speaker's intuitions.'

If linguistics is indeed based on intuition, then it is not a science. The quotation from Chomsky just given is self-contradictory: whatever an 'intuition' is, it is not an *empirical* datum – not the sort of thing that can be checked by reference to experience. If a woman 'intuitively knows' that her fiancé is honest, and bases her decision to marry him on that intuitive feeling, one cannot quarrel with the feeling – she either has it or she does not, and if she says she feels it then nothing counts as evidence that she really does not feel it. One might, however, suggest that intuition without evidence is a poor basis for belief, and point out that there is plenty of empirical evidence that her fiancé is a crook.

Science relies exclusively on the empirical. The data for a scientific theory – say, a theory about electricity – consist not of statements like 'At time t it appeared to John that the voltmeter registered 100 volts', but of statements like 'At time t

the voltmeter registered 100 volts'. The latter is empirical: if anyone doubts that the report is accurate, one can find out who wrote it, inquire whether his eyesight is good and whether he is usually truthful, check that he does not call the ammeter the 'voltmeter', and so on. The former statement is uncheckable: if that is what John thought was happening, then that is what John thought.

It is fairly obvious why science refuses to use introspective data: they are hopelessly unreliable. Anyone who has studied a little psychology knows that what we see depends very largely on what we want or expect to see. Until a few centuries ago, men intuitively knew, as certainly as they knew anything, that the Earth is fixed and that the sun moves round it. If anyone doubted it, one could take him to a hill at sunset: he would see the sun dropping below the horizon, while the Earth remained steady. If his report 'I saw the sun move' counted as evidence for physics, there would be no question of adopting a theory which says that the sun stands still; if he saw things that way, then that is how he saw them. But the physicist will listen to him only if he reports, 'The sun moved': and then it is open to the physicist to reply, 'How can you be sure?', 'Might it not have been the Earth that was moving?', and so on.

Someone who advances a scientific theory commonly has a certain emotional commitment to it; by a very normal process of wishful thinking, the theorist is likely to interpret his perceptions in ways that are favourable to his theory, and to overlook or distort unfavourable evidence. There is nothing dishonest about this; we all act in this way, even though we try not to. Conversely, when a theory is well established there is glory to be won by overthrowing it, so the young scholar is under emotional pressure to see counter-examples where, perhaps, none really exist.

If we ask scientists to avoid succumbing to these pressures, we ask the impossible. The only solution is to insist that all the statements occurring in science – the statements used as evidence for a theory, as well as the theory itself – be statements about external reality rather than about an individual's inner mental world, so that if any datum is doubted it can be checked. This means that scientific data are 'provisional' and open to criticism, just as scientific theories are; but that cannot be helped. To borrow a metaphor of Popper's, knowledge is an edifice built on piles driven into a swamp; nowhere does it touch bedrock certainty, but if any of the supports are unsteady they can always be driven in deeper.

The methodology of psychology and related disciplines, then, must be 'behaviourist' rather than 'mentalist', in the sense of chapter 2. If Chomsky's linguistic theories are really based on nothing more reliable than people's intuitive beliefs about their languages, then the theories are worthless. Chomsky and other contemporary linguists certainly think that linguistics could not do without introspective data. Fortunately, when we examine their reasons for thinking this, we find that they do not stand up. Although much of current linguistics is claimed to rest purely on intuitive data, the same results can be justified from empirical evidence.

Why, then, do linguists believe that they need the evidence of introspection?

In the first place, there is a problem about negative instances. A grammar is a system of statements which classify strings into a grammatical set and an ungrammatical set. If we hear an Englishman utter some string, we know that string must be in the grammatical set; but we cannot infer that a string is ungrammatical just because we have not heard it – perhaps we have not waited long enough. In view of this asymmetry, would our best move not be to choose a grammar which treats *all* strings as grammatical? The statement 'Every string of the following formatives is grammatical in English' (followed by a list of the English vocabulary) is a very simple grammar; and it can never be refuted. We discover that a grammar is wrong only by hearing an utterance which the grammar does not permit; this grammar permits everything, so it is quite secure against refutation. Yet an English speaker knows full well that not every sequence of English words is English; to continue with our previous example, we all know that **Of of the of** is not English. There seems to be an impasse here. The suggestion is that we should solve it by requiring the grammar to declare ungrammatical the strings which English-speakers know to be ungrammatical, so that we have a motive for making the grammar exclude **Of of the of**.

But we have no need of this 'solution' to the impasse. We

have seen that scientific theories in general are required to be as strong as possible, and a grammar of English is no exception. If we refute a grammar by hearing an utterance which the grammar forbids, then a 'strong' grammar is one that permits few utterances. In other words, we want a grammar of English that defines the narrowest possible range of strings as grammatical, providing it permits everything we actually hear; and this gives us a motive for excluding **Of of the of** independently of our intuitions.

However, in solving one problem we may appear to have created a new one. If our aim is to construct the strongest possible grammar permitting the strings we have observed, will our best move not be simply to list the strings we have heard and to say that they and only they are grammatical in English? However much data we have collected, we will never have observed every possibility. To take a simple if banal example, perhaps we have heard utterances of **Boys like girls, Boys like pets, Girls like boys**, but we happen not to have heard, say, **Girls like pets**. Any English-speaker knows that the latter sentence is fully as grammatical as the other three, but what motive can we have for constructing our grammar accordingly? A grammar which permits the string **Girls like pets** is that much less strong than one which forbids it; apparently we are justified in treating **Girls like pets** as grammatical only if we require the grammar to permit all the sentences which the native speaker 'knows' to be grammatical.

Not so. There is a general principle of scientific methodology which bids us choose *simple* theories; one can almost define 'science' as the process of reducing apparently complex phenomena to simple patterns. Consider, for instance, a physicist investigating the relationship between two measurable quantities (elapsed time and temperature in some physical process, or the like). He takes several measurements and plots the results on a graph, and finds that the points lie almost but not exactly on a straight line. Now the physicist will draw a straight line passing as near as possible to the various points, and will adopt a theory which states that the quantities are related by the simple equation corresponding to the line he has drawn. He will explain away the slight deviations of the points from the line as due to inaccuracies in the experimental situation – perhaps

63

his clock or his thermometer are slightly imperfect. The physicist is not forced to do this. Mathematically, it is always possible to find a complex equation defining a curve which passes through the points exactly; so the physicist might choose a theory embodying that complex equation rather than the linear equation. Such a theory would actually be stronger than the 'linear' theory. The complex theory allows the physicist to predict that future points will lie exactly on the curve; the linear theory permits him only to predict that they will fall near the line (since previous observations were close to rather than exactly on it). But, provided the points fall fairly near the line, the physicist will invariably regard the simplicity of the linear theory as outweighing the slightly greater strength of the complex theory.

Now let us return to the sentences about boys, girls and pets. We can describe the sentences we intuitively feel to be grammatical by saying something like 'A sequence of noun, **-s**, transitive verb, noun, **-s** is grammatical; **boy, girl**, and **pet** are nouns; **like** is a transitive verb.' To rule out **Girls like pets**, which we have not observed, we must insert a further clause after the word 'grammatical', say, 'except when the first noun, verb, and second noun are respectively **girl, like**, and **pet**'. To add this clause to the grammar is a considerable extra complication, which would be justified only if it made the grammar very much stronger; since it affects only one string, the loss of simplicity is too great to tolerate.

There is nothing mysterious about this notion of 'simplicity'. When we say that we want linguistic descriptions to be as simple as possible, we are using the word in a perfectly everyday sense; one does not need to be a philosopher to agree that one body of statements is simpler than another, if the second contains all the clauses of the first together with an extra one. To say precisely what makes a scientific theory simple, and just how we are to trade theoretical simplicity and theoretical strength off against one another, is a very difficult problem; but it is not one that the linguist need concern himself with, since it is a general problem of the philosophy of science. For the practising scientist, whether physicist or linguist, it is sufficient to trust his intuitive judgement to tell him how to balance strength and simplicity. This is where intuition is admissible in science: in deciding how best to account for the facts, not in deciding what the facts are.

Chomsky has made some confusing and contradictory remarks, to the effect that *a priori* notions of 'simplicity' or 'elegance' are not relevant to the choice between scientific theories, and that the only concept of 'simplicity' relevant in linguistics will be a concept to emerge from empirical linguistic research. But Chomsky is wrong. The standard sciences depend crucially on an *a priori* notion of simplicity of theories, and the same is undoubtedly true for linguistics. (Cf. p. 104, below.)

So far, then, we have seen two cases where the data of speech seemed to be inadequate as evidence for the grammar of English, so that English-speakers' intuitions had to be used instead; and in each case it turns out that, when we take into account standard methodological considerations about what makes one theory better than another, the empirical evidence is quite adequate after all.

However, linguists who defend the use of intuitive data have a stronger argument. So far we have assumed that the grammar must permit everything which is actually observed, and we have seen that methodological considerations justify us in treating some of the strings that we have *not* observed as grammatical, others as ungrammatical. But my opponents may point out that all linguists (including the present author) also treat as *ungrammatical* some strings which they *have* observed; in other words, sometimes we ignore refutations. Here the criteria of strength and simplicity seem irrelevant, since we want theories to be strong and simple only so long as they are not refuted (otherwise no scientist would ever need to look at any evidence at all).

A particularly straightforward example would be, say, someone who spots a saucepan boiling over and breaks off in mid-sentence to attend to it. She was going to say **If the phone rings, could you answer it?**, but she only gets as far as **If the phone**. One does not usually think of **If the phone** as an English sentence, and a linguist's grammar of English will not treat it as grammatical; but why not, since it was after all uttered? We cannot assume that every utterance which is

65

immediately followed by a flustered grab at an overflowing saucepan is ungrammatical; sometimes, a speaker will notice an emergency just as he reaches what would in any case have been the end of his sentence.

Again, the orthodox linguist answers that, if the evidence for a grammar is behaviour, then we have no grounds for excluding from the set of grammatical strings anything that is uttered; if we want to call **If the phone** 'ungrammatical', then we must base our grammar on our 'intuitive knowledge' that **If the phone** is incomplete. But, again, this attitude represents a misunderstanding of the nature of science.

The misunderstanding in this case has to do with the way in which the various branches of knowledge are mutually inter-dependent. Our grammar says that **If the phone** is ungram-matical, and thereby predicts that, *other things being equal*, **If the phone** will not be uttered. But other things are not equal. Our theories confront reality in a body, not one by one; each individ-ual branch of knowledge makes predictions about observable facts only when we take into account other relevant pieces of knowledge. Now, quite apart from linguistics, we know as a fact about human behaviour that we often interrupt one task when a higher-priority task intervenes. Given this knowledge, we can predict that we will sometimes hear strings which constitute the beginnings of grammatical sentences with-out their ends. As long as the grammar treats **If the phone rings, could you answer it?** as grammatical, we *do not care* whether it also treats **If the phone** as grammatical. Given the longer string, we can predict, from non-linguistic (but perfectly empirical) knowledge, that there are circumstances in which we will hear the shorter string, whether or not it is grammatical. And, if it does not matter whether the grammar does or does not permit **If the phone**, then it will be simpler not to permit it.

This case is particularly clear, because we could see the boiling saucepan. Sometimes we shall want to discount uttered strings as 'incomplete' or as 'mistaken', without being able to point to an external factor disturbing the speaker's behaviour. But this is all right. It is a matter of empirical, non-linguistic observation that people sometimes interrupt what they are doing for no apparent reason, and that people make mistakes when performing complex tasks. We do not need linguistics to tell us that the same will be true of speaking. If an Englishman utters a string which we can treat as grammatical only at the cost of greatly complicating a grammar that accounts well for other data, then we are free to say that he has made a mistake – as long as we do not use this escape route too often. Of course, we predict that this deviant behaviour will be rarer in writing or in formal public speaking than in informal chat, just as more false notes are played at rehearsals than in the concert itself.

There will also be cases where the grammar permits strings which we know will never be uttered. One of the rules of a standard English grammar, for instance, says that a noun may have a relative clause in apposition to it; and the definition of 'relative clause' implies that a relative clause may contain nouns. In this respect the standard grammar of English is *recursive*: main clauses have subordinate clauses upon their backs to bite 'em, and subordinate clauses have sub-subordinate clauses, if not *ad infinitum*, then at least *ad libitum*. For instance:
This is the dog, that chased the cat, that killed the rat, that ate the malt, that lay in the house that Jack built. But, although the grammar imposes no limit to this process, there certainly is a limit in practice: the nursery-rhyme about the house that Jack built is already something of a *tour de force*. That rhyme, when it reaches its climax, has about a dozen levels of subordination; we would surely be safe in predicting that one will never get more than, say, twenty levels. So, is our standard grammar, which fails to distinguish between strings with two levels of subordination and strings with two hundred levels, not intolerably weak? Should we not either add a rule limiting the process of subordination, or else recognize that the standard grammar is justified because we intuitively know that sentences with many levels of subordination remain 'grammatical' (even if they are not 'acceptable' in practice)?

Once more, no. It is again part of our general knowledge, quite independent of linguistics but perfectly empirical, that behaviour-patterns are less and less likely to be executed as they become more and more long and complex. Many people whistle the latest pop tune, few try to whistle a Bach fugue. From this knowledge we predict that relatively long strings are relatively improbable in practice. To incorporate a rule to this effect in the *grammar of English* would be simply to duplicate within linguistics this piece of extra-linguistic knowledge. There is no reason to do so. It is quite difficult enough to construct linguistic theories which do the tasks that only they can do – e.g. that of distinguishing between **The child seems sleepy** and **The child seems sleeping** – without taking on extra work unnecessarily.

We can sum up the situation I have been describing in a diagram:

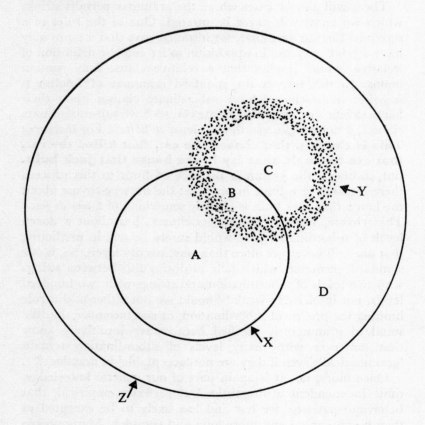

Here, the large circle Z represents all possible strings of English formatives. The circle X represents the set of strings which some grammar of English defines as grammatical. But the grammar is only one of the factors which jointly determine what is actually uttered: Y represents the set of strings which are predicted to be possible when we take into account both the grammar and all the knowledge that we have apart from linguistics. Since they overlap partially, X and Y divide the complete set of strings into four subclasses: A, B, C, and D. Strings in B are both grammatical and utterable: e.g. **This is the dog that chased the cat**. Strings in A are grammatical but will not be uttered in practice: e.g. a sentence like the 'house that Jack built' one, but with two hundred rather than a dozen levels of subordination. Strings in C are ungrammatical, but may be uttered: e.g. **If the phone**. Finally, strings in D are neither grammatical, nor will they be observed: e.g. **Of of the of**.

The border of Y is drawn 'fuzzy', because the non-linguistic factors that help settle whether a string is likely to be uttered are many and various, and many of them are intrinsically 'gradient' rather than yes-or-no factors. For instance, **Of of the of** is not likely to occur as a mistake in place of some grammatical sentence (as one might say **The bus we made all the trips in are outside** as a careless slip for . . . **is outside**), and accordingly I assigned **Of of the of** to set D. But **Of of the of** becomes quite a likely utterance in the context of a book or lecture on linguistics, and accordingly it should perhaps be assigned to set C. (Some strings really will be in D, of course. For instance, the string consisting of the word **of** repeated one thousand times will not occur in full even in a book on linguistics.) Although grammatical sentences become more and more implausible as their length increases, there is no sharp cut-off point below which they are possible but above which they are impossible.

Since the set Y, of strings which can occur in practice, is 'fuzzy-edged', it follows that B, the set of strings which are both possible and fully grammatical, will also be fuzzy-edged. The members of B are often called the *acceptable* sentences of English. We see, then, one reason why one might object to Chomsky's assumption that a grammar should define a set of strings in a sharp, yes-or-no way. If we identify 'English' with the set of *acceptable* English sentences, this assumption will lead to quite the wrong results. However, if we draw the distinction between what is predicted by the grammar alone and what is predicted by the conjunction of the grammar with extra-linguistic knowledge, then we realize that the set B of accept-able strings may be fuzzy even if the set X of grammatical strings is sharp. This is the answer to one of Hockett's objec-tions to Chomsky. (As we have seen in chapter 3, though, Hockett also had more serious objections concerning syntactic creativity; and furthermore it remains possible to distinguish grammaticality from acceptability and insist that *both* are gradient properties.)

The foregoing has shown that Chomsky is quite unjustified in claiming that linguistics rests on introspective evidence. The sort of considerations which make Chomsky think linguistics needs intuitive data can in fact be explained perfectly well on the basis of exclusively behavioural data, provided we impose on our grammars quite standard methodological requirements of strength and simplicity, and provided we realize that the predictions made by our grammars are affected by the rest of our knowledge. We do not need to use intuition in justifying our grammars, and, as scientists, we must not use intuition in this way.

Let me add, for completeness, that the same methodological considerations that decide which is the best *grammar* compatible with given data apply equally to the choice between general *theories of language*. At the lower level of linguistic theorizing, we look for the strongest and simplest grammar that permits all the English sentences we have actually observed: the set of strings defined by this grammar will be the stringset we call 'English'. Having constructed grammars for a number of attested human languages, we then look for the strongest and simplest general theory of language (i.e. definition of a range of 'natural languages') which counts all the attested languages we have examined as natural.

When I introduced the prime-number language and the odd-token language, I appealed to the reader's intuition in asking him to agree that they were not the kind of languages humans speak. But I am not suggesting that the general theory of language relies on intuitive knowledge that certain languages are unnatural, any more than that the grammar of English relies on intuitive knowledge that certain strings are ungrammatical. Rather, the strongest theory of natural language which includes the attested languages will exclude the prime-number and odd-token languages.

The strongest theory of all will in fact say that the attested languages are the only possible natural languages, although intuitively one imagines that there are many languages, only trivially different from the attested languages, which humans might equally well speak but for the accidents of history. For instance, suppose we use the name *noun-first English* for the stringset like English, except that adjectives follow the noun (as in French): surely 'noun-first English' is as natural as ordinary English? But, if the theory of language must treat both English and French as natural, then it will be simpler for it also to permit noun-first English than to rule it out; this gain in simplicity will outweigh the slight loss of strength, and again our intuition merely reiterates what normal scientific methodology tells us in any case.

All this is not to deny that we have intuitive knowledge, if one wants to call it that, about our own language or about language in general. I am concerned only to emphasize that the intuitions we have must not and need not be used to *justify* linguistic theories. Certainly we have opinions about language before we start doing linguistics, and in many cases linguistics will only confirm these pre-scientific opinions. But then we have opinions about very many subjects: for instance, one does not need to be a meteorologist to believe that red sky at night means fine weather next day. In some cases our pre-scientific opinions about language come from what we are taught in English lessons at school (the division of our vocabulary into parts of speech, for instance); in other cases they are worked out by individuals independently (as when a non-linguist judges that **Of of the of** is not English and that **Three zebras stayed behind** is English, for instance). Our pre-scientific opinions, both about the weather and about English, may well be right; but it is the job of meteorology and linguistics to find out *whether* they are right or wrong, to explain why they are right if they are right, and to show where they are wrong if they are wrong. What we are taught about English at school, and what we work out for ourselves, is rudimentary linguistics, just as the proverb about red sky is rudimentary meteorology; but it is the job of a science to attempt to *improve* on the rudimentary theories of Everyman, not simply to *restate* them in novel jargon.

One may object that the analogy between linguistics and meteorology is unfair. If there are links between red evening sky and future fine weather, these links have to do with the physics of air, water-vapour, and the like, and are quite independent of human beings: any opinion that a human has about meteorology is one he has formed solely as an observer. On the other hand, whether such and such a string of words is English or not depends on our own behaviour as native speakers of English. So it may be reasonable to suggest that we may have 'infallible intuitions' about what is or is not English, in a way that our opinions about the weather clearly cannot be infallible. To put it figuratively, the part of our brain which makes conscious judgements about the English language perhaps has a 'hot line' to the part of our brain which controls our actual speaking, so that we know what we can and cannot say in English in the same direct, 'incorrigible' way that, say, I know I have toothache.

This might be so, and it would be very convenient for linguists if it were. The very fact that we can ask the question shows that behaviour is the ultimate criterion: to decide whether we have such a 'hot line', we have to construct a description of English *based on behaviour,* and then see whether it coincides with our 'intuitive' opinions about English. And in fact the empirical evidence is negative: it is easy to show that people believe quite sincerely that they say things which they never do say, and, more strikingly, that they never say things which they in fact frequently say. Even with respect to the basic issue 'Are such and such strings grammatical for me?', though people's opinions tend to be fairly accurate, they are very far from infallible. As for subtler intuitive abilities which have been attributed to the native speaker, such as the ability to parse his sentences, one can only suppose that linguists who state that this is an innate endowment have forgotten the struggles their less language-minded class-mates went through in the English lessons of their childhood.

If we lack infallible intuitions about the grammar of our

native language, still less do we have such intuitions about the naturalness of languages in general. To take an example at random: it is surely intuitively rather obvious that no natural language would interpret past tense as future and vice versa whenever a verb was preceded by the word for 'and', so that 'and' followed by, e.g., the word for 'he spoke' meant 'and he will speak', while 'and' followed by 'he will speak' meant 'and he spoke'. Yet Hebrew had just this feature.

Someone wishing to defend the use of intuition may object that all linguists, including the pre-Chomskyan descriptivists as well as those, like the present author, who aim to reconcile Chomskyan linguistics with behaviourism, have in fact relied heavily on intuition in formulating their grammars. The descriptivists in many cases took great pains to gather an objective 'corpus' of data before commencing analysis, even when investigating their native language; one thinks, for instance, of Charles Fries, whose grammar of American English was based on a series of bugged telephone conversations made in Ann Arbor, Michigan. But even Fries could not move from data to grammar without using intuitive 'guesses' (if you will) about the status of strings not in his corpus. And the present author freely admits to having published analyses of points of English syntax based exclusively on his intuitions about his mother tongue.

This objection again misses its mark through failure to appreciate how science works. We do not care where a scientist gets his theory from, only how he defends it against criticism. Any scientific theory is sure to incorporate many untested assumptions, guesses, and intuitive hunches of its creator. All that matters is that any feature of the theory which is doubted can be confirmed or refuted on empirical grounds. It seems to be true in the case of language that people's pre-scientific intuitions tend to be more reliable on the question of grammaticality of individual strings than on the structure of grammars. That being so, it is a sensible research strategy for a linguist to assume that his opinions about what is or is not English are correct, and to use these grammaticality-judgements as evidence for or against grammars of English. But, should his grammaticality-judgements about individual strings be challenged, the thing to do is to see whether English-

73

speakers actually utter strings like that – not to quarrel about whose intuitions are clearest.

What one must never do is to say: 'I intuit that the string is grammatical/ungrammatical in *my* kind of English; and my idiolect is an attested language too, so the theory of language must be able to handle my idiolect even if all other English-speakers speak differently.' Short of following the author of such a comment round with a tape-recorder for a few months, there is simply no way of checking his claim. If what he claims is awkward for one's general theory of language, it is much more sensible to reject his claim for lack of evidence than to change one's theory of language. This is why we said in the last chapter that it is better to choose the speech of nations rather than that of individuals as the subject of linguistics; it is easy to check a claim about English, but hard to check a claim about Sampsonese. One of the unfortunate consequences of Chomsky's mentalist view of linguistics is that in recent years a number of younger linguists have indulged very heavily in arguments based on their intuitions about quirks of their personal idiolects.

Since the arguments against mentalism in science are very strong, it is natural to wonder why Chomsky and other linguists have been so willing to embrace mentalism. We have seen that lack of familiarity with general methodological considerations might lead one to think that mentalism is inevitable in linguistics. However, the average meteorologist, say, is no better informed about the philosophy of science than the average linguist; yet no meteorologist supposes that the aim of his science is to record people's pre-scientific opinions about weather forecasting. Furthermore, many linguists seem to espouse mentalism, not as an unavoidable last resort, but readily and eagerly.

One cause of linguists' confusion is an ambiguity in the way we talk about linguistic behaviour in English. Gilbert Ryle has pointed to a distinction between two uses of the word 'know', which he calls 'knowing how' and 'knowing that'. If I say that someone, say John, 'knows that p', then p is a proposition or fact which John knows to be the case. But English (unlike some other languages) also uses the same word 'know' as in 'John knows how to *a*', where *a* is an activity which John is capable of performing: 'know how to' in this sense is just an idiomatic alternative to 'can' or 'be able to'. If I say that John knows how to ride a bicycle, for instance, I do not imply that John knows any *facts* about bicycle-riding: I just mean that he can cycle. If John is at all self-aware, then he will no doubt have worked out for himself some truths about cycling; but that he has done so is no part of what I mean when I say that he knows how to cycle. (There is also a third use of 'know', as in 'John knows my father', but this is irrelevant here.)

Now we commonly refer to the ability possessed by a speaker of English by means of phrases such as 'John knows English', 'John knows how to speak English', 'John's knowledge of English'. Here we are using 'know' purely in the 'know how' sense. However, someone not alert to the ambiguity might interpret these phrases in the 'know that' sense, so that if John has 'knowledge of English' then John knows various things to be the case about English. Once we make this confusion, it becomes natural to think that the evidence for a grammar of English should be the set of facts which one knows by virtue of having native-speaker knowledge of English.

Chomsky has been charged with this confusion by Hockett, and by Gilbert Harman. His reply is that 'it does not seem to me true that the concepts "knowing how" and "knowing that" constitute exhaustive categories for the analysis of knowledge'. But this is surely just a pun, as if one were to say that 'blond' and 'equitable' are not exhaustive categories for the analysis of fairness. The only things that can be used to confirm or refute a theory are facts; the statement that 'John knows English' concerns a relation not between John and facts but between John and actions. In the 'know that' sense, as Steven Stich has put it, 'speakers, *qua* speakers, know nothing'.

There is more to Chomsky's adoption of mentalism than a mere verbal confusion, though. We have seen that one of the points on which Chomsky differs from his predecessors is that Chomsky believes linguistic theories to correlate in some way with properties of human minds, rather than being merely concise summaries of human behaviour. On the realism *v.* descriptivism issue, I suggested, few would now disagree with

Chomsky: if the theories are accurate, then there are surely *some* features of reality which cause linguistic behaviour to be as Chomsky's theories say it is. The claim that these features are properties of people's psychological machinery is less obviously true; in chapter 6 we shall consider alternative interpretations that have been proposed. But it is at least a reasonable hypothesis that the theories of linguistics represent facts about people's minds. Now, if one devotes a great deal of effort to persuading the sceptical that linguistic theories are about minds rather than about behaviour, it is easy to slip into the habit of thinking that the *evidence* for those theories also consists of mental rather than behavioural facts – particularly if one is not careful to distinguish the two issues.

If one takes the descriptivist position on the status of scientific theories, then the issues are not distinct. But, for a realist, the questions (i) 'What sort of facts count as evidence for linguistics?' and (ii) 'What aspects of reality does linguistics tell us about?' are quite separate. Chomsky and his followers argue strongly for scientific realism, so it is ironic that they fail to distinguish the issues consistently. In the classic defence of mentalism in linguistics, Jerrold Katz slides between these two senses of 'mentalism'. Chomsky falls into the same trap. In a discussion of the linguist W. F. Twaddell, Chomsky actually begins by drawing the distinction between the two questions; but he goes on to support a (true) claim that Twaddell is an empiricist with respect to question (ii) by referring exclusively to Twaddell's behaviourist statements on question (i).

I take it that questions (i) and (ii) are genuinely distinct; and, although we may agree with Chomsky in thinking that the theories of linguistics tell us about minds, I cannot see how we can accept anything other than publicly-observable behaviour as evidence for those theories. Nor can I see anything undesirable about linguistics being in this position. Anyone can come up with theories about the workings of the mind by using introspection, imagination, and guesswork; the only trouble is that different thinkers come up with incompatible theories. Surely it is much more worth while and exciting to pursue a subject which promises to tell us something of how the mind works, but which is based on evidence as concrete and reliable as the evidence to which physics and the other 'hard sciences' appeal?

The main danger in admitting introspective data, we have said, is that linguists are likely to have intuitions which are convenient for their pet theories. If this happens, then there may be no point in arguing that the findings of linguistics have implications for our understanding of Man, since these findings may themselves rest on false premises. Are there cases where important parts of the Chomskyan theory of language depend in this way on wishful thinking?

There does seem to be one case. Recall our discussion of recursion, in which we suggested that one of the rules of English permits nouns to take relative clauses in apposition, and that relative clauses may themselves contain nouns. We saw that these two statements, taken together, imply that any degree of subordination can occur, although in practice sentences become increasingly improbable as their levels of subordination (and hence length) increase.

The example we gave was one in which the antecedent noun of each relative clause is always the last word in its own clause:

This is the dog [that chased the cat [that killed the rat [...]]].

Dog is the last word of the main clause, **cat** is the last word of the next clause down, etc., and in each case it is these words which are followed by a relative clause (written here in square brackets, to make the point clearer). But we can attach relative clauses also to nouns which are not final in their clause: **The dog [that chased the cat] was barking.**

However, if we again use the recursive property of the quoted rules to form many-layered subordinations, this time with subordinate clauses occurring in the middle of their superordinate clauses (as in the example just quoted) rather than at the end, we very quickly run into trouble. With three levels of subordination we get strings like:

(1) **The dog [that the girl [whom John employed] called] chased the cat.**

This is a very peculiar sentence indeed. Intuitively, it seems not to be the sort of thing that English speakers say, and one can only understand it after some deliberation. Yet this is not simply because it is too long to say conveniently. If (1) is English, it means the same as (2), which is actually a rather longer sentence; yet (2), though pedestrian, seems much more acceptable:

(2) **The cat was chased by the dog [that was called by the girl [who was employed by John]].**

These differences are even more striking with four levels of subordination (**The man whom the girl that the boy whom the film amused met admired wrote those books**). There seems to be a general principle by which we avoid more than one or two levels of subordination clause-internally, while allowing subordination to occur much more freely at the ends of clauses. To use the terminology that has become standard in linguistics, we avoid *self-embedding*.

It happens that this principle can be incorporated in Chomsky's theory of language only by considerably complicating that theory. Chomsky's theory predicts that, if subordination can happen at any point in the clause, it should be equally possible at every point. (I have not yet expounded Chomsky's theory, so this will not be obvious to the reader; for the time being, let us take it on trust.) Accordingly, Chomsky and other linguists 'intuit' that self-embedded strings such as (1) are just as grammatical as strings like (2), although they do not quarrel with the statement that multiply self-embedded strings are rare or nonexistent in practice. Chomsky even offers an explanation for the difference in acceptability between (1) and (2). For him, this is a particular linguistic consequence of a general property of the machinery of the brain, which he specifies; this brain feature is not intrinsically connected with language, and its consequences are therefore to be discounted when constructing a theory of language.

However, although Chomsky's hypothesis about the brain does not refer specifically to the language-processing aspects of our psychological make-up, there is not a scrap of *evidence* for this hypothesis other than the linguistic facts already discussed. The rarity of (1) is not like the rarity of very long sentences, which can be explained without reference to linguistics and therefore need not be explained within linguistics. Nobody other than the linguist can offer any explanation for why (1) is less acceptable than (2), therefore the linguist must do so. (A precise statement of what makes a string unacceptably 'self-embedded' in fact involves even more detailed syntactic properties than those mentioned above, making it all the clearer that this unacceptability is a fact about language.)

A theory, like Chomsky's, which predicts no difference between (1) and (2) is thus, to that extent, an unsatisfactory theory. The fact that Chomskyans intuit (1) to be as grammatical as (2) may simply be an illustration of how our beliefs determine our perceptions. Chomsky may be right in suggesting that the oddity of (1) is to be explained by an *ad hoc* hypothesis independent of the rest of his theory; but, if one can find an alternative theory of language which *predicts* that languages avoid self-embedding, then the new theory will in that respect be an improvement on Chomsky's.

Such a theory has recently been put forward by Peter Reich. For Reich's theory, it would be awkward if (1) and (2) were equally acceptable: it is predicted that self-embedding should lead to difficulties after one or two layers. In this sense, Reich's theory represents a clear improvement over Chomsky's. Why, then, is this book devoted principally to Chomsky's views? Because one does not adopt a theory which explains one fact well, unless it is satisfactory in other respects also. Reich's and Chomsky's theories differ on many empirical issues, of which the matter of self-embedding is only one. On balance, I judge that Chomsky's theory is clearly superior to Reich's in its present form. However, it may be that in the future some modification of Reich's views will eliminate their current weak points while preserving their advantages with respect to self-embedding and certain other matters; in which case we shall have to ask whether the new theory carries the same psychological and philosophical implications as Chomsky's theory.

The question of clause-internal subordination is the only important case known to me in which linguists' intuitions have diverged from what can be empirically established in a direction which is convenient for the linguists' theories. Perhaps surprisingly, the opposite situation is rather commoner: there are many cases where linguists have been led by erroneous intuitions to adopt theories which are much *less* attractive than the theories which the empirical facts support.

What I have in mind is linguists' treatment of contradictory or nonsensical sentences. As we have seen, in his first book, *Syntactic Structures*, Chomsky argued that a grammar should distinguish between grammatical and ungrammatical strings, but should *not* distinguish, among the grammatical strings, between sensical and nonsensical strings. Strings like **The books is on the table** or **Of of the of** should be forbidden by a grammar of English, but **Sincerity is triangular**, like **Sincerity is admirable**, should be permitted – even though no one ever says **Sincerity is triangular**.

The principle is by now familiar: it is not for linguistics to tell us things that we know independently of linguistics. If someone asks why Englishmen never utter the string **Sincerity is triangular**, one can reply, 'Sincerity is a character trait and as such has no shape.' This is a statement about sincerity and triangularity, not about words, but it implies that there will be no point in uttering **Sincerity is triangular**: we do not also need the grammar of English to tell us that the sentence is odd. On the other hand, if one asks what is wrong with **The books is on the table**, the reply has to be along the lines: 'The verb does not agree with the subject': in other words, it has to use linguistic terminology, and no non-linguistic knowledge will rule this string out. Similarly, what is wrong with **Of of the of** is that it 'simply is not English' – again we have to refer to a linguistic notion, namely 'English'.

If the linguist relies on his intuition to tell him what his grammar should permit, then we can understand that he may decide to rule out **Sincerity is triangular** along with **The books is on the table**. Our intuition does not seem particularly sensitive to the distinction between nonsensicality and ungrammaticality, but simply registers a general feeling of 'oddity'. Here is a case where intuition lets the linguist down; if linguistics is an empirical science, we have excellent reasons to distinguish the two kinds of 'oddity'.

To make clearer the idea that sentences like **Sincerity is triangular** should be treated as 'good' sentences by our grammar, let me give an analogy. Suppose the Highway Code were revised so that, in order to indicate one's intentions at a cross-roads, one simply pointed in the appropriate direction. (This might be sensible if we drove horse-drawn carriages rather than sitting behind windscreens.) Now the revised Highway Code would not need explicitly to exclude the gesture of pointing up in the air, or pointing left and right with both hands simultaneously. As a signal of one's intentions, the former is patently false, and the latter contradictory; this is a quite adequate explanation of why drivers do not use these signs. Indeed, it is only because these signs *do* fit the system as defined that we can recognize them to be respectively false and contradictory; a sign outside the defined system (say, folding the arms) is not 'false' or 'contradictory' but simply 'not in the Code'. Similarly, it is only because it *is* a sentence of English that we can recognize **Sincerity is triangular** to be contradictory. We cannot call **Of of the of** 'false' or 'contradictory': it is not an English sentence, so the question of its meaning does not arise.

One might add that, if we agree (as I have suggested we may) with Wittgenstein, when he argues that the use of words is a creative process, then it would in any case be hopeless to try to state a fixed borderline between 'sensical' and 'nonsensical' strings. Someone may well extend the use of **sincerity** or **triangular** tomorrow in such a way that **Sincerity is triangular** becomes a sensible thing to say. The main point I am making, however, is that even if there were a clear distinction to be drawn between sense and nonsense, it is no business of a grammar to draw it.

In *Syntactic Structures*, as we have said, Chomsky recognized this point. Unfortunately, by the time he published *Aspects of the Theory of Syntax* eight years later, Chomsky changed his mind. Chapter 2 of *Aspects* is largely concerned with the problem of how to reorganize linguistic theory so as to allow grammars to exclude nonsensical as well as ungrammatical strings. Chomsky does not present this as a change of mind. Rather, he claims that, while a grammar should permit genuinely contradictory but grammatical strings such as **Both of John's parents are married to aunts of mine**, the oddity of strings such as **The book dispersed** (to use one of his examples) is a fact about the English language and must therefore be stated in the grammar of English. But this distinction is quite unfounded. **The book dispersed** is an odd thing to say because only aggregates which are not physically linked can disperse, whereas a book is a single continuous physical object: this is a statement in the 'material mode' of speech, referring to books and to dispersing but not to English. One *can* recast it in the 'formal mode' by saying, 'The verb **disperse** cannot be predicated of the noun **book** in the singular,' but it is not necessary to do so. (The oddity of **The books is on the table**, by contrast, can be explained only in the formal mode.) The only difference between the oddity of **The book dispersed** and that of **Both John's parents ...** is that it takes a slightly longer chain of reasoning to spell out the contradiction in the latter case.

This mistake on Chomsky's part has two important consequences. First, his new version of English grammar becomes much more complicated. Whether a grammatical string is sensical or not has very little to do with its syntax, so in order to define the set of sensical strings – even assuming this can be done at all – one has first to define the set of grammatical strings and then add extra clauses to the definition in order to eliminate the nonsensical strings. No one has yet claimed to have provided a complete definition of the set of *grammatical* strings for any attested language; but people's opinions about how close we are to that goal correlate well with how clear they are about the ungrammatical/nonsensical distinction. One man who claimed that the task of constructing an English grammar is almost finished was the logician Richard Montague, before his tragic death in 1971; and Montague is particularly good at drawing the distinction carefully.* On the other hand, the younger linguists whom I criticized earlier in this chapter for describing their personal idiolects rather than full-scale languages are linguists who confuse nonsensicality

* Thus Richmond Thomason, a follower of Montague, mentions that strings such as **John lends Mary that a woman finds her father** are grammatical in English. The string quoted is very bizarre; but that is because a woman's finding her father is a fact, and one cannot lend a person a fact, although one can tell a person a fact or lend him a book. This is a truth about facts and lending, not about English. To treat strings like this as grammatical greatly simplifies English grammar: this string is syntactically quite parallel to **John tells Mary that a woman finds her father**, so that it would be relatively awkward to permit the latter while ruling out the former.

with ungrammaticality much more thoroughly than Chomsky does; and these people are also deeply pessimistic about the possibility of constructing complete grammars of natural languages. Paul Postal, for instance, has recently characterized the Chomskyan programme of grammar construction as 'naïve' and 'unrealistic'. Wittgenstein, who also failed to distinguish grammaticality from sensicality, would have agreed with Postal; but if, as Chomsky originally claimed, the job of a grammar is to delimit the boundaries of grammaticality rather than those of sensicality, then Postal's comments seem unjustified.

The decision to deal with sensicality leads to a more complex grammar of (e.g.) English. But this is a minor point. More important is the fact that it leads to a less strong *theory of language*; in other words, to a weaker account of universal constraints on natural languages. The modifications which Chomsky makes to English grammar in order to rule out strings like **The book dispersed** do not merely amount to choosing a more complex grammar from the same general class of grammars which he envisaged in his earlier work. Rather, Chomsky adds machinery of a quite novel type to the existing grammar, so that the general class of grammars from which his new grammar is drawn is much wider than before; which is the same as to say that Chomsky's new theory of language, or theory of universal constraints on natural languages, is much weaker than before.

It is noticeable that the group of younger linguists whose methodology I have twice had occasion to criticize are also linguists whose general theories of language have in many ways been very much weaker than those advocated by any other linguists working in the Chomskyan framework. It would be inappropriate to go into detail in a work such as the present book; I shall content myself with mentioning George Lakoff's theory of 'global rules', which constitutes a gross weakening of Chomsky's theory of language.

The question of the weakness of the general theory of language is very important. We seek the strongest possible theory of language that can be empirically supported. Only if the theory of language is very strong, that is, if there exist relatively narrow constraints on the diversity of natural languages, can we draw any of the general psychological or philosophical conclusions discussed in chapter 2.

We have seen that salient cases where linguists have replaced a stronger theory of language by a weaker one have been associated with errors of methodology. This does not prove, of course, that the stronger theory is necessarily correct. Perhaps the type of machinery which Chomsky invokes in order to rule out **The book dispersed** is needed in any case to distinguish genuinely ungrammatical from grammatical strings (though I do not believe it is). Perhaps Lakoff's global rules really are unavoidable, even though Lakoff is a linguist who advocates reliance on intuitions about one's personal idiolect and who consistently fails to distinguish nonsensicality from ungrammaticality. (This seems to be a more serious possibility.) However, it is at least heartening to find that the *a priori* undesirable (because weak) theories are so often also the methodologically ill-founded theories. Methodology is certainly a point on which many linguists are open to criticism; but when we revise linguistic theory in the light of these criticisms, the result seems to be a theory which provides more rather than less strong support for Chomsky's nativist and rationalist views.

5

Rules and Languages

After looking at the scope of Chomsky's linguistic theories, at the evidence on which they are based, and at the implications Chomsky draws from them, it is now time to turn to an examination of their substantive content.

Consider first the question of producing a grammar of English. In quite traditional terminology, one might describe one common class of English sentences along the following lines: 'A sentence may consist of a subject nominal phrase followed by a predicate. A nominal phrase can be an article followed by a noun. **A** and **the** are articles; nouns include **boy**, **girl** and **fact**. A predicate can be an intransitive verb followed by the third-person suffix **-s**, or a transitive verb, **-s** and a nominal phrase. **Run** and **muse** are intransitive verbs; **kick** and **believe** are transitive verbs.' A Chomskyan linguist will express the same statements by choosing symbols to stand for the categories *nominal phrase, predicate, article, noun, intransitive verb* and *transitive verb* (say, 'A', 'B', 'C', 'D', 'E', 'F'), and writing:

S → A B
A → C D
C → **a**
C → **the**
D → **boy**
D → **girl**
D → **fact**
B → E **-s**
B → F **-s** A
E → **run**
E → **muse**
F → **kick**
F → **believe**

(By convention, 'S' is always used for the category *sentence*.) Both of these statements, the traditional one written in plain English and the Chomskyan one written in symbols, imply that, e.g. **The boy kicks the girl** and **The girl muses** are sentences, while e.g. **Muses the boy** or **Believe believe the** are not. (If these were proposed as complete grammars of English, they would imply also that, e.g. **The boy is smoking** or **Does the girl run?** are ungrammatical; obviously, however, what is written above will be only a tiny part of a complete grammar of English.)

A natural and very reasonable reaction to what we have done so far is to ask 'Why bother with the symbols?' Chomsky's symbolic notation says no more and no less than what is said in a perfectly straightforward way by the ordinary English statement which preceded it. The symbolic notation may seem to be an unnecessary complication. True, the symbolic grammar has the virtue of a certain conciseness; but the advantage of taking up less space on the page is more than outweighed by the unfamiliarity of the symbolic format.

This objection misses the point. Certainly, we cannot express anything in the symbolic notation that we could not equally well say in plain English. Obviously not, since we can only understand the symbolism if we are given some way of translating it into English. The 'translation manual' for Chomsky's notation runs like this: 'Start by writing down "S". If one of the symbols you have written down occurs as the left-hand side of some rule, replace it by what occurs on the right (making a random choice if there is more than one rule beginning with the same symbol). Go on doing this as long as possible. When you are left with a string of formatives, that string is one of the strings permitted by the grammar.' Thus a grammar of Chomsky's kind can be viewed as a set of instructions for constructing formative-strings; the stringset defined by the grammar will contain the various strings which can be constructed by following the rules and making different choices at the choice-points. The symbolic grammar is meaningless until we have specified the translation into plain English, so to adopt the symbolic format cannot extend our powers of expression. But the point of the symbolism is not to *increase* what we can say but rather to *limit* it.

Remember that our ultimate aim is to produce a strong theory of language. That is, we aim to define a class of 'natural' stringsets which is required to include any attested human language, but should exclude as many other stringsets as possible. In order to define a class of natural stringsets, we have to proceed indirectly by defining a class of 'natural' grammars (i.e. definitions of stringsets); then we can say that any stringset defined by one of the 'natural' grammars is itself natural and may be attested, but we predict that a stringset which fits none of the defined grammars is 'unnatural' and will never be found as a human language. If our 'grammars' were sequences of statements in plain English, then it is not clear how we could proceed. Any stringset that can be defined at all can be defined in plain English: what we aim to do is to define a class of stringsets much *smaller* than the class which can be defined at all. In order to do this, we must lay down a canonical format for grammars: then we can specify that only grammars which meet the constraints of the canonical format count as 'natural' grammars. If we choose our format appropriately, it may provide grammars for only a minority of the stringsets which can be defined when we allow ourselves all the resources of plain English. If so, then by deciding to restrict our grammars to the canonical format we are adopting a strong, refutable theory of language.

The symbolic grammar given above exemplifies one such canonical notation system, which I shall call *constituency grammar*. (The usual but unnecessarily long-winded term is 'context-free phrase-structure grammar'.) A constituency grammar is a set of *constituency rules*, where a constituency rule is any sequence made up of some symbol followed by the arrow '→', followed by any number of symbols (which may include both formatives of the language being defined and *auxiliary symbols* such as the 'S', 'A', 'B' used above). Thus 'S → A B' is a typical constituency rule with the 'sentence' symbol followed by the arrow and two auxiliary symbols; 'C → **the**' is a special case in which only one symbol (in this case a formative) appears to the right of the arrow.

The significant of constituency notation is that it corresponds to the traditional notions about syntax which we are taught at school. According to our received ideas, words are divided into

87

a small set of *parts of speech* (noun, verb, etc.); sequences of words form *phrases* of different categories (nominal phrase, adjectival phrase, etc.); groups of phrases form *clauses*, and subordinate clauses are contained within superordinate clauses in hierarchical fashion. We may interpret the auxiliary symbols 'A', 'B', 'C', etc. of a constituency grammar as representing the parts of speech and the different categories of phrase. Thus, in the grammar presented above, 'A' corresponds to the traditional category of 'nominal phrase', 'D' to the category 'noun', and so on.* For each string which it permits, the constituency grammar defines a hierarchical structure which can be represented by a *constituency tree* diagram. For instance, **The girl kicks the boy** will have the following structure:

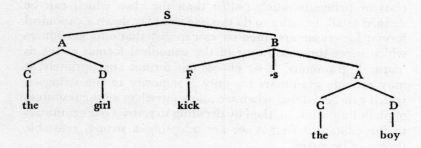

in which the successive branchings, moving away from the 'root' S, correspond to applications of the various constituency rules.

As we expand the grammar to take account of more English sentences, we shall incorporate rules containing the sentence symbol 'S' to the right of the arrow. Consider e.g. the sentence **The boy believes that the girl runs**. The easiest way to modify the grammar to permit this sentence will be to add a rule 'A → **that** S'; i.e. a nominal phrase may consist of **that**

---

* It is usual in linguistics to write 'NP' instead of our 'A', 'N' rather than 'D', etc. However, this is only a matter of mnemonic convenience; the grammar makes exactly the same empirical predictions, whatever auxiliary symbols are used. Grammars using standardized auxiliary symbols have a superficial air of similarity even when the rules in which the symbols occur are quite different; accordingly, in this book we deliberately use arbitrary, non-standard auxiliary symbols. (Cf. p. 110, below.)

followed by a sentence. The quoted sentence will thus be assigned the structure:

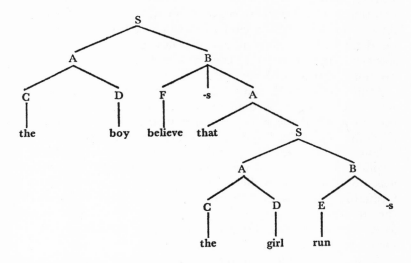

in which the symbol 'S' occurs in an intermediate position as well as at the root. This gives us the notion 'clause': a clause will be any sequence of formatives dominated by the sentence symbol 'S', so that in this tree **the girl runs** will be a subordinate clause within the main clause dominated by the root 'S'. As soon as we allow 'S' to appear on the right-hand side of one of the rules, the grammar acquires the property of 'recursiveness' which causes it to permit infinitely many strings; thus the grammar we now have permits e.g. **The boy believes that the girl believes that the boy believes that ... the girl runs**, in which the **believe** clauses can be repeated to any degree of subordination.

Our grammar will clearly permit many strings that no one ever says, for instance **The boy kicks that the girl runs**. But, as we saw in the last chapter, that is quite all right. A proposition, for instance the proposition that the girl runs, cannot be kicked although it can be believed: this is a fact about kicking and propositions, not about English. **The boy kicks that the girl runs** is just as *grammatical* as **The boy kicks the girl**.

Constituency notation, then, seems to correspond well with our pre-scientific ideas about language. But this in itself is scarcely significant, unless we can show that constituency notation is restrictive, by comparison with plain English, as a format for defining stringsets. Let us call stringsets which can be defined by means of constituency grammars *constituency stringsets*. The question is: can we specify any stringsets which are not constituency stringsets?

Mathematically, it can be shown that there are many stringsets which cannot be defined in constituency notation, even though some of the non-constituency stringsets are quite easy to define in plain English. In other words, the claim that attested languages are constituency languages – which is implicit in our received views on syntax, although the question was not discussed explicitly before Chomsky – is indeed a falsifiable claim about human language. And this is essentially the universal property which Chomsky's theory of language attributes to human language, although the claim will be modified in some respects below.

As a very simple example of a non-constituency stringset, suppose that (to guard against fraud or mistakes, say) we adopted a system of numerals in which any number is written in its usual Arabic style but repeated, so that 'two' is written **22**, 'fourteen' as **1414**, and so on. Now the set of possible numerals in this new notation constitutes a well-defined stringset, to which **22**, **1414**, **936936**, etc. belong, but from which **3**, **97**, **506507**, etc. are excluded. This stringset (let us call it the *double-number language*) cannot be defined by any constituency grammar, because it exhibits what are called *overlapping dependencies*: thus, in a string such as

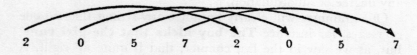

the choice of item occurring in fifth place depends on the item occurring in first place, choice of sixth item depends on second item, and so on. Stringsets embodying overlapping dependencies cannot be defined by constituency grammars, unless there is a sharp limit to the extent of overlapping; since there is no largest number, there is no limit on overlapping in the double-number language. The non-constituency nature of the double-number language will be unaffected if we make it superficially more similar to the attested languages by using as its vocabulary, not the ten digits of the Arabic numeral system, but the several thousand formatives of, say, Chinese (so that, e.g., **Wo ni wo ni** is grammatical, **Ta chi fan wo chi fan** ungrammatical).

The double-number language is particularly easy to describe, and intuitively it certainly seems quite unlike the attested languages with which we are familiar; so a theory of language which asserts that it is unnatural may well be correct. This result may, however, not seem very impressive. The double-number language is just a language in which one has to say everything twice over, and clearly time is too valuable for us to use such languages as our native tongues. However, non-constituency stringsets are not necessarily repetitious. Imagine a stringset which has categories of, say, A-phrase, B-phrase, and C-phrase, as in English we have nominal, verbal, and adjectival phrases; and let there be a rule which says that sentences may contain a sequence of A-, B-, and C-phrases in any order, as long as the latter part of the sentence has A-, B-, and C-phrases in the same order as the earlier part. Thus, a sentence may consist of two A-phrases; a sequence of A-, C-, C-, A-, C-, and C-phrases; etc. etc. Now there may be many different A-, B-, and C-phrases, so that a grammatical sentence will not necessarily contain a repetition of any individual formative; yet still the stringset cannot be defined by a constituency grammar. The stringset just described again seems quite unnatural; but now it is very hard to give a *reason* why human languages cannot be constructed in this way. This is just not the sort of structure natural languages possess. Agreed; but *why* is it that nested subordinations are an appropriate device for humans to use in communicating with each other about themselves and about the world they live in, while overlapping dependencies are quite inappropriate?

By defining a particular canonical format for grammars (in this case, constituency notation), we define a particular class of stringsets. Thus, a choice of a canonical format for grammars constitutes choice of a theory of natural language. We seek the strongest theory of language compatible with our observations of the languages that exist in the world, in other words we want our canonical format to be as restrictive as possible.

Constituency notation is intermediate in restrictiveness between two other particularly important systems of notation. A constituency rule, remember, always contains a single auxiliary symbol to the left of the arrow, while permitting any number of auxiliary symbols and/or formatives to the right. This particular format was invented as a specialization of a more general kind of rule, called *unrestricted rewrite rules*, in which the left-hand side is also allowed to contain more than one symbol. Thus, e.g., 'AB → CDE' counts as an unrestricted rewrite rule, though it is not a constituency rule. The 'translation manual' given above for constituency notation can be extended in an obvious way to unrestricted rewrite notation: thus, if we are faced with a string of symbols 'FGABKL', we can use the rule just quoted to turn this string into 'FGCDEKL'. Notice, though, that unrestricted rewrite rules do not define hierarchical tree structures for the strings they permit: if we tried to construct a tree representing the way a string is derived from an unrestricted rewrite grammar, we would not know (in this case) whether to show 'CDE' as dominated by 'A' or by 'B'.

Any constituency stringset is an unrestricted rewrite stringset, since a constituency grammar is simply a special case of unrestricted rewrite grammars; but the reverse does not hold – an unrestricted rewrite stringset is not necessarily a constituency stringset. Unrestricted rewrite notation is in fact important because there is a proof that *any* stringset which can be defined at all can be defined in unrestricted rewrite notation. It is only by restricting the left-hand side of rules to single symbols that the constituency theory makes a falsifiable claim about natural language.

Some readers may object that the notion 'any stringset that can be defined' seems too woolly to be the subject of a mathematical proof, unless we lay down exactly what is to count as a definition. Surprising as it may seem, mathematicians are prepared to distinguish 'all stringsets that can be defined' (in mathematical terminology, 'all *recursively enumerable* stringsets') from 'all stringsets whatever', and to use the former notion in their proofs, without needing to specify what counts as a definition.

It is easy to imagine that there could be stringsets which are undefinable. For instance, if an immortal forms a stringset by tossing a coin once for each of the infinitely many possible strings of (e.g.) Chinese words, including the string in the set whenever the coin comes down heads, then the resulting string-set will be impossible to represent in any definition framed by mortal man (unless the fall of the coin happens to follow a specifiable pattern, which is infinitely improbable). But we need not concern ourselves with these mathematical day-dreams; what counts as English or Chinese depends on the behaviour of finite English- or Chinese-speaking humans, so, if natural languages are stringsets at all, they are certainly definable stringsets.* Since the distinction will not be a crucial one, in what follows we shall frequently understand the term 'stringset' to mean 'definable stringset'; although we must be careful to remember that the fact that a set is definable in principle does not imply that anyone has succeeded in framing a definition for it.

While constituency grammar is a special case of unrestricted rewrite grammar, the third particularly important grammatical notation we shall consider, *finite-state grammar*, is a special case of constituency grammar. A constituency rule is a finite-state rule if its *right*-hand side has at most one auxiliary symbol, which must be in the last place in the sequence. Thus 'A → **the** B', or 'D → **dog**', are finite-state rules; but 'A → B C', or 'E → **the** F **of** G', are not. Again, all finite-state stringsets clearly must be constituency stringsets, but the reverse does not hold: there are many constituency stringsets which cannot be defined by a finite-state grammar.

Notice that, although a finite-state grammar can be thought of as assigning hierarchical structure to the strings it permits,

---

* The term 'definable' has a technical sense of its own in mathematics, but that usage is irrelevant here. I use 'definable' purely as an informal paraphrase of 'recursively enumerable': a set is recursively enumerable, or 'definable' in my sense, there is *some* finite way of specifying all and only its members.

it does so only in a trivial sense. A string **a b c d e . . .** will
always have the structure:

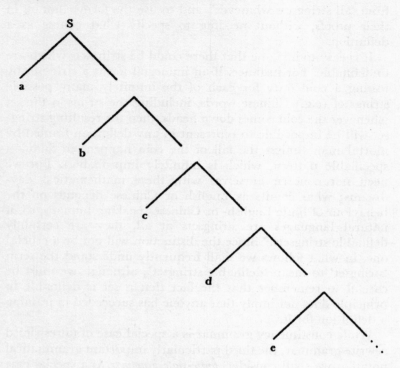

since the definition of 'finite-state rule' allows the tree to 'grow'
only at its rightmost end. Of the three kinds of grammar discussed – unrestricted rewrite, constituency and finite-state –
only constituency grammar groups formatives into phrases and
clauses in the non-trivial way which corresponds to our received
notions of 'parsing'.

The special significance of finite-state grammar is that it
goes with an *a priori* rather plausible and appealing view of
how humans might speak. Somehow, we have the ability to
utter grammatical sequences of words while avoiding ungrammatical sequences. One explanation of how this is managed
would run as follows. Some part of our psychological machinery
is capable of being in a large number of different states,

depending on what words it has uttered. Before speaking, it is in an 'initial state': in this state it has the option of making various moves, corresponding to the different words that can begin a sentence. One possibility is to say **the**; if the speaker does so, he moves to a new state corresponding to having begun a sentence with **the**. Now there are rather fewer options open: one is to say **quick**. It is not necessary for him to change state now – he can go on uttering adjectives indefinitely and the string will be grammatical if a noun follows eventually. So he says **brown**. However, at any point he has the option of moving on to a new state by uttering a noun, e.g. **fox**. – And so on, until on eventually uttering **dog** the speaker reaches an 'end state' calling for no more moves.

By using auxiliary symbols to stand for the different states, we can represent psychological machinery of this sort in terms of finite-state rules (hence the name). A finite-state grammar corresponding to the scenario just sketched would look like this:

S → **the** A
A → **quick** A
A → **brown** A
A → **fox** B
B → **jumps** C
C → **over** D
D → **the** E
E → **lazy** E
E → **dog**

One sees why finite-state rules are limited to a single auxiliary symbol on the right; a rule like 'A → B C' would imply that one was able to move from state A into both state B and state C simultaneously, but this is a contradiction – the mechanism can be in only one state at a time, by definition.

A finite-state grammar for English would clearly need to have a lot of states, but then human beings are complicated organisms. One might well suppose that English and other attested languages will be definable in terms of very large finite-state systems. This would then explain in a rather straightforward way the mechanics of the process by which we are able to utter grammatical strings while avoiding un-grammatical ones.

D*

However, Chomsky argues that English and other attested languages are not definable in finite-state notation. Finite-state grammars cannot group sequences of words at the beginning of a sentence together as constituents. In the example quoted, we are brought up to feel that **the quick brown fox** and **the lazy dog** are constituents of the same type, and this feeling seems to be well founded in fact: wherever one of the sequences may occur, the other is equally possible (e.g. **The lazy dog jumps over the quick brown fox** is also a grammatical string). But a finite-state grammar has no means of classifying the two sequences together as nominal phrases: in the grammar cited, different auxiliary symbols have to be used to produce **the quick brown fox** from those which come out as **the lazy dog**, in order to capture the fact that the sentence is complete after **dog** but cannot be terminated after **fox**.

This is an intuitive argument against treating English as a finite-state stringset. It is not conclusive: the finite-state grammar can generate the sentence in question, if apparently rather inelegantly. We cannot take it for granted that the ways in which attested languages are handled by the psychological machinery of their speakers necessarily reflect the elegant grammars which the linguist imposes on those languages. It might be that the brain works in a relatively uneconomical way.*

Chomsky's argument would be more conclusive if he could show that attested languages belonged to the class of stringsets which are in principle impossible to define in finite-state terms. A characteristic known to put stringsets into this class is the presence of what are known as *nested dependencies*. Consider the sentence:

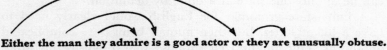

Either the man they admire is a good actor or they are unusually obtuse.

*If it turned out, though, that the 'grammars' implied by speakers' psychological apparatus were regularly more complex than the grammars which linguists construct for the same languages, then one would want some *non*-psychological interpretation of the linguists' grammars. Provided the linguists' grammars fitted the data, one could not simply dismiss them as artificial constructs not corresponding to any aspect of reality, or one would cease to be a scientist.

Here there are dependencies between subject and verb (singular and plural subjects must be followed by singular or plural verbs, respectively) and between **either** and **or** (given **either, or** must follow).* The notion of 'nesting' is rather clear: the dependencies occur one within the other, like Russian dolls. It can be proved that, if there is no limit to this nesting of dependencies, then the resulting stringset is impossible to define in finite-state notation. Since the kind of dependency-nesting we have quoted seems to be a common characteristic of attested languages, Chomsky argues that natural languages are not in general finite-state stringsets.

This is an important point, for Chomsky. The over-all pattern of Chomsky's argument, remember, consists of inferring innate psychological machinery from the existence of constraints on the diversity of natural languages. Since the theory that all natural languages are finite-state stringsets is even stronger than the theory that all natural languages are constituency stringsets, one might feel that Chomsky's nativist arguments would be all the more compelling if the former theory were true. But Chomsky's nativism depends on the existence not merely of constraints on natural language, but of *arbitrary* constraints: that is, the constraints must be ones which cannot be inferred from existing knowledge. If we could predict, before studying linguistics, that natural languages might be expected to have some property *P*, then we can hardly infer novel psychological or philosophical theories from the linguistic finding that the attested languages do indeed have *P*! Now, quite apart from questions of language, it seems *a priori* very plausible that humans might be (extremely complex) finite-state machines; indeed, the reason why Chomsky discusses finite-state grammar is that a number of psychologists have discussed human behaviour in terms which *presuppose* that it is to be explained in finite-state terms. Therefore the finding that attested languages are the kind of languages which finite-state machinery can handle would be no use to Chomsky. It would be merely a confirmation, from language data, of some-

---

* The situation is complicated by the fact that, in addition to the conjunction **either**, English has a homonymous adjective **either** (as in **Either hand will do**) which does not call for a following **or**. A clearer illustration is provided e.g. by German, in which the conjunction **entweder** has no homonyms.

thing which was regarded as likely in any case. The theory that natural languages are constituency but not finite-state stringsets, as our received notions of syntactic structure suggest, is a theory of just the right strength for Chomsky's purposes: it is not as weak as the theory of unrestricted rewrite grammar, which imposes no constraints on the diversity of languages (and thus seems unfalsifiable), while on the other hand it is not so strong as to confine natural languages to a class (finite-state stringsets) which could be expected *a priori* to contain them.

It is unfortunate, then, that Chomsky's claim that English and other attested languages permit unlimited nesting of dependencies is far from cogent. We have seen (in the discussion of self-embedding in chapter 4) that certain sorts of syntactic recursion which give rise to nested dependencies are sharply restricted in English, and several scholars have argued that the attested languages may well be finite-state. Peter Reich's work is significant because it suggests that precisely the restrictions on embedding observed in the attested languages are predicted if we assume that these languages are the output of finite-state machines of a particular kind. I have suggested (in the review referred to on p. 205) that Reich's arguments are not as yet satisfactory; and we may also note that Reich argues for a *particular kind* of finite-state grammar, i.e. for a theory of language even stronger than finite-state theory, so that a version of linguistic nativism might follow even from Reich's theory of language. However, it is worth bearing in mind, as we continue to examine Chomsky's ideas, that this is one point at which his theory is quite vulnerable.

We have discussed a number of different kinds of rule used in various categories of grammar, and we shall introduce rules of a yet further kind shortly. At this point, we must digress briefly to discuss the general notion of 'grammatical *rule*'. We made no special comment on the term 'rule' when we first introduced it into the discussion, yet it is a quite controversial term for philosophers and social scientists.

'Rule' was made a salient term in philosophy by Wittgenstein. According to Wittgenstein, one of the features which distinguish *meaningful* acts such as waving a white flag, or saying **I surrender**, from acts such as eating an orange, which simply are what they are and have no 'meaning', is that the former are instances of 'rule-governed behaviour' (the phrase is not Wittgenstein's own). Since Wittgenstein, a number of philosophers have devoted considerable effort to the analysis of the concept 'rule'; and philosophers often complain that linguists misuse the term.

For one thing, a rule (e.g. the rule of the Highway Code which bids us indicate before turning right) is something to which given behaviour either conforms or fails to conform; but it is not clear that the 'rules' of a constituency grammar relate to any particular kind of actions. The 'translation manual' we have quoted interprets, e.g., 'S → A B' as 'if the last line contains "S", replace it with "A B" '; but no one supposes that before we utter a sentence we inscribe symbols on some cerebral blackboard, erase them, and substitute other symbols. The 'translation manual' interprets a grammar as a set of instructions that an automaton could use to construct random sentences, as a convenient way of explaining what set of sentences is defined by the grammar. No one, least of all Chomsky, assumes that the human mind contains such an automaton.

Secondly, for something to be a rule rather than a scientific law, we must have the option of disobeying: I can choose to turn without indicating, though I cannot choose to disobey the law of gravity. What would it be to disobey the rule 'S → A B'? We can utter ungrammatical strings such as **Of of the of**; but these strings do not seem to violate any *particular* rules, rather they conflict with the entire grammar as a body of rules. Furthermore, as we shall see below, linguists often claim not only that the format of their rules is a linguistic universal, but that many individual rules are shared by all natural languages; this makes it even harder to see how they can be disobeyed.

These criticisms involve a fundamental misunderstanding of Chomsky's position. The philosophers who raise objections of this kind assume that the shape of Chomsky's argument is something like the following: 'I have discovered that natural languages may be defined by means of rules, and, since we already have a rich theory of the nature of rules, this discovery tells us a great deal about the nature of language.' If Chomsky

99

were to argue in this way, it would be appropriate to criticize him by attacking his account of rules. But the truth is that, for Chomsky, 'rule' is a technical term to which he attributes a precise meaning *by definition*. Chomsky is saying this: 'It is a mathematical theorem (*not* an empirical discovery) that any definable stringset may be specified by a finite set of formulae each of the form "$\varphi \rightarrow \psi$", where φ and ψ are sequences of symbols; I choose to call such formulae "rules". I have found that the attested languages all fall within a special subset of the class of definable stringsets, and this subset may be specified in terms of particular subtypes of these "rules"; *this* is an empirical discovery.' The formulae serve only to define the stringsets corresponding to the languages we speak, and it is no part of Chomsky's claims that the formulae describe or regulate whatever psychological processes result in our uttering individual sentences of our languages (though it would perhaps be surprising to discover that the psychological processes bore no relation whatsoever to the formulae).

If this were all the controversy amounted to, it would be a trivial verbal case of mistaken identity – as if a physicist were to object to the use of the term 'police force' on the grounds that it misrepresents the rather precise sense which the term 'force' bears in physics. There is a little more to it than that. Chomsky's use of 'rule' is a natural extension of one philosophical use of 'rule'; namely, the use current in formal logic. Chomsky's 'constituency' and 'transformational' rules (the latter will be discussed shortly) are closely analogous to the logician's 'formation rules' and 'rules of inference', respectively; and these, particularly rules of inference, may well be viewed as behaviour-governing rules – they are rules which the logician follows or fails to follow when constructing a logical 'derivation'. (Concepts of formal logic will be explained when we discuss semantics in chapter 7.)

However, although Chomsky's rules of syntax are so called by analogy with a category of philosopher's rules, the analogy refers to *form*, not to function. The formation rules of standard logics define tree structures (usually represented in logic by bracketing) in just the same way as Chomsky's constituency rules, for instance; but it does not follow that syntactic rules describe a series of actions which issue in speech, in the way that logical rules describe the series of actions by which a logician builds up a derivation on paper. Therefore the criticism of Chomsky still misses its target. The philosophers who object to Chomsky's use of 'rule' tend to be just those who stress Wittgenstein's argument that there are no fixed limits on the ways in which the use of a word can be extended; so they can hardly object to Chomsky's rather minor extension of the use of 'rule'!

The theory that natural languages are constituency languages is a theory strong and arbitrary enough to serve well as the basis for nativist views of the sort Chomsky advocates. The constituency theory accords closely with received ideas about language; and it can be argued that those of Chomsky's predecessors who discussed syntax presupposed, more or less explicitly, the correctness of the constituency theory.

Unfortunately, it turns out (according to Chomsky) that constituency notation alone is not sufficient for the description of attested languages. The grammar of, e.g., English will contain a series of constituency rules; but these must be supplemented by rules of a new kind, called *transformational rules*.

A transformational rule acts in a quite different way from the various classes of rewrite rule we have examined above; rather than creating strings by replacing symbols with other symbols, a transformational rule converts the trees defined by a constituency grammar into trees of a different structure. It will be best to illustrate by example. One English transformation will be responsible for converting active sentences into their passive counterparts. The Passivizing transformation might be represented by means of the following diagram (top of p. 102). The 'translation manual' for rules of this form runs as follows: 'If the upper part of a given constituency tree has the pattern shown on the left of the diagram, construct a new constituency tree whose upper part has the pattern shown on the right, adding the lower parts of the old tree at appropriate places in the new tree as indicated by the dotted lines.' This rule will convert active sentences into passive sentences. For instance,

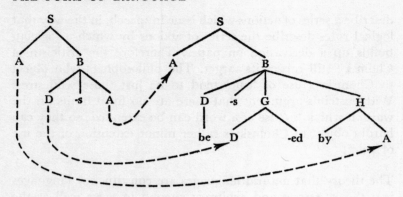

our constituency grammar will assign the following structure to the string **A girl kicks the boy**:

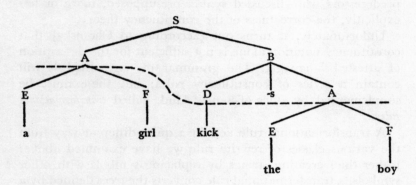

The part of this tree above the dotted line is identical to the left-hand side of the transformational rule; so, that rule gives us the new tree corresponding to the string **The boy is kicked by a girl** (see opposite). Other actives will lead to other passives, as different substitutions are made for the A and D nodes.

Transformational rules, then, give us an extra means of constructing sentences. Rather than producing every grammatical string by constituency rules, we may write a constituency grammar for only certain of the sentences, and use transformations to derive the other sentences from these

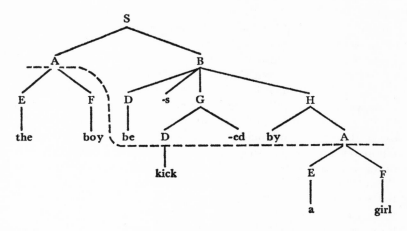

sentences, as here we have derived passive sentences from active ones. In fact transformations are even more central than this in Chomsky's grammars. The Passivizing transformation is optional (active and passive sentences are both grammatical), but grammars will include also transformations that apply obligatorily to trees which fit them. Indeed, for Chomsky, *no* English sentence – not even apparently simple sentences like **A girl kicks the boy** – will be produced directly by constituency rules. A Chomskyan grammar consists of a set of constituency rules called the *base*, together with an ordered series of transformations. The structured strings defined by the base are required to undergo in order each of the transformations applicable to them, unless these are optional (there will usually be a good many obligatory transformations applicable); the strings defined as grammatical are those strings which are dominated by the trees that finally emerge at the end of the series of transformations.

In other words, Chomsky agrees with the traditional notion that sentences have hierarchical structures, but he claims that they have more than one such structure each. The parsing we learn at school consists in stating the structure which a sentence ends up with at the end of the series of transformations – what Chomsky calls the *surface structure* of the sentence. The surface structure is only the last of a series of progressively altered structures associated with the sentence, beginning with the structure defined directly by the base rules and input to the earliest transformation, which Chomsky calls the *deep structure* of the sentence in question. The series of trees associated with a given sentence, beginning with the deep structure defined by the base and ending with the surface structure produced by the last transformation, is called the *derivation* of the sentence.

As we have seen, there are stringsets which cannot in principle be defined by means of constituency rules alone: those with overlapping dependencies, for instance. However, although Chomsky and others suggested at one time that English and other attested languages might have characteristics making them undefinable in constituency terms, these suggestions have been rather unconvincing; probably we could define English with a large number of constituency rules. The real argument for transformational rules is an argument of simplicity. Chomsky claims that, if we allow ourselves to use transformational as well as constituency rules, we shall be able to specify attested languages much more economically than if we restrict ourselves to constituency rules alone.

This is not obvious from the single example I have given. We could produce passive sentences directly, by dint of increasing somewhat the number of constituency rules in our grammar. Why regard the addition of the Passivizing transformation as preferable to the addition of the extra constituency rules needed to produce passive sentences without the transformation? I have given no reason. But Chomsky's argument does not concern the simplest way of handling individual constructions such as the passive; rather, it concerns which grammars are simplest over all. The claim is that, as we take more and more of the various sentences of English into account, the complexity of a pure constituency grammar will grow in a runaway, exponential fashion; while, if we use transformations, we will find that transformations posited to handle one construction turn out also to serve other purposes, so that the returns from expanding the grammar will increase rather than diminish.

Notice that the concept of 'simplicity' appealed to here is a purely intuitive, *a priori* one: we prefer a grammar that occupies ten pages rather than twenty, other things (e.g. the size of the print) being equal. As we have seen (p. 65), Chomsky suggests that what makes a grammar 'simple' is an empirical question to be answered within linguistics: we have to discover what kinds of 'generalization' typically occur in attested languages, and then prefer grammars which contain generalizations of those kinds. But this is to pick ourselves up by our own bootstraps. If we choose to use pure constituency notation for grammars, then the grammars of attested languages will contain the kinds of generalization expressed by constituency rules, and we shall prefer constituency grammars; if we use transformations, then grammars of attested languages will contain transformational generalizations, so that transformational theory will be correct. To escape the circularity, we must rely on an (admittedly vague) *a priori* criterion of simplicity.

It is in some ways unfortunate that Chomsky chose terms as evocative as 'deep structure' and 'surface structure' for the constituency trees at either end of a transformational derivation. No aspect of his theories has attracted wider attention or been so frequently misunderstood. We must therefore stress that the two phrases are purely technical terms, and are not intended to imply anything more than has been said here. Chomsky is claiming merely that the simplest formal device for defining any attested stringset will consist of a set of constituency rules together with a sequence of transformational rules, from which it follows that any sentence will be associated with a series of tree diagrams; he chooses to use the terms 'deep' and 'surface' structure to name the first and last tree in the sequence associated with each sentence. 'Deep' is certainly not being used, for instance, in the sense in which we call some people 'deep thinkers': Enid Blyton's sentences have structures as deep as Bertrand Russell's. To the philosopher it is worth pointing out that Chomsky's terms were not modelled on Wittgenstein's distinction between 'depth grammar' and 'surface grammar' (*Philosophical Investigations*, §664); here, as elsewhere, Wittgenstein used 'grammar' to refer to sensicality, not to grammaticality in the linguist's sense.

These remarks will become particularly relevant later, when we shall suggest that Chomsky's 'deep structures' do in fact have a special relationship with the meanings of their respective sentences. It will be important to bear in mind that this is a purely empirical finding; there is nothing in the *definition* of 'deep structure' to imply that the deep structure of a sentence is any more or less closely related to its meaning than is the surface structure of the sentence.

One of the misunderstandings to which Chomsky's account of 'deep structure' has led is that many people have taken the finding that attested languages contain transformations as a great positive advance in our appreciation of the nature of human language. Jerrold Katz, for instance, compares Chomsky's replacement of pure constituency grammars by transformational grammars with the idea of the ancient Greek, Democritus, that apparently-continuous physical objects are composed of discrete atoms. Both Democritus and Chomsky improved on their predecessors' ideas, according to Katz, because both of them saw an 'underlying reality' beneath the surface appearance of things.

It is not clear to me that one can characterize views as speculative as those of the Greek atomists as scientific advances, even though modern empirical science might be said to have vindicated them in this instance. But, even if we accept Katz's view of Democritus, his comparison with Chomsky is misleading. Chomsky's transformational theory is preferable to the constituency theory because the latter is false, perhaps; but the move from constituency grammar to transformational grammar is not a triumphant advance, it is rather a necessary but unfortunate retreat. Constituency theory is much stronger than transformational theory (a constituency grammar is a special case of transformational grammar, in which the number of transformations is zero); in other words, constituency theory imposes much narrower constraints than transformational theory on natural language, so that psychological and philosophical arguments based on linguistic universals would be more cogent if constituency theory were correct.

To say that transformational theory is weaker than constituency theory is not to say that it is empty. Transformational notation still seems to be quite restricted as a format for writing grammars, by comparison with the full range of possibilities provided by ordinary English. Let us return to the case, introduced in chapter 3, of the child who is trying to solve the proportion **Mary is coming : Is Mary coming? :: John's**

mother must be asleep : X? I gave three logically-possible hypotheses: front the second word; front the shortest word; front the main verb; and I suggested that, of these three alternatives, only the third will be tested out by the child. Transformational theory offers a way of formalizing this suggestion, since the third hypothesis can be expressed as a transformational rule. If we assume that the structure of **Mary is coming** is, say:

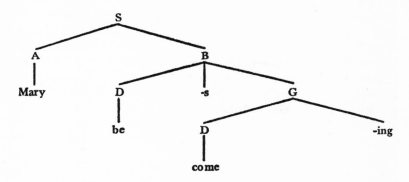

then we can express the rule 'front the main verb' in transformational format as, for instance:

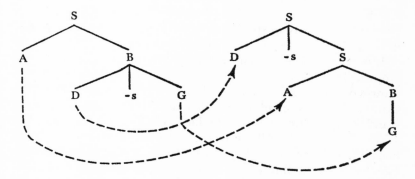

This rule takes **Mary is coming** into **Is Mary coming?**; and, if we assume that **John's mother must be asleep** also has the structure shown on the left, then by substituting **John's mother** for **Mary** under A, **must** for **be** under D, and **be**

asleep for **coming** under G the same rule will take the latter string into **Must John's mother be asleep?** (At least, the rule will work in the latter case provided we overlook the third-person suffix **-s,** which never occurs with **must.** We have seen that we shall need some extra clauses in the description of English to tidy up sequences of formatives into words; just as we shall need a rule that **be -s** comes out as **is,** so we may have a rule which realizes **must -s** as **must.**)

I do not claim that the rules quoted here are in fact the rules that will appear in our ultimate 'best grammar' for English. If we went on to examine more facts about English, we should soon find reasons to believe that the underlying structures, and hence also the transformations, involved in the sentences under discussion are other than suggested here. (For instance, the question corresponding to **John goes home** is **Does John go home?**, not **Goes John home?**) The point is, though, that the rule just given is *a* transformational rule which expresses the hypothesis 'To form a question, move the main verb to the front'. It should be fairly clear that there are *no* transformations which would express the rules 'Move the second word to the front' or 'Move the shortest word to the front'. In the **Mary is coming** case, since the A constituent, **Mary**, is only one word long, the second word of the sentence is dominated by D; but if A happens to be longer than one word, then its second word will be the second word of the sentence. The transformational format has no way of specifying how many words occur under its auxiliary symbols, or what their lengths are.

Intuitively, then, transformational theory does seem to be empirical: it permits us to say some things but not others. However, the reader may find this argument specious. We cannot observe the rules a speaker uses to form his sentences, if indeed syntactic rules are the kinds of thing speakers can be said to 'use' at all. All we can observe is the stringset which constitutes the speaker's language. (Indeed, even this has to be inferred from the limited set of examples speakers are observed to utter.) In order to demonstrate that transformational theory is empirical, we must surely show that there are stringsets which cannot be defined in transformational terms; to show that there are individual rules which cannot be stated as transformations seems inadequate.

The question whether there are non-transformational stringsets is a complex one. Obviously it depends on saying precisely what we count as a transformational grammar; I have done no more than sketch the notion of 'transformational grammar' here. In practice, there are a wide range of competing and slightly differing hypotheses about what is to count as a transformational grammar, and the question has to be asked separately for each version. However, the answers coincide in many cases: for quite a number of plausible alternative versions of transformational theory, it has been proved that any string-set which can be defined at all can be defined by a finitely large transformational grammar. Even such unnatural stringsets as the prime-number and odd-token languages can be specified in transformational terms.

This seems to rob Chomsky's theory of any empirical content. If *any* stringset can be defined transformationally, Chomsky cannot be said to have discovered anything by finding that attested languages can be defined transformationally. Chomsky's transformational theory of language, it would seem, amounts to a highly elaborate and esoteric way of making the assertion that Joos expressed in a dozen words in 1957: 'languages [can] differ from each other without limit and in unpredictable ways'.

This negative evaluation is unjustified. There are two arguments against it. I begin with the less forceful.

The first point is that, in claiming that all natural languages can be defined by transformational grammars, Chomsky is not claiming that all transformational grammars necessarily correspond to natural languages. It is accepted, by all Chomsky-an linguists, that the current theory of transformational grammar is clearly far too weak, in the sense that it provides for structures and structure-changing operations which seem never to occur in attested languages, as well as for those which do occur. One of the tasks facing linguists is to impose constraints on the definition of 'transformational grammar' so as to rule out the unrealized possibilities while allowing all the situations which are observed. A large proportion of day-to-day technical research in linguistics, in fact, consists of making proposals about constraints on grammatical notation which seem to hold for attested languages (or of refuting such proposals by citing languages which do not obey particular constraints).

One widely-canvassed suggestion, for instance, is based on the observation that, as transformational analysis of various attested languages proceeds, the deep structures hypothesized for sentences in different languages seem to be coming more and more to resemble one another. The suggestion is that, while a 'transformational grammar' is defined as a constituency base together with a sequence of transformations, it may be that all attested languages in fact share one particular constituency grammar as their base, so that natural languages differ only in their transformations (and in their vocabulary). Clearly this suggestion, if correct, greatly reduces the range of entities which count as 'transformational grammars'. Chomsky himself, although not explicitly an advocate of the *universal-base hypothesis*, seems to support it implicitly by arguing that the set of syntactic categories – noun, verb, nominal phrase, etc. – is a linguistic universal. The syntactic categories correspond to the auxiliary symbols A, B, C etc. occurring in the base; but we have seen that the particular symbols used have no empirical import: I make exactly the same claims about English if I replace every occurrence of 'A' in an English grammar by an occurrence of, e.g., 'NP'. Chomsky's remark seems to make sense only as a claim that the *pattern* of occurrence of auxiliary symbols in constituency rules is constant: i.e. that if a grammar using 'A' has three rules with 'A' on the left, then a grammar using 'NP' will have three rules with 'NP' on the left, and so on.

Another suggestion, made by Emmon Bach, is that, although the definition of 'transformational rule' allows for infinitely many different examples, it may be that only a finite number of transformations ever actually occur in natural languages; each individual language would pick an assortment from the finite permitted set. For instance, English has a question-forming rule which moves an item from the middle of a sentence to the front, and many other languages use 'fronting' transformations either to form questions or for other purposes; but there are no known examples of languages with rules moving an item to the *end* of its sentence. 'Backing' transformations can be defined as readily as fronting transformations; but perhaps backing transformations are not permitted in natural languages.

If the theory of transformational grammar is restricted in such ways, it may be that the restricted theory will no longer provide a grammar for each stringset. Indeed, this is known to be the case. Stanley Peters and R. W. Ritchie have recently proved that much weaker constraints on transformational grammar than those suggested here are sufficient to render some stringsets undefinable.

Furthermore, the very fact that children invariably succeed in mastering their mother tongue gives us good reason to suppose that the correct theory of language will ultimately turn out to be stronger than Chomsky's transformational theory. We may view the task facing an infant who has to learn the language surrounding him as that of working out, presumably by trial and error, which of the range of possible human grammars fits the data with which he is confronted. Obviously this task is easier if the range of possible grammars is relatively restricted and if the data are relatively complete. However, the data are in fact quite limited; it is not clear that the infant is even given negative instances. (It is rare, except in the most pedantic of households, for children's errors of syntax to be corrected; parents are usually too concerned with the *content* of what their children say to bother with its syntactic *form*.) Yet children always do suceed in learning their mother tongue. We have no idea what procedure they use; but, recently, Henry Hamburger and Kenneth Wexler have proved some interesting mathematical theorems based merely on the observation that there must exist *some* procedure guaranteed to succeed in the long run. The details of their findings are too complex to discuss here, but, essentially, they appear to have demonstrated that the range of possible human grammars must be considerably narrower than the range of transformational grammars if children are to succeed in the task of language-acquisition.

This, then, is one answer to the objection that transformational theory fails to forbid any stringsets: much current work in linguistics consists of arguing for constraints on the theory which do lead it to forbid some stringsets. But the sceptic may not be very happy with this reply. Although linguists agree that we want to constrain the definition of 'transformational grammar', there is as yet no consensus on what the correct constraints are likely to be. The sceptic may reasonably say to the linguist: 'You tell me that you can infer important conclusions about the nature of Man from the finding that there are limits to the diversity of human languages. When I ask you to state those limits, you tell me that you have not yet worked out what they are, though you are confident of being able to do so soon. I suggest you stop bothering me until you have actually come up with a concrete theory of linguistic universals.'

Indeed, even if linguists agreed on a theory of language which could be shown to rule out some stringsets, one would not know how to take this unless one knew how numerous the 'forbidden' stringsets were. The mathematical proofs usually run: 'There is *at least one* recursively enumerable stringset which cannot be defined by a grammar of class X'; but, if a theory of language rules out only one or a few freakish stringsets, the fact that those stringsets do not occur as attested languages will scarcely provide overwhelming support for the particular theory in question.

All this is less grave than it may seem. In my view even the unconstrained transformational theory, which fails to forbid any stringset, is a perfectly empirical, refutable theory of language, and quite sufficient as a basis for Chomsky's nativist arguments. I suggest that the lesson to be drawn from the *omnipotence* of many plausible versions of the theory of language (i.e. from the fact that these theories permit all stringsets) is that 'naturalness' of stringsets may be a gradient rather than an all-or-none property. We have already discussed the question of gradience in connection with grammaticality of strings in a language, in chapter 3; I argued there that linguists have assumed grammaticality to be an all-or-none property, and that, while this assumption cannot be taken as an *a priori* truth, there is little evidence against it. Those linguists who have concerned themselves with the problem of dividing natural from unnatural stringsets have assumed that naturalness is also an all-or-none property; but again there is no *a priori* reason to believe this, and if plausible theories of language are omnipotent then we shall do well to take it that the all-or-none assumption is false in this case.

What I am suggesting is as follows. Every stringset that can be defined at all can be defined by means of a transformational grammar, assuming we impose no special constraints on transformational theory. However, the simplest transformational grammar for some stringset A may be much more complex than the simplest transformational grammar for another stringset B (using 'simplest' in the *a priori* sense, as always). If that is the case, then the theory of transformational grammar asserts that A is *less natural* than B. The theory assigns each stringset to a point on a scale of relative naturalness; and now we may interpret the theory as making the empirical assertion that the attested languages will be concentrated near the 'natural' end of the scale.

Notice that, although different theories of language may each permit the same range of stringsets, they may make quite different assertions about naturalness. Both plain English and transformational theory permit all stringsets to be defined; but, whereas the prime-number language is particularly easy to define using plain English (I defined it in a few words in chapter 3), in transformational notation it is presumably rather difficult to define. ('Presumably', because I have no idea how to write a transformational grammar for the prime-number language; it is only because of the theorem about transformational omnipotence that I know it must have some – surely rather complex – transformational grammar.) Therefore transformational theory asserts that the prime-number language is relatively unnatural, and thus relatively unlikely to be attested, in a way that the use of ordinary English as our linguistic metalanguage would not. (Likewise, the theory of unrestricted rewrite rules, which I suggested to be vacuous earlier in this chapter, does in fact make empirical predictions about relative naturalness of stringsets; the reason for dismissing the unrestricted rewrite theory is that its predictions are less accurate than those of transformational theory, not that it is vacuous.)

One may justly reply that attested languages also do not seem particularly easy to define in transformational notation.* But this is merely to say that the current transformational theory is not yet the correct theory of language, which is much less grave than the charge that it is vacuous. As we impose con-

---

* I am indebted to Eva Szoffer for pointing out this objection.

straints on the definition of 'transformational grammar', whether or not we render some stringsets absolutely undefinable we radically alter the naturalness-ordering of those stringsets which can be defined transformationally. For instance, if we adopt a universal-base hypothesis, then many stringsets which previously had very simple transformational grammars will become much less 'natural' – their strings will now have to be derived, presumably by a complex series of transformations, from deep structures very different from the surface forms of the strings.

This, then, is the real goal of research in linguistics: to reorder stringsets along the naturalness gradient in such a way that the attested stringsets come ever closer to the natural end, while as many other stringsets as possible are moved away from that end of the scale. If some stringsets can be shown to be absolutely 'impossible', well and good; but this is in no way necessary. There is nothing 'unscientific' in abandoning all-or-none predictions in favour of predictions about the relative likelihood of various stringsets being attested; many, if not most, scientific theories make probabilistic rather than yes-or-no predictions.

Interpreted in this fashion, Chomsky's theory of language clearly has some way to go before it can be regarded as perfected, in the sense that Chomsky's definition of 'transformational grammar' still treats as natural (and therefore relatively likely to be attested) many stringsets which we would confidently predict will never be observed. However, though we are still a good way from the end of our journey, we have also come a long way from the beginning. Chomsky's theory does succeed in condemning, as unnatural, many stringsets which are easily defined in plain English. Although Chomsky's theory will certainly be improved on, there is little reason to suppose that it will be flatly rejected. Better theories are likely to incorporate Chomsky's theory rather than contradicting it, as, for instance, Einstein's theory in physics incorporated Newton's theory as a special case.

Before concluding, we should mention a further objection which is sometimes voiced against Chomsky's theory of linguistic universals. Chomsky claims that all attested languages are appropriately described by means of transformational grammars, and we have now seen that this is an empirical claim. But the claim is premature (the objectors suggest) until linguists have looked at all, or at least a large proportion, of the attested languages. Chomskyan linguists are far from having done this; in fact linguists often suggest modifications to the general theory of language based merely on their experience of English or one or two other European languages.

The objection has no force. Like any other scientific theory, a claim about linguistic universals is a *prediction* about possible future observations, not a *report* on an exhaustive set of completed observations. When the chemist claims that iron dissolves in sulphuric acid, he does not pretend to have tested all pieces of iron in the world – if the claim is a novel one, he may have asserted it on the basis of only one or two experiments, but he predicts that it will hold true for any future experiment. There are only finitely many attested languages (how many depends on what counts as one 'language', but the figure often quoted is between three and four thousand); this finitude of the subject of linguistics deceives people into thinking that linguists ought to make exhaustive observations before theorizing. But there is no reason to impose more rigid requirements on the theoretical linguist than on the theoretical chemist. If we did require the linguist to survey all or most languages before making any pronouncement, then clearly in practice we would have no theory of language.

What we do expect, in linguistics as in chemistry, is that the theorists should search for refutations of suggested theories. If a theory of language not only were constructed on the basis of English data but were never tested against the data of exotic languages, then one would be entitled to a sceptical attitude. But this is not normally the case. Certainly a disproportionate amount of linguistic research deals with English, for unavoidable practical reasons. (It is much easier to do fruitful syntactic research on one's mother tongue than on a language one has learned later, even if one is very fluent in the latter; the mother tongue of a majority of Chomskyan linguists is American English.) However, the imbalance is not as extreme as it appears to those observing linguistics from the outside: the fact is that work on English syntax tends to be published in journals and books which are readily accessible to the non-specialist. There is plenty of research on other languages going on. To take the language in which the present author happens to have a special interest, a scholarly journal recently began publication which is devoted exclusively to the linguistics of Chinese. Another happy development is that the handful of countries in which Chomskyan linguistics is pursued on a large scale, which until a few years ago were all countries whose national language is English or a closely-related European language, has recently expanded to include Japan. We may look forward to severe testing by Japanese linguists of universal claims based on English data, and vice versa.

Although Chomsky's theory of language must be regarded as provisional and liable to modification in the way that all scientific theories are provisional, we have as much reason to believe in the reality of the universal traits Chomsky attributes to natural language as we have to believe in the statements of other sciences. The central linguistic universal of Chomsky's theory is the hierarchical structure represented by constituency diagrams: according to Chomsky, each sentence of a natural language has, not just one constituency tree (as constituency theory asserts), but a whole series of them. If any abstract scientific finding can be regarded as needing explanation, the prevalence of hierarchical structure in natural language also needs to be explained.

Whether Chomsky's explanation will hold water is, of course, another question. In the next chapter we consider some counter-arguments to Chomsky's nativist explanation of constituency structure.

6

Objections to Linguistic Nativism

According to Chomsky, the languages which humans use as their mother tongues are stringsets of a particular kind: namely, they are stringsets which are relatively easily defined by some version of transformational notation. It can hardly be a coincidence that the attested languages are all of a kind. Chomsky explains the similarities between the attested languages by saying that humans are capable of acquiring and/or using languages only because they are genetically endowed with some specific neural equipment, and that transformational notation correlates with the properties which a language must have if it is to fit this inherited neural machinery.

It is not excluded that a human might succeed in mastering some non-transformational language-like system. For instance, it might conceivably be that one could equip the sentences of the prime-number language with some function or meaning, and that humans could learn, as a *tour de force*, to operate with the prime-number language as we operate with English. (Of course, this is scarcely a practical experiment. Even if we knew what it would be to assign meanings to the prime-number sentences and to teach people to use them, the test would be fair only if we tried to teach infants the prime-number language as their first language – which would clearly be unethical.) But in any case, the languages which people speak naturally, rather than as a virtuoso intellectual performance, will be those which are relatively easy to describe in transformational notation.

One obvious objection to Chomsky's account, which I have heard advanced by Sir Alfred Ayer, is that Chomsky only defers the problem rather than solving it. Chomsky explains the *individual's* acquisition of language by treating language as an inherited trait of the human species, but he says nothing about how the *species* acquired language. This is very true; indeed, not only does Chomsky fail to offer an explanation of the origin of human language, but he attacks the suggestions of others (e.g. Popper's evolutionary account) as misguided. Chomsky's attitude on the question of how human language originated has been justly described (by Stephen Toulmin) as 'agnostic'. Not only do we not know how humans using transformational languages evolved from languageless apes (Chomsky suggests), but we probably never can know.

Whether Chomsky has 'failed to solve the problem', though, depends entirely on what one takes 'the problem' to be. If one seeks an account of how individual humans manage to learn and/or to use a given language, then one will surely regard it as an advance if one can pick out certain properties of the language as genetically determined. The psychologist constructing a model of learning mechanisms, for instance, will be interested exclusively in the relative contribution of inheritance and environment to the individual's abilities; he would not regard questions about how the inherited factor originated in the species as falling within his purview. Chomsky is perfectly consistent in his refusal to offer an explanation for the latter problem, since Chomsky's emergentist view of biological evolution implies that there are no answers to questions about how species acquire new traits. In other words, if Chomsky's view of biology is correct, he has shown that what appears to be a rather *sui generis* psychological question ('Why does the linguistic behaviour of humans always have form X?') is really just one more of a large class of biological questions known to be unanswerable ('Why does species Y have trait Z?'). No one can do more than this.

Ayer is neither a psychologist nor a biologist but a philosopher. The burden of his complaint may well be that Chomsky's findings have no *philosophical* consequences, even if they are of interest to various of the empirical sciences. But again, whether this is so depends entirely on what one counts as philosophically problematic. Even more than most subjects, philosophy has to be defined question-beggingly as 'that with which philosophers concern themselves'. Many philosophers clearly do find Chomsky's work relevant to their interests. This is partly because Chomsky himself claims his work to have philosophical importance (so that philosophers feel bound to examine it if only in order to dismiss that claim), but it is not wholly for this reason. Some philosophers view language as a more or less adaptable medium through which we describe the world, and their concern is with the world rather than with the medium through which we describe it. Man's ability to speak is of course part of the world, but for these philosophers it is simply one more contingent fact, alongside the ability to digest or to ride a bicycle. A philosopher of this turn of mind may have no more interest in Chomsky's work than in the fact that digestion is an innate capacity and cycling a learned skill. However, many philosophers, particularly since Wittgenstein, have shifted language to a more central position in their field of view, and have not felt it possible to distinguish so sharply between the world and the linguistic medium through which the world is described (if indeed 'describe' is an appropriate term). Chomsky's work tends to have much more appeal to philosophers of this latter class. (Indeed, Wittgenstein's own early book, *Tractatus Logico-Philosophicus*, is strikingly similar in flavour to Chomsky's work, although much less empirical.) Ayer himself happens to stand rather apart from the Wittgensteinian tradition dominant in modern British philosophy; hence, perhaps, his view of Chomsky.

It is no part of my task to stipulate who should and who cannot be expected to find Chomsky's work relevant to their interests. I am concerned simply to state and criticize the inferences Chomsky draws from linguistics. The reader is in the best position to decide whether or not the discussion interests him.

Assuming that we are interested in whether Chomsky's nativist account of linguistic universals is well founded, the next objection to that account which we must face may be called the 'What else?' objection. Hilary Putnam, for instance, suggests that Chomsky's argument for linguistic nativism boils down to the rhetorical question '*what else* could account for language learning?' If we have not eliminated alternative explanations for linguistic universals, then there is no reason to believe that the nativist explanation is the correct one.

The trouble with this is that it seems to be an objection to science in general, rather than to Chomsky specifically. *All* scientific explanations are 'What else?' explanations. It would be satisfying if scientists, like Sherlock Holmes, could proceed by eliminating all but one explanation for given facts, so that 'whatever remains, *however improbable*, must be the truth'. But we have seen that there is no limit to the range of scientific theories; and this surely applies even to the range of conceivable explanations for a given set of facts. All any scientist can do is to offer *an* explanation, and invite the onlooker either to refute his explanation or to offer a better one. This is just what Chomsky has done.

Serious objections to Chomsky's nativism will consist either of arguments that the universals are vacuous or fail to apply to some attested languages, or of refutations of Chomsky's explanations for the universals, or of counter-explanations. There have been a number of attempts to construct such objections, and we shall examine these in turn.

In the first place, since Chomsky argues that our ability to acquire and use human languages is due to innate psychological machinery, it seems to follow that our species should be the only one capable of acquiring or using human language. Certainly, other species have rudimentary communication systems – the danger calls of birds, the dancing of bees; but Chomsky's point is precisely that human languages are sharply distinct from these systems, which do not (for instance) involve recursive constituency grammars. Intuitively it seems acceptable to regard human languages as different in kind from these systems: the bees, for instance, can tell each other only how to find nectar, while in English or Chinese we can tell each other anything whatsoever.

If, then, it were possible to teach an individual of another species to use a human language, this would seem to be a refutation of Chomsky's nativism. Two experiments in recent years have attempted to do just this.

In both cases, the subject has been a chimpanzee. It is obviously sensible to use a closely-related species for an experiment of this kind; since chimps are so like us, if they could talk at all they are likely to want to talk about some of the same sorts of thing as we talk about, so that there will be relatively few barriers to communication *other* than the hypothesized fact that chimps lack the innate human *faculté de langage*. (Imagine trying to make conversation with an ant – what would one have in common?) If it makes sense to rank species in terms of intelligence, then the chimpanzee would commonly be ranked second or third to Man (although, as we have seen, this may be nothing more than a roundabout way of repeating the point that chimpanzees are similar to men). However, chimps in the wild state have only the rudimentary kind of signalling system – calls for 'Danger', 'Food', and so on – found in many other species. According to Jane van Lawick-Goodall, 'whilst chimpanzee calls do serve to convey basic information about some situations and individuals, they cannot, for the most part, be compared to a spoken language'.

It is clearly impossible to teach a chimp a spoken human language, since, as we saw in chapter 2, chimps cannot produce (or, probably, hear) the range of sounds involved in human languages. Written human languages involve very subtle manual and visual skills which are difficult even for human children to acquire, so they would not provide a fair test of a chimp's ability to learn. But the features of natural language which Chomsky uses as the basis for his nativist arguments are features of our linguistic messages, not of the media in which we express those messages. Perhaps chimpanzees could learn languages similar to ours if we chose a more suitable medium.

The first experiment we shall examine, organized by R. A. and B. T. Gardner with the chimpanzee Washoe, involves a gesture language used by the deaf and dumb, called American Sign Language. This is not the finger-spelling by which the deaf spell out English words letter by letter, but is an independent language which uses gestures (some 'onomatopoeic', others not) to stand for units of meaning – signs correspond to words or formatives rather than to letters or sounds. American Sign Language has no special relationship with English; in fact American 'signers' can understand French signers more easily than British (because sign language was introduced to America from France, by Thomas Gallaudet and Laurent Clerc in the early nineteenth century). However, the various versions of sign language used in different Western nations apparently are related closely enough that signers can usually communicate after a fashion. Sign language seems to serve its users just as well as spoken languages serve normal humans; one writer, for instance, mentions observing a vigorous political meeting (concerned with the chairmanship of a centre for the deaf) conducted entirely in sign language.

The Gardners, with a number of assistants, began to teach Washoe American Sign Language in June 1966, when she was about one year old. The teaching situation was as close as possible to the situation in which a human learns his mother tongue: Washoe lived in an environment filled with adult humans signing to each other, she was played with and made much of as a human baby would be, signs were repeated to her and her attempts to imitate them were encouraged, and so on. Washoe proved a good learner; by 1971 she used a vocabulary of some 140 'words', and she was taking part in quite complicated conversations with humans. Seeing the Gardners' films of Washoe, one certainly has the impression of a creature as articulate as a human child would be at the same age. In a more recent related experiment, a group of seven chimps taught the sign language have begun to use it among themselves.

Let us assume, for the sake of argument, that chimps can learn to become as proficient in American Sign Language as humans. (Washoe has not reached this stage, but she is still only a 'child'.) Would this refute Chomsky?

To answer this we must presumably ask how far American Sign Language, as used by human signers, counts as a fully-fledged 'natural language'. Certainly it shares many of the obvious features of more normal languages: it contains a large number of symbols, many of which are arbitrary, including both proper names and general terms applying to classes of objects; Washoe has no difficulty in using the sign language to refer to objects not physically present, in generalizing the use of a word (e.g. the word for 'key') from the situation in which she first met it to other instances of keys and of locks for which keys are needed, and so on. And, as already mentioned, signers seem to be able to use sign language to perform the same tasks for which speakers use spoken languages. However, the features of natural languages on which Chomsky bases his arguments do not involve the nature of their vocabulary, or the uses to which they are put, but their syntactic structure.

Does sign language have structural properties akin to those with which constituency and transformational theories are concerned?

The Gardners themselves are not interested in this question. They argue that, if sign language serves the same purposes as spoken human languages, then mastery of sign language by chimps would establish that chimps share any intellectual characteristics involved in the human use of spoken languages. But, since spoken human languages do in fact have very particular, arbitrary syntactic properties, it is surely worth asking whether sign language is similar; and the answer is unequivocally 'no'. Sign language seems to be a language virtually without syntax of any kind: there are very few 'structure-marking' elements akin to English **the, of, is, to,** etc., and word-order seems to be either random, or else used in a quite *non*-arbitrary way to mark relative salience of items mentioned, or ordering in time of the parts of an action or process. A typical sign-language 'sentence' is one cited by B. T. Tervoort, with which a young man asked his girlfriend out for the afternoon: **You me downtown movie fun?** I. M. Schlesinger has conducted experiments showing that users of Israeli Sign Language (which exemplifies the same general system as American Sign Language) are incapable of expressing in signs the difference between pictures of a boy giving an apple to a girl and of a girl giving an apple to a boy, and the like. Sign language is very *unlike* the kinds of system which occur as spoken languages.

The Washoe experiment does not therefore seem to provide clear evidence against Chomsky. It does raise an obvious problem: if signers can get by in life without syntax, why do spoken languages always contain syntax, and syntax of a particular kind? This is a perplexing problem, which might become clearer with more research on how signers use their language. The only suggestion I can offer is the frequently-expressed notion that language is akin to, say, a power station whose output is used most of the time merely to run an electric doorbell – in other words, that in everyday speech we normally exploit only a fraction of the expressive potential which natural spoken languages offer us. If this view is correct, then perhaps sign language seems functionally equivalent to spoken language only because the situations in which one needs the extra expressive power or precision of spoken language are so infrequent. I do not find this explanation at all satisfying; but I certainly see no reason to abandon the claim that transformational theory represents psychological structure innate in our species on the grounds that members of another species can master a *non*-transformational language.

However, this reply may be irrelevant in view of the second experiment, by Ann and David Premack with the chimpanzee Sarah. The Sarah experiment also started in 1966; by 1972 Sarah had a vocabulary of about 130 words. Sarah's language is completely artificial, using coloured plastic shapes which adhere magnetically to a metal blackboard; and Sarah's language is a much more formal affair than Washoe's language. For one thing, Sarah's language is rich in abstract logical concepts: 'same', 'different', 'not', 'name', etc. The language contains a question-forming element **?**, and it is possible to ask questions such as 'What colour are bananas?' (literally, **? colour banana**), to which Sarah will reply 'Yellow.' (The word for 'banana' is a red square, and that for 'yellow' a black T-shape; Sarah apparently has no difficulty in distinguishing 'use' and 'mention' of words – i.e. she would not say that bananas are red just because **banana** is red – although this is a fairly subtle point even for humans, judging by the frequency with which inverted commas are misused.) Sarah's language also has a rigid syntax, from which she is not permitted to depart; thus, to ask Mary to give her an apple, Sarah has to say **Mary give apple Sarah**, and may not use a different word-order or omit words.

Although Sarah's language clearly has syntax, we have not yet shown that the syntax resembles that found in human languages. We might well take the material cited so far as evidence *for* rather than against Chomsky: Sarah's language is one which permits quite abstract, subtle concepts to be expressed, yet it is not clear that the language involves constituency structure or transformational rules – so one cannot explain away the prevalence of constituency and transformational rules in human languages by asserting that any language used to express abstract ideas must of necessity involve such rules.

However, the Premacks claim that Sarah's language does indeed employ rules of the kind typical of human languages, and that Sarah understands the use of these rules. Thus, one of Sarah's words represents the logical connective ⊃ (as in **p ⊃ q** for 'if **p**, then **q**'). A language using ⊃ will clearly possess constituency structure; the rule controlling the use of ⊃, namely 'S → S ⊃ S', is a clear case of a constituency rule (in fact it is a rule which makes the grammar containing it recursive). Sarah understands pairs of sentences such as **Sarah take apple ⊃ Mary give chocolate Sarah**; **Sarah take banana ⊃ Mary not give chocolate Sarah**, and acts accordingly (Sarah is indifferent as between bananas and apples but much prefers chocolate to either, and therefore takes the apple in this case). Admittedly, the structure of the compound sentences is made plain by setting out, e.g., **Sarah take apple**, ⊃, and **Mary give chocolate Sarah** in three separate columns (whereas in English we have to infer the structure of a compound sentence from a continuous sequence of words); but the fact remains that, given the structured sentences, Sarah can make sense of them.

Sarah's language even contains an example of a transformational rule. In English we have a transformation of 'Co-ordination Reduction' which amalgamates partially similar sentences by deleting the repeated material: thus **John ate fish** and **John ate meat** become **John ate fish and meat**.* Sarah's language works in the same way: **Sarah insert apple dish apple banana pail** means 'Sarah is to put an apple in the dish and Sarah is to put an apple and a banana in the pail', and Sarah responds by doing all these things.

What can the Chomskyan say to these findings? Sarah's language is rather simple by comparison with English or other human languages, and there are indications that its more complex sentences (such as the last one quoted) are at the limit of Sarah's powers of comprehension. But, if Sarah's language exemplifies in its small way the kind of structure typical of human languages, its simplicity seems irrelevant – after all, seven-year-old humans do not use particularly complex examples of English sentences. Just as we suggested that a human might succeed in learning an 'unnatural' language as

---

* The transformations we discussed previously changed single constituency trees into other trees; however, in general a transformation may derive a new tree from any number of 'input' trees.

an intellectual *tour de force*, so one might suggest that Sarah's mastery of the plastic-shape language is equally irrelevant to the basic psychological organization of chimpanzees. But to make this move is surely to reduce the empirical claim that transformational syntax is specific to Man to a dogmatic article of faith – if Sarah's abilities do not refute the claim, what could?

Another conceivable way out would be to suggest that the psychological machinery which enables one to use a transformational language is specific, not to Man alone, but to a group of closely-related species including both Man and the chimpanzee. But this is grossly implausible, since men are the only animals which do in fact acquire and use such languages outside the psychologist's laboratory. The hypothesis that animals other than Man possess a highly specific psychological trait which is never exploited in any way in practice is surely a desperate defence of Chomsky's theory.

It may be that further examination of Sarah's language will make it look less like human languages than it now appears. But, on current evidence, I see no way in which one can reasonably continue to accept the assertion that Man speaks languages of a certain class because of an idiosyncratic genetic trait. There is no doubt that this is part of what Chomsky asserts, and in this respect Sarah has surely shown Chomsky to be wrong.*

However, this is far from refuting Chomsky's nativist claims in their entirety. The key word in the preceding paragraph is 'idiosyncratic'. The reason why human languages are hierarchically-structured transformational languages is not, apparently, because of a genetic trait *peculiar to our species*; but it may still be because of a genetic trait shared by many or all other species. We may look at the situation as follows. Two things are true of Man: (i) he alone commonly uses fully-fledged languages (as opposed to the limited signalling systems of other species), and (ii) the languages used by Man are of a certain type. Our original exposition of Chomsky's ideas suggested that both (i) and (ii) are consequences of some genetic

---

* The chimpanzee experiments may indeed have more than merely academic implications. After reading about Washoe's and Sarah's linguistic proficiency, it is difficult to forget that they will reach voting age in about 1984.

trait distinguishing Man from the other species. This view cannot be maintained. However, suppose we assume that (i), at any rate, follows from a distinctively human genetic trait, if not necessarily a surprising one (it is after all true that humans have more complex nervous systems than other species, and perhaps this is a sufficient explanation of the fact that we commonly use complex languages while other species normally use, at most, finite systems of signals). Then we may still assert that (ii) is also a consequence of our genetic make-up, even though the genetic feature which among other things causes our languages to be as they are may well be a feature shared by many other species that do not use languages. This is a somewhat weaker version of linguistic nativism, but it seems scarcely less interesting than the original claim.

To clarify the position being argued here, let us consider a further class of objections that have been raised against Chomsky. Many people have suggested that the properties which Chomsky claims characterize human languages – the role of hierarchical structure, for instance – are by no means restricted to language, but probably relate to many other aspects of the psychology of humans or other species. It may be argued (e.g.) that the machinery of visual perception, whereby the impression of a solid object is abstracted from a complex two-dimensional pattern of retinal stimulation, involves a hierarchical processing system. Again, L. Jonathan Cohen points out that any decision-making situation is appropriately represented in terms of a hierarchical tree of choices. C. R. Peters even sees constituency structure in the copulatory behaviour of rhesus monkeys, and concludes that 'the evolutionary capacity for syntax may have its roots in much broader aspects of mammalian behaviour than has been previously recognised'.

Cohen has also suggested to me that, as science advances, it may well happen that the hierarchical structure of human syntax will turn out to be an automatic consequence of much more general facts about biochemistry, neurobiology, or the like. Just as finite-state languages are associated with the kind of abstract mechanisms known as finite-state automata, so constituency languages are the kind of stringset defined by what are known as *non-deterministic push-down storage automata* –

127

'push-down storage' because they involve 'memory' units which work on the principle that the only element that can be retrieved at any time is the element which was stored most recently. Possibly, if we knew more about the biology of the nervous system, it might turn out that this is organized quite generally into units which act as push-down storage automata – which would explain constituency structure, if not transformations. Conceivably, one might somehow ultimately even be able to show, say, that if a life-form is based on carbon chemistry then its language, if it has one, must be transformational.

It is not suggested that we can at present infer transformational theory from more general facts in this way. But I would concede quite readily that this is a very real future possibility. It seems a very plausible idea that we will one day be able to infer the statement 'All human languages must be transformational languages' from some statement p which is not specifically about humans or about language; it may indeed be that p is a statement which we already know to be true, and we lack only the inferential steps allowing us to move from p to the transformational theory of human language.

However, although this kind of suggestion has been intended as an objection to Chomsky, I cannot see that it counts as such. It would seem very strange if Chomsky's theory of linguistic universals were correct and yet were completely independent of the rest of scientific knowledge. Theories which exist in a vacuum, isolated from the main body of science, are not usually regarded as having any special virtue; rather the reverse.

It *would* be an objection to Chomsky if one could show that the transformational theory of human language *already* follows from known facts by familiar patterns of inference. But this is certainly not so; in fact, as we saw when discussing finite-state grammar, Chomsky's work is important because, among other things, it *contradicts* the theory of language which appears to follow from first principles.

Chomsky's discoveries are important because they show that human speech and (we shall suggest in the final chapters) human thought, flexible though they seem, in fact conform to structural constraints which might, logically, be other than they are. The fact that these constraints turn out to follow from, say, the fact that life is based on carbon chemistry (and hence apply to other species in so far as these have languages at all) will surely not detract from their intrinsic interest. As for the suggestion that the genetic trait which causes our languages to be transformational may also have consequences for non-linguistic aspects of psychology, this seems to increase rather than diminish the importance of Chomsky's work. It is linguistics which has first led us to posit such a trait; if, as we come to understand it better, we discover that the trait has implications beyond the area of language, then so much the more interesting.

The chimpanzee experiments seem to be the nearest thing yet produced to a *refutation* of linguistic nativism, but are not in fact such. Another category of argument against Chomsky consists of constructing equally plausible *alternative explanations* for the linguistic universals.

Bruce Derwing attempts to construct one such argument. According to Derwing, Chomsky assumes without warrant that the linguistic universals are part of the innate *contents* of the human mind. Might it not rather be (Derwing suggests) that the universals are merely an automatic consequence of the nature of the learning *process*?

Derwing's process/content opposition seems to the present author to be a distinction without a difference. I have thirty teeth, though I started life with no teeth at all. Should I say that my genetic blueprint *contained* a specification of (among other things) a set of thirty teeth, or rather that my body was innately programmed to *process* the nourishment that came my way from conception onwards in a way which caused the growth of thirty teeth? Either way of speaking seems equally appropriate; and to shift the discussion from acquisition of teeth to acquisition of language does not make the process/content distinction any more relevant.

A weightier argument occurs in the article by Putnam already referred to in connection with the 'What else?' objection. Putnam in fact makes two further important points. He begins by arguing that Chomsky's universals are scarcely empirical; but he goes on to suggest that, even if the universals are regarded as objective facts in need of explanation, they can easily be explained without resorting to nativism.

Putnam questions the empirical status of the universals by arguing that Chomsky's claim about the universality of syntactic categories is vacuous, or nearly so; let us deal with this point first. According to Putnam:

'If a language contains nouns . . . it contains noun phrases, that is, phrases which occupy the environments of nouns. If it contains noun phrases it contains verb phrases – phrases which when combined with a noun phrase . . . yield sentences. If it contains verb phrases, it contains adverb phrases – phrases which when combined with a verb phrase yield a verb phrase. Similarly, adjective phrases, etc., can be defined in terms of the *two* basic categories "noun" and "sentence". Thus the existence of nouns is all that has to be explained.'

True enough: given constituency structure, then there is little room for falsifiable claims about the particular categories of constituent (i.e. the particular auxiliary symbols) our grammars are to contain. This book has made no claims about universality of syntactic categories, although (as mentioned in chapter 5) Chomsky has cited these as a universal. But the passage quoted from Putnam *presupposes* just what I have treated as the central linguistic universal, namely that human languages exhibit constituency structure. It is only within the framework of constituency theory that phrases like 'a noun phrase combined with a verb phrase yields a sentence' make sense. So far Putnam has not touched our argument.

Putnam realizes this, and goes on to explain the prevalence of constituency rules ('phrase-structure rules') in terms of the relative simplicity of computing machines designed to work with them:

'phrase-structure rules are extremely simple algorithms . . . The fact is that all the natural measures of complexity of an algorithm – size of the machine table, length of computations, time, and space required for the computation – lead to the same result here, quite independently of the detailed structure of the computing machine employed. Is it surprising that algorithms which are "simplest" for virtually any computing system we can conceive of are also simplest for naturally evolved "computing systems"?'

In other words, Putnam regards the human brain as a problem-solving device analogous to artificial digital computers (an *algorithm* is the explicit, step-by-step procedure into which a task has to be analysed before a computer can be instructed to do it); if artificial computers work best with constituency languages, then we do not need any explanation for the fact that human brains use languages of the same type.

Here I would take issue with Putnam on a point of fact. The 'language' with which a digital computer operates is called its *machine code*; and the machine codes of standard computers contain nothing akin to constituency structure. True, in practice a programmer writes programs not in machine code but in a so-called *high-level programming language*, and high-level languages commonly *are* constituency languages. A computer executes a program in two stages, first translating the high-level program into a machine-code program (using a translation manual written in machine code), and then obeying the translated program. But high-level languages are used not to suit the computer's convenience but to suit the human programmer: humans find it difficult to work directly with machine code, and high-level programming languages are a compromise between machine language and human language. If constituency structure is present in high-level programming languages but not in machine codes, this is a good pointer to the notion that constituency structure is a distinctively human contribution to the general activity of problem-solving engaged in by both people and computers!

Constituency structure is indeed an arbitrary, surprising property of human language. How much more so the transformational rules, which affect strings only in ways which relate to their constituency structure. Putnam suggests that it is natural enough that we should use devices to abbreviate sentences, and many transformations (e.g. the transformation of Co-ordination Reduction, mentioned above) do abbreviate the strings to which they apply, though others (e.g. the Passivizing transformation) do not. But why, in any case, should we modify strings only in ways which depend on their constituency

131

structure? For instance, is the question-forming rule 'Move the main verb to the front' *simpler* in any absolute sense than 'Move the second word to the front', or, say, 'Reverse the order of words in the string'? Surely not.

Putnam fails, then, in his attempts to deduce the linguistic universals *a priori*. However, he offers a non-nativist explanation for the universals even if these are treated as unpredictable empirical facts. His explanation is in terms of common historical origin.

We know that families of languages descended from a common ancestor language resemble each other much more closely than they resemble unrelated languages. Indeed, it would be surprising if this were not so. French, Spanish, Rumanian and the other Romance languages are all descended from Latin, and they are much more similar to one another than any of them is to, say, Chinese. Much earlier, the language called Proto-Indo-European (cf. chapter 1) split into the ancestors of Latin, Greek, the Germanic languages, the languages of Northern India, and so on: the contemporary Indo-European languages as a whole have many features in common, though their mutual resemblance is not as great as that within the Romance subfamily, which was a single language until relatively recently. Now, Putnam argues, if we could trace the history of languages far enough back, we might well find that *all* attested languages have a single ancestor. This first language had to have *some* particular properties; perhaps the properties common to all contemporary languages merely reflect properties which the first language happened by chance to possess.

The linguist's reaction is to pooh-pooh the suggestion of a single historical origin. This is because, within linguistics, diachronic linguists have in the past been very eager to find more and more inclusive family relationships between the languages of the world; the onus has been on the linguist who would assert the existence of a single ancestor language to prove it, and the linguistic evidence is quite insufficient. (Every linguist knows how the search for a common origin became such a mare's nest that, when a Linguistics Society was founded in France in 1866, the statutes of the society expressly vetoed papers on the origin of language!) However, the situation here is the reverse: it seems that the onus is on the Chomskyan to refute Putnam by proving that the languages of the world do *not* have a common origin, and this is even less possible.

The real answer to Putnam is that the arguments for linguistic nativism are unaffected if we grant the common-origin hypothesis. We know that languages change over time in many respects; and, since the languages of the world are very diverse, if they all descend from a single ancestor then some of them must have undergone even more radical changes than were previously suspected. If languages can change in so many other ways, then why can they not change also with respect to the properties described by transformational theory? The common-origin hypothesis does not *explain* the universal constraints on human languages, it merely alters them from synchronic into diachronic constraints: rather than 'No natural language may lack property *P*', they now read 'No natural language may *lose* property *P*'. Replacing 'lack' by 'lose' does not make linguistic nativism any less or more appealing than before.

The final objection we shall consider is one that has been expressed most explicitly by Stephen Toulmin, though Toulmin regards himself as doing no more than confronting Chomsky with an argument implicit in the work of Wittgenstein and of his Viennese contemporary, Karl Bühler. In Toulmin's words:

> 'we need no[t] . . . explain the universal forms of linguistic behaviour by simply invoking correspondingly detailed forms in their underlying "native capacities" or "physiological endowments": the existence of these universal forms need . . . reflect no more than the universality of the "objective tasks" which language is everywhere used to perform.'

In other words, linguistic structure depends on linguistic function: transformational languages are simply the most suitable languages for the job at hand.

If this could be spelled out in detail so as to be convincing, it would make an excellent argument against Chomsky. Whatever else it may be, language is among other things a skill that has been passed down from generation to generation over many millennia, undergoing frequent modifications in the process. If the features common to the attested languages were features which made those languages more efficient than conceivable alternatives, there would be no case whatever for explaining the presence of those features in terms of a genetic predisposition. If we observe that farmers everywhere rotate their crops annually and thus improve their harvests, we do not infer that farmers must be born with an instinct for annual crop-rotation!

The trouble with Toulmin's argument is that we are given no account of what the 'objective tasks' are which language is used to perform, or why those tasks should be best performed by transformational languages. Wittgenstein and Bühler, the authorities to whom Toulmin appeals, offer no guidance here; and this is unsurprising – they wrote long before anyone had thought of the notion that there are constraints on the syntactic diversity of natural languages. The nearest Wittgenstein comes to explaining the adoption of a language by reference to its functions is his account of how a builder and his mate might evolve a language consisting of sentences such as **Block!**, **Slab!**, etc., which the builder could use to ask his mate to pass him different objects. But a language of this kind, limited to a finite set of 'atomic' sentences, will be the sort of rudimentary signalling system used by non-human species; it is quite *unlike* the kind of language characteristic of Man. So, although Wittgenstein's scenario seems plausible enough, as far as it goes, it is in no sense an alternative to the Chomskyan, nativist account of human language.

We have already suggested (in chapter 2) that language is unusual among the various behavioural and anatomical properties of Man in that, although it is obviously very useful to the species – language is not merely a useless left-over like the appendix, which we would be better off without – it is very difficult to say, in non-circular terms, *what* use language is. Toulmin does nothing to clarify this problem.

The stock one-word answer to the question about the function of language is 'communication'. Many passages in this book have presupposed that the use of language is to communicate. But the notion of 'communication' is much obscurer than that of 'language'; if one asks what 'communication' is, the obvious answer is 'that which one achieves by using language'. One can try to be more precise. Thus, to communi-

cate with another is to change his state in some way. Not every
act of changing a person's state counts as communicating with
him: for instance, I do not communicate with someone by
killing him. However, we might try saying that communication is that type of mutual state-changing which leads to
greater co-operation between members of a species; one
psychologist has characterized language as the trait of human
behaviour which enables human societies to attain a relatively
sophisticated level of division of labour. Or we might suggest
that communication means changing a person's state in ways
which correlate with properties of the outside world – we tell
someone **Dinner is ready** because dinner is indeed ready.
But now the futility of this attempt to account for Chomsky's
universals becomes apparent: why should division of labour
be promoted particularly efficaciously by hierarchical trees,
or what is it about the outside world which makes tree structures specially appropriate as a representational device? If I
see that dinner is ready, I see steaming plates scattered over a
table: I do not see a branching diagram with nodes labelled by
auxiliary symbols.

Of course, one can say that communication consists of
predicating properties of individual entities, of asserting relations between pairs of entities, and the like. Now it will follow
that sentences must have something close to the structure they
in fact have: nominal phrase followed by copula and adjective
to handle the first case, two nominal phrases separated by a
transitive verb for the second case, and so on. But this is quite
circular: we have no independent definition of 'entity', 'property', etc., other than 'that which is denoted by a nominal
phrase', 'that which is ascribed by an adjective', and the like.
As we saw in our discussion of Kant in chapter 2, it is not by
empirical observation that we discover that the world is composed of individuals, properties, and relations.

That human languages are based on constituency structure
is an empirical finding: there is no logical contradiction in the
notion that, say, the inhabitants of Mars might exchange
utterances for which the best grammar is that of the prime-
number language. If we hope to explain human linguistic
structure from the functions of human language, then we must
have some account of those functions from which it follows

that constituency structure is an appropriate device for fulfilling them, but which does not ascribe constituency structure
to language by definition. Toulmin offers no such account;
therefore his alternative to Chomsky's explanation of the
linguistic universals amounts to explaining the obscure by
reference to the more obscure. Essentially, Toulmin's objection to Chomsky is a version of the 'What else?' objection.
Toulmin suggests that, if we knew more, we might be able to
construct a functionalist alternative to Chomsky's nativist
explanation of the universals: but until such an alternative is
actually produced, we have no reason to take the possibility
seriously.

There is a serious point hidden here, though. Let us return
for the moment to the notion that Martians might speak the
prime-number language. The obvious intuitive objection to
this notion is 'What could their sentences *mean*?' Indeed, I
suspect many readers may have lost patience with me several
chapters ago for omitting to discuss meaning: after all, the
meaning of a sentence is normally the reason for uttering it.
One might well suggest that the proper account of the function
of language is that 'we speak in order to mean' (although this
turn of phrase is somewhat strange in English). Might it not
be – indeed, is it not almost obviously the case – that it is
their role as bearers of meaning which imposes constituency
structure on our sentences?

I would not object to this remark; I would only point out
that it is far from clear what it is for a sentence to 'mean'
something. In the following chapter we shall consider this
question. We shall find that the syntactic structure of natural
language is indeed determined by its semantic structure; however, an understanding of the relationship between syntax and
semantics will not decrease but, if anything, increase the
cogency and interest of Chomsky's nativist arguments.

7

Syntax and Meaning

So far, we have deliberately chosen to treat sentences of a natural language as mere sequences of spoken or written words. But they are much more than that: they are *meaningful* sequences. We should like to expand our theory of language to deal with the semantic aspect of language. But what exactly will this involve?

The area of semantics is unusual within linguistics as being a part of the subject where linguists are frequently unclear, not just about how best to achieve their goals, but even about what their goals should be. The aim of syntactic description is fairly plain: to specify all and only the grammatical strings of formatives. But what should semantic description set out to do? The answer is by no means obvious, and the theories of linguists who have discussed semantics contain many deep-rooted confusions. The present book aims to concentrate principally on the positive achievements of linguistics. However, in the semantic area confusion has spread so widely that we shall have to spend much of this chapter untangling false leads. We apologize in advance for what may seem to the reader at times to be unnecessary complexities; the author can only plead that these are not (he hopes) of his own making.

Thus, one way of looking at the notion of semantic description, which has had great appeal for linguists though it is quite wrong, runs as follows. A language is a system that connects two aspects or 'planes' of reality: speech-sound, and meaning. (For simplicity of exposition we discuss only spoken language.) A sentence, like a coin, consists of the linking of two faces: on one hand it has a pronunciation and on the other a meaning. Therefore a complete description of an individual language should portray sentences not simply as strings of sounds but as pairs: on the one hand a specification of the pronunciation (a *phonetic representation*), and on the other hand a specification of the meaning (a *semantic representation*). Likewise, a general theory of language should provide not only a *universal phonetic alphabet* of symbols to be used in phonetic representations, but also a *universal semantic alphabet* of symbols to be used in semantic representations. The universal phonetic alphabet will include symbols for all the sounds men are capable of uttering; the universal semantic alphabet will include symbols for all the 'units of meaning' men may wish to express.

Although this view has been influential in linguistics, a little consideration shows it to be very deeply in error.

The notions of 'phonetic alphabet' and 'phonetic representation' are clear enough: a phonetic representation is a sort of symbolic *picture* of the actions of the vocal organs. We have quoted English sentences in standard spelling rather than in phonetic symbols, but there is no great mystery about the latter. In the usual phonetic alphabet, a sentence such as **Bitter beer is best** comes out as **bĭtəbiərīzbɛst**. The fact that the phonetic representation begins with the symbol **b** corresponds to the fact that the speaker begins by pressing his lips together, and so on. The symbols 'represent' the speaker's actions in the stylized way that a map, rather than an aerial photograph, represents a piece of territory; but the relation between representation and represented is straightforward enough.

Now suppose we are given some second array of symbols and are told that this is the 'semantic representation' of **Bitter beer is best**. Never mind what the semantic representation looks like: what is it that it is claimed to represent? Acts of uttering speech-sounds are quite concrete, tangible events, and there is no problem in the notion of representing such events symbolically; but where are the entities called 'meanings' which our semantic alphabet is supposed to symbolize? Is the semantic representation of **Bitter beer is best** a symbolic picture of the observations which make the sentence true? – say, of a scene in which a man drinks bitter beer with a satisfied smile on his face? This is absurd: apart from anything else, the very same scene is also evidence for the truth of, e.g., **Someone is having a drink**, yet the meanings of the two sentences are quite different.

Perhaps one might suggest that the semantic representation of **Bitter beer is best** is a symbolization of some process occurring in the brain of the speaker or hearer when the sentence is uttered. Maybe, but then why suppose that semantic representations are different from phonetic representations? We have no direct access to the mechanisms of the brain, and the only *evidence* we have is that the speaker uttered the string of words **Bitter beer is best.** Clearly there must be some brain-process which causes these sounds to be pronounced in this order; why imagine that there is also some second, quite distinct brain-process corresponding to 'holding the belief' or 'wanting to express the idea' that bitter beer is best? Still more remarkable, on what grounds could people argue about whether given semantic representations for given sentences were right or wrong, since we cannot see into the workings of the mind?

For people do state their opinion about the semantic representations of different sentences, and there is even a fair measure of agreement on the subject. Let me give a simple example. It is often suggested that the semantic representation of a sentence such as **They want to win** will have **they** as subject of the subordinate clause as well as of the main clause: the semantic representation will be something like:

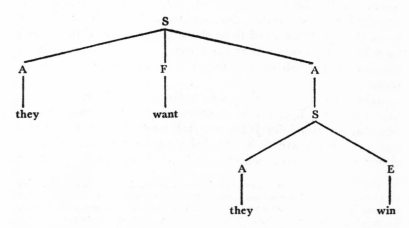

(using the same kind of constituency notation that we used earlier for syntactic structure). Intuitively it seems reasonable

139

to say of **They want to win** that 'to is a meaningless syntactic particle which should not appear in a semantic representation of the sentence', while '**they** is meant as the subject of both verbs, though it in fact occurs only with the first'. Yet what *facts* can these intuitions correspond to? How can we tell whether they are right or wrong?

The answer is that statements about the 'meaning' of a sentence are statements, not about properties of that sentence in itself, but about the relationships of *inference* which hold between that sentence and other sentences of the language. We say that **they** is 'meant' or 'understood' as the subject of **win** in the sentence quoted, because there are inference-relationships linking **They want to win** with sentences in which the clause **they win** does occur overtly. For instance, if it is true that **They want to win**, then it follows that **If they win, they will be glad.***

In other words, the facts which a semantic description of a language aims to predict are of a different order from the facts which a syntactic description predicts. A syntactic description of English makes predictions of the form 'Sentence X may be uttered by an English-speaker'. A semantic description of English makes predictions of the form 'Sentence X may be inferred by an English-speaker from the set of sentences $\{ Y, Z, \ldots \}$'. In the case just cited, for instance, the semantic description must predict that we are liable to infer **If they win, they will be glad** from the single sentence **They want to win**: if we assume that the latter sentence is true, then as speakers of English we feel that the former sentence must be true.

Inferences are not always from single premisses.† Thus, to take up a trivial example mentioned earlier in another connection, we may infer **John ate fish and meat** from the two sentences **John ate fish** and **John ate meat**, but not from either of these two sentences alone. Sometimes we make

---

* One might argue that my example is a poor one: it is common enough, after all, for something which has been ardently desired to seem worthless as soon as it is attained. For the sake of argument, however, let us assume that the example works. There is little point in hunting for a better example, since, later in this chapter, we shall argue that *no* example of 'lexical inferability' is perfect.

† The term 'premiss' is used for a sentence from which an inference is drawn; the term 'consequent' denotes the sentence which is inferred.

inferences from much larger sets of premisses. A particularly clear (because artificial) case is the sort of puzzle which begins 'Tom, Dick, and Harry are (not necessarily respectively) a teacher, a salesman, and a farmer, and Jane, Elizabeth, and Mary are their wives', and ends, say, 'Which man is married to Jane?' Someone who succeeds in solving the puzzle has inferred a sentence such as 'Tom is married to Jane' from a large set of premiss sentences, each of which is needed for the inference to go through. Of course, most of the inferences we make are simpler than this.

As a limiting case, there are sentences which we may treat as being inferable from no premisses at all. These are the *analytic* sentences, to use Kant's term: sentences such as **Either John is here or he is not**, or **Water is wet**, which are 'true by virtue of their meaning' – we do not need to know anything *else* to be true to infer that water is wet, since, if something were not wet, we would not call it 'water'.*

A syntactic description of English defines a set of sentences: we test the grammar by trying to observe an utterance not in the set. A semantic description of English, on the other hand, defines a set of pairs, where the first member of each pair is a set of zero or more sentences (as premisses) and the second member is a single sentence (as consequent).† Thus a semantic description of English must permit, among others, the pairs ({**John ate fish**, **John ate meat**}, **John ate fish and meat**); ({**They want to win**}, **If they win, they will be happy**); and (∅, **Water is wet**).

The strings involved in inferences will be restricted to the grammatical sentences. We cannot infer the truth of any sentence from the truth of an ungrammatical string such as

* The term 'analytic' and its converse, 'synthetic', were used by Kant in some-what narrower senses than suggested here; the broader usage is by now standard.

† I apologize for the use of mathematical jargon such as 'pair' and 'set'; this is one point at which the demands of precision do seem to require a certain amount of mathematical terminology. The words contain no hidden implications; in fact they are deliberately chosen to be as abstract and devoid of substantive content as possible. Thus, a *pair* is any two things, and a *set* is any collection of things, where a 'thing' can be any entity whatsoever, including sentences or sets. We write the members of a pair between round brackets, and those of a set between curly brackets, separated by commas. For instance, the set of English vowels would be symbolized '{**a, e, i, o, u**}'. Mathematically, a collection with no members is a special case of sets, called the *empty set* and symbolized '∅'.

Of of the of, and likewise we cannot infer the truth of **Of of the of** from any premisses, since it means nothing to call **Of of the of** 'true' (or 'false').

What of the grammatical but nonsensical sentences discussed in chapter 4, such as **Sincerity is triangular**? These will be premisses from which we can infer each of two contradictory consequents. Thus, from **Sincerity is triangular** we can infer **Sincerity has a shape** (anything triangular *a fortiori* has a shape); yet **Sincerity has no shape** is analytic, and therefore we can infer this sentence too from **Sincerity is triangular**. (If *A* is true come what may, then *A* is certainly true given the truth of *B*; in other words, we may infer any analytic sentence from any premiss.) **Sincerity has a shape** and **Sincerity has no shape** are mutually contradictory, and this is what it means to call **Sincerity is triangular** 'nonsensical': it leads to contradiction.

We test a semantic description by trying to find a case of an English speaker inferring some consequent *c* from some set *P* of premisses such that the pair (*P*, *c*) is not allowed for by the description. As usual, we want the description to be as strong as possible; so we want it to permit as few inferences as possible, given that it must permit any inference that English-speakers actually make (allowing for the fact that speakers may get confused when the premisses are very complex – we may tolerate a few forbidden but observed inferences, just as we may tolerate a few ungrammatical but observed utterances).

There are some obvious problems in this account of the task of a semantic description.

For one thing, although it seems intuitively acceptable to say that we make inferences from sentences to other sentences, it is not clear that we can *observe* an inference being made in the same concrete way that we can observe a string being uttered. Some inferences are made explicitly; a court of law is a good place to hear the fine implications of various sentences being drawn out aloud. But if we hear someone say '*p*, and *q*, therefore *r*', we cannot know that this constitutes an inference of *r* from premisses *p* and *q* unless we already know what the words **therefore** and **and** mean; so there seems to be something circular in the idea that inferences are the objective data which a semantic description has to account for. Apparently we must rely on our 'native speaker's intuition' that certain sentences follow from certain other sentences. But I have laid great stress in earlier chapters on the need for linguistics to base itself on empirical observation, so what am I doing now accepting the 'evidence' of intuition?

A second problem is that the notion of 'inference' seems to apply only to statements, yet many sentences are not statements. Sentences like **Shut the door after you!** or **Is John here?** are neither 'true' nor 'false'; so they can play no part in inference, if this consists of recognizing that a consequent is true given that certain premisses are true. Is a semantic description satisfactory if it ignores sentences other than statements?

Thirdly, the 'meaning' of a sentence is not just a question of its relations with other sentences; it also, and crucially, involves a relationship with the outside world. **John's car is red** is, among other things, a premiss from which one can infer **John's car is not blue**; but it is also a statement about the hunk of metal out in the street, which is not a sentence or a collection of sentences.

These are valid objections to my account as it stands so far. They can all be answered, and the answers to the three objections are closely related. However, it would be unnecessarily confusing to deal with these issues now. For the purpose of this chapter, let us pretend that we have infallible intuitions about the inferences made by native speakers, and let us ignore sentences other than statements, together with the relations between statements and the world. In the final chapter we shall see that these assumptions can ultimately be dispensed with.

Let us call any pair (P, c) in which P is some set of zero or more sentences, and c is some single sentence, an *inference-pair*; and we shall say that (P, c) is *valid* if c follows from P for speakers of the language in question. Just as a grammar has to divide the class of all possible strings into a grammatical and an ungrammatical set, so a semantic description has to divide the class of all possible inference-pairs into a valid and an invalid set. Just as a natural language will have infinitely many grammatical sentences, so it will no doubt have infinitely many valid inference-pairs. To describe the semantics of English, we must find some finite body of statements which defines an infinitely large set of valid English inference-pairs.

How are we to go about doing this? The syntactic formalisms we have discussed earlier in this book – constituency grammar, etc. – do not at first sight seem much help; they define sets of *strings*, not sets of *inference-pairs*.

Historically, inference has been studied not by linguists but by philosophers: the study of inference is called *logic*. At one time, philosophy and linguistics were scarcely counted as separate disciplines; but, since linguistics has been a subject in its own right, logic has been studied by scholars whose background is very different from that of linguists studying the syntax of natural languages. Only in the last five years or so have the two subjects begun to merge again. As we shall see, this historical split between semantics and syntax has led to some strange developments.

The logician defines an infinitely large set of inference-pairs by means of a system called a *logic* (or *logistic*, or *calculus*). However, the logics studied by logicians in practice deal with artificial languages, not with natural languages such as English. A logic consists of two things: a set of *formation rules* and a set of *rules of inference*. The formation rules are simply a grammar which defines the grammatical sentences (in logical terminology, the *well-formed formulae*) of the artificial language with which the logician is concerned; the rules of inference are rules specifying an infinitely large class of inference-pairs involving those well-formed formulae.

Let us consider a very simple example, namely a version of the logic called the *sentential calculus*. This logic uses a large stock of 'primitive formulae', represented by the letters, **p**, **q**, **r**, **p′**, **q′**, **r′**, **p″**, etc., etc., and its formation rules permit complex formulae to be built up from the primitive formulae by means of two symbols ⊃, ∼. The formation rules for the sentential calculus form a simple constituency grammar:

$$S \rightarrow S \supset S$$
$$S \rightarrow \sim S$$
$$S \rightarrow \mathbf{p}$$
$$S \rightarrow \mathbf{q}$$
$$S \rightarrow \mathbf{r}$$
$$S \rightarrow \mathbf{p'}$$
$$\vdots$$

The grammar is recursive, so there are infinitely many well-formed formulae – thus, one such may be represented by the constituency tree:

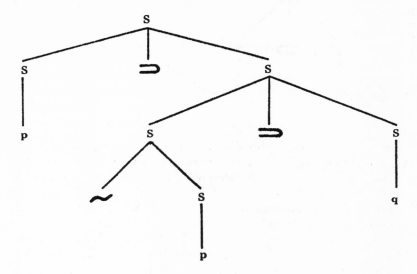

When the formula is written as a string, brackets are used to mark the constituency structure defined by the grammar: $p \supset [[\sim p] \supset q]$. There is no need to add any information about the auxiliary symbols dominating the constituents, since these are always S.

The rules of inference of the sentential calculus define a number of *immediate inferences*: for instance, there is an immediate inference from premisses $p \supset q$ and p to q. This immediate inference is one instance of a rule called *modus ponens*, which can be represented in transformational notation (see p. 146): In other words, given a premiss of the form $S_1 \supset S_2$ together with the premiss S_1, one may infer S_2.*

The *modus ponens* rule permits the inference from $p \supset q$ and p to q, together with infinitely many other immediate infer-

---

* The dotted line with the 'equals' sign indicates that the two constituents must be identical. This piece of notation is needed also for syntactic transformations in natural languages, and it is not as *ad hoc* as it looks; but the matter is too technical to expand on here.

premisses   consequent

ences; for instance, it also allows the move from $[\sim \mathbf{p}] \supset [\mathbf{q}' \supset \mathbf{q}']$ and $\sim \mathbf{p}$ to $\mathbf{q}' \supset \mathbf{q}'$. However, the rules of the sentential calculus permit us to derive many inference-pairs which are not immediate inferences. We do this by constructing *derivations*. A derivation is a column of formulae beginning with a set of premisses: we may add a new formula at the end of the column whenever that formula may be immediately inferred from formulae earlier in the column (whether the earlier formulae were premisses or were themselves inferred from still earlier formulae). Consider, for instance, the derivation:

1	$\mathbf{p} \supset \mathbf{q}$	⎫
2	$\mathbf{q} \supset \mathbf{r}$	⎬ premisses
3	$\mathbf{p}$	⎭
4	$\mathbf{q}$	by *modus ponens* from 1 and 3
5	$\mathbf{r}$	by *modus ponens* from 2 and 4

Since the last formula in the column is $\mathbf{r}$, this counts as a derivation of $\mathbf{r}$ from $\{\mathbf{p} \supset \mathbf{q}, \mathbf{q} \supset \mathbf{r}, \mathbf{p}\}$: the existence of such a derivation means that $(\{\mathbf{p} \supset \mathbf{q}, \mathbf{q} \supset \mathbf{r}, \mathbf{p}\}, \mathbf{r})$ is one of the inference pairs defined by the sentential calculus, even though there is no *immediate* inference of $\mathbf{r}$ from these premisses.

Other rules of inference of the sentential calculus hinge on the properties of these derivations. For instance, there is a rule which says that if a formula S_1 may be derived from a set of premisses including a formula S_2, then the formula $S_2 \supset S_1$ may be derived from the same set of premisses excluding S_2. This rule enables us among other things to derive certain formulae from no premisses at all. Thus, the one-member column:

1 **p**   premiss

is a derivation of **p** from {**p**} (since **p** is both premiss and last member of the column); so the rule just mentioned permits us to derive **p** ⊃ **p** from that set of premisses (namely, the empty set) which results if we exclude **p** from {**p**}. Formulae, such as **p** ⊃ **p**, which can be derived from no premisses are called *theorems* of the calculus; there are infinitely many theorems, some much more complex than **p** ⊃ **p**.

For completeness, we should add the rules dealing with the symbol ~. Any formula S may be immediately inferred from ~ ~ S; and, if we can derive both formulae S₁ and ~S₁ from some set of premisses including a formula S₂, then we may derive ~S₂ from the same set of premisses, excluding S₂.

We mentioned earlier that **p** ⊃ **q** is customarily read 'if **p**, then **q**'; and ~ is commonly understood as the sign of negation – ~**p** is read 'not **p**' or 'it is not the case that **p**'. We can now see why this is so: these interpretations of the symbols are not arbitrary stipulations by logicians, rather the interpretations 'if . . . then' for ⊃ and 'not' for ~ impose themselves, given the formal derivations of the calculus on the one hand, and the inferences actually made by English-speakers on the other. Suppose we take **p** and **q** to represent arbitrary English statements (say, **Oranges contain vitamin C** and **Pigs can fly** respectively). Now we may derive, e.g., **q** from [~**p**] ⊃ **q** and ~**p**; and, sure enough, on the (false) assumption that **If oranges do not contain vitamin C then pigs can fly** and **Oranges do not contain vitamin C** are both true, then **Pigs can fly** follows. The formula **p** ⊃ **p** is a theorem and, sure enough, **If oranges contain vitamin C then oranges contain vitamin C** is analytic for English speakers. And so on. The sentential calculus gives us many inference-pairs, each of which can be tested against the inferences actually made by English speakers given the interpretation 'if . . . then' for ⊃ and 'not' for ~ ; and in each case (I claim) the prediction is borne out. On the other hand, we soon run into trouble if we try alternative interpretations for ⊃ or ~. For instance, suppose we interpret ⊃ as 'either . . . or'. Now, **q** ⊃ **q** is a theorem, but **Either pigs**

can fly or pigs can fly is certainly not an analytic truth in English; in fact, it is a contingent falsehood (pigs, as it happens, cannot fly).

We are now in a position to say what it is to give a semantic description of a natural language, assuming that we know the inference-pairs valid in that language. To describe the semantics of, say, English, we must construct a logic (i.e. a set of formation rules and a set of rules of inference), and specify rules correlating the logical formulae with the sentences of English, and the entire system must obey the following constraint: whenever the English speaker infers sentence s_0 from the set of sentences $\{s_1, s_2, \ldots, s_n\}$, then (if f_0 is the formula correlated with s_0, f_1 the formula correlated with s_1, and so on) the inference-pair $\langle\{f_1, f_2, \ldots, f_n\}, f_0\rangle$ must be permitted by the logic. As a limiting case, when $n = 0$, i.e. if s_0 is analytic in English, then f_0 must be a theorem of the logic. Given such a system, we may call the formula paired with a sentence the 'semantic representation' of that sentence; but we shall remember that there is no entity called the 'meaning' of the sentence which is represented by a semantic 'representation'. A semantic description will normally assign any individual sentence a single semantic representation; but we can allow ambiguous sentences to be correlated with more than one logical formula. The task of semantics is to find the simplest semantic descriptions of the various natural languages which are faithful to the inferences actually made by speakers of the languages.

This still does not answer the question why we posit that 'semantic representations' of natural sentences are distinct from their overt syntactic forms. Nothing in the foregoing definition of 'semantic description' prevents us using sentences as their own semantic representations. That is, why do we bother with this apparatus of formation rules defining artificial formulae, together with correlation rules relating the artificial formulae to the sentences of the natural language; why do we not simply give rules of inference applying directly to the natural-language sentences?

One might do this; the argument against it is purely one of over-all simplicity of description. It might seem simplest to define rules of inference for sentences directly, since then our semantic description need contain only rules of inference – we will not also need formation rules defining semantic representations and correlation rules relating semantic representations and natural sentences. However, we can make the rules of inference considerably simpler if we define them for artificial formulae; the claim is that the simplicity gained in connection with the rules of inference outweighs the additional burden of formation and correlation rules. Consider again the notion that the semantic representation of **They want to win** is of the form **they want [they win]**. Our semantic description needs to predict that we can infer **If they win, they will be glad** from this premiss; if the semantic representation is as given, we may use a rule such as:

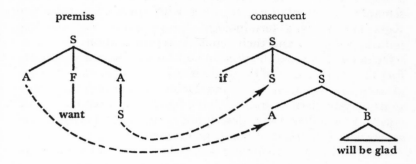

Notice that this rule is of very general application. In the present case it works by substituting **they** for A and **they win** for S, but the rule is not sensitive to the particular items filling these slots: it will equally well take, e.g., **The women want John to win** into **If John wins, the women will be glad**. However, the rule works only on the assumption that **They want to win** has **[they win]** in its semantic representation, just as **The women want John to win** has **[John win]**. If we wished to write rules of inference for the natural sentences directly, we should have to provide a separate rule for the **They want to win** case, where the subject of the subordinate clause does not appear overtly. (We also have to complicate the rules to handle the automatic syntactic alteration between, e.g., **John wins** and **John to win**, but this is true in either case.) It is arguments like these which justify logicians' and linguists' intuitive feelings that semantic representations of sentences are different from the sentences themselves.

Both logicians and, more recently, linguists interested in semantics can be regarded as engaging in the task of constructing semantic descriptions in the sense we have defined. However, because of the split that has developed between mathematically-minded logicians and linguists interested in natural language, the attempts of both groups have been inadequate.

Semantically-minded linguists (for instance, Jerrold Katz and Jerry Fodor in their influential article 'The structure of a semantic theory') have provided a set of formulae to act as semantic representations, together with correlation rules (in Katz and Fodor's terminology, 'projection rules') relating natural sentences and their semantic representations, but they have not appreciated the need to add rules of inference controlling the construction of derivations. As a result there is no way of knowing which of Katz and Fodor's semantic representations may be derived from which others, and hence no way of checking whether their description accurately portrays the semantics of the natural language in question.

Katz and Fodor are among those who see semantic representations as 'pictures of meanings'. For them, the semantic representation of an English sentence will break the sense of the sentence down into primitive 'units of meaning', or 'semantic markers': thus a sentence such as **John kills Bill** will come out as something like **John** CAUSE **[Bill** DIE], where the items in small capitals are drawn from the universal alphabet of semantic units.* But this tells us nothing about the meaning of the English sentence: it merely amounts to offering a *translation* of the English sentence into a more long-winded, artificial language which we might call 'Universal Semantic Markerese'. This is like the promise on a pound note: 'I promise to pay the bearer on demand the sum of one pound.' If one asks a bank clerk to redeem the promise, he merely gives one another pound note in exchange: but this gets one nowhere. If one really wants to know what a pound is worth, one needs to

* This concept of semantic description has subsequently been repudiated by Fodor.

know, e.g., that it is equivalent to twenty shillings, or to an hour's labour. Similarly, if one wants to know what **John kills Bill** means, it is no use merely giving a synonymous sentence in a less familiar language (such as Universal Semantic Markerese): one needs to know the inference relations holding between **John kills Bill** and other English sentences, and, ultimately, between **John kills Bill** and the facts about the world which make the sentence true or false.

Katz and Fodor do offer devices for predicting which English sentences are analytic and which nonsensical. As we have seen, however, this is only a small part of the task of semantic description; and there is no reason to believe, as they do, that it is fruitful to treat the special properties of analyticity and nonsensicality in isolation from the more general relation of inferability.

If we treat the writings of formal logicians as essays in semantic description of natural languages, on the other hand, they exhibit an inadequacy which is precisely the converse of the linguists' failing. The linguists provide formation rules and correlation rules, but no rules of inference. Logicians have spent much time designing logics containing sets of formulae and rules of inference defined over those formulae, but they do not explicitly state correlation rules relating the formulae of their artificial systems to natural sentences. Therefore, unless the reader can supply this deficiency from guesswork and from the informal hints thrown out by the logician, the work of the latter is equally untestable as a semantic description of a natural language.

The reason for this gap is that logicians tend to lack interest in natural languages, which they regard as irregular, woolly and imperfect systems. Some logicians claim to be interested exclusively in the intrinsic mathematical properties of their artificial logics, and not at all in *interpreting* the formulae occurring therein. With these scholars one can have no quarrel. There is no reason for them to prefer to study logics which could as a matter of fact be used in the semantic description of natural languages. There have been logicians, on the other hand, who envisage their task as that of *improving* on everyday languages. Philosophers of the inter-war years, such as Rudolf Carnap, wanted to provide a language for science which should be more precise and determinate than the fluid, woolly languages of everyday life. This project seems more questionable; although these writers could equip their systems with their own formulae and rules of inference, they could hardly hook their formulae on to observable reality except via the everyday languages which they, like we, in fact speak; and in that way their artificial languages would fail to escape the 'imperfections', if such they are, of everyday language.

In any case, whether or not it is feasible to construct relatively perfect artificial languages, in the present book we are concerned with the description of natural languages, imperfect though they may be. While both the linguists' and the logicians' work lacks components which are needed in a complete semantic description, fortunately their deficiencies are complementary. There is every reason to suppose that both sets of scholars are working along the right lines in many cases, so that logicians' rules of inference may supply the gap in linguists' semantic descriptions and (even more probably) linguists' correlation rules will apply to logicians' artificial formulae.

The sentential calculus discussed above may be treated as a first tiny step towards the construction of a semantic description of English: it handles just those inferences which are valid by virtue of the meanings of **if** and **not**. That is, suppose we provide rules specifying one of the primitive formulae **p**, **q**, **r**, etc., for each English sentence not involving **if** or **not**, together with rules relating formulae containing $\supset$ and $\sim$ with complex English sentences built up from simpler sentences by using **if** and **not**: then the logic will correctly predict any English inference which is valid because of the use of these words, though it has no means of predicting other English inferences. (For instance, in English **All apples are round** implies **This apple is round**; but the sentential calculus provides only primitive formulae, say **p′** and **q′**, for these sentences, and $(\{p'\}, q')$ is not an inference-pair permitted by the sentential calculus.) More complicated artificial logics familiar to logicians provide means for predicting also inferences valid by virtue of the senses of **or**, **and**, **all**, **some** and many other English words. Ultimately, one may feel, we should be able to construct a rather complex semantic description which succeeds in predicting *all* inferences valid in English.

However, just as we asked in chapter 3 whether the goal of syntactic description was attainable, so we must ask here whether it will be possible in principle to give a complete semantic description of a natural language such as English. In the syntactic case, we saw that there were two objections to the notion that strings could be divided into grammatical and ungrammatical classes: the distinction might be gradient rather than sharp, and, because of the creativity of linguistic behaviour, the distinction might not even be determinate. Exactly the same objections may be levelled against the notion of classifying the possible inference-pairs of English sentences into a valid and an invalid class. It may already be apparent from the discussion in chapter 3 that, in the present author's view, these objections are more justified for the semantic than for the syntactic case.

In the syntactic case, the question was 'Is it appropriate to assume that an arbitrary string of English words either definitely is or definitely is not grammatical?' The analogous question for semantics runs 'Is it appropriate to assume that an arbitrary English sentence either definitely follows or definitely fails to follow from an arbitrary set of English sentences?' The simplest cases are where the set of premisses is empty: are we to presuppose that any given English sentence either clearly is or clearly is not true by virtue of its meaning alone? In Kant's terms, is there a fixed borderline between analytic and synthetic sentences?* To simplify our discussion, let us restrict it to the special case of analyticity – my remarks could easily be extended to the general case of inferability.

A number of philosophers of logic, e.g. Morton White and W. van O. Quine, have argued that the analytic/synthetic distinction is a gradient rather than a sharp one. **Mothers are female** and **Bachelors are untidy** are rather clearly analytic and synthetic, respectively: nothing seems to count as evidence for or against the first, but it is a purely contingent matter whether bachelors are as a rule untidy – we have to find out, we cannot know in advance. However, White and Quine would argue, these are merely extreme cases. What of, for

---

* A 'synthetic' sentence is one such as **Bachelors are untidy** (as opposed to **Mothers are female**) which may be true or false, depending on how the world happens to be arranged.

instance, **Chairs have legs?** It seems to be part of what it means to call something a 'chair' (as opposed to 'stool', 'bench', etc.) that it has legs as well as a seat and a back; yet conceivably some modernistic house may have seats suspended from the ceiling, say, and it is not obvious that we would refuse these novel objects the name **chair** merely because of the absence of legs. Perhaps different sentences possess different degrees of analyticity for different people: **Chairs have legs** will seem more analytic to someone used to traditional furniture than to someone familiar with modern design. **Mothers are female** is special because it is close to completely analytic for almost everyone; however, if sex-change operations become commonplace, even this sentence might seem less analytic.

Linguists who discuss semantics have commonly presupposed that it is possible in principle to construct complete semantic descriptions of natural languages; those linguists who are aware of White's and Quine's arguments have accordingly had to try to counter them. But their attempts have been unimpressive. Katz, for instance, argues that there are objective tests which can be used to establish whether a dubious sentence is in fact analytic. Thus, one can write sentences on cards, including a number of clearly analytic and a number of clearly synthetic sentences as well as the sentence(s) whose status is in doubt, and one can ask an English speaker to sort the cards into separate piles. The linguist then observes whether the doubtful sentence is put on the 'analytic' or the 'synthetic' pile. However, though Katz confidently predicts the results of such experiments, he does not say that he has carried them out himself. Assuming that the subject even realizes that analyticity is the relevant variable (he might, after all, sort the sentences according to their length or their aesthetic properties), I would predict that speakers would be hesitant about the crucial cases and would make inconsistent decisions on different occasions, that they might assign such cases to an 'intermediate' pile unless explicitly told to form only two piles, and so on. Such experiments as have been carried out seem to support Quine's rather than Katz's view.

If the analytic/synthetic distinction is at all determinate, then, it is certainly a more/less rather than a yes/no distinction. This in itself might not be a fatal argument against the possibility of complete semantic description: it might suggest merely that the rules of inference in such a description should be *probabilistic* rather than sharp ones. Thus the rules which define the meaning of **chair** would include not 'A **is a chair** ⇒ A **has legs**', but something like 'A **is a chair** ⇒ (with probability $n\%$) A **has legs**'. The figure n would be allowed to vary from speaker to speaker. Writers such as Yehoshua Bar-Hillel have advocated the notion of probabilistic semantics.

However, the real death-blow to the idea of complete semantic description comes with the notion that inference is *creative*; and we have already accepted Wittgenstein's argument that this is so. We simply cannot predict which features of an object will be seized on as grounds for applying a given word to it. For instance, given that flat-topped mountains are called 'tables', if some such mountains have lower peaks surrounding them perhaps we might start referring to these as 'chairs' – in which case it may be analytic that **Chairs surround tables** but will be simply false that (**All**) **chairs have legs**. If language use is normally creative in this way, then it will be impossible in principle to describe the semantics of a natural language in terms of a fixed set of rules of inference – whether these are probabilistic or absolute.

The process of scientific advance may be viewed as, among other things, a process of altering the rules of inference of our language. A sentence such as **Hydrogen atoms are each composed of two particles** was once contradictory – an 'atom' *by definition* had no parts – and is now analytic – a 'hydrogen atom' *by definition* contains one proton and one electron – having passed through a synthetic stage, when 'hydrogen' was defined in some independent way and the constituency of the hydrogen atom was regarded as an open question. The naïve view of science assumes that the meaning of scientific terms (and hence the division of sentences into analytic, synthetic and contradictory) is fixed, and that progress consists of discovering which of the various synthetic sentences are true and which false. But in fact the borderlines between analytic, synthetic and contradictory fluctuate constantly; 'what today counts as an observed concomitant of a phenomenon will tomorrow be used to define it', to quote Wittgenstein. And 'science' is of course not a specialized activity divorced from the everyday mental life of the man in the street; we are all scientists, constantly evolving theories in order to understand and control the phenomena of our ordinary lives. The theories which are dignified by the title 'science' differ from, e.g., my mini-theory that heavy meals in hot weather make me lethargic, partly by being more general, but also by being relatively formalized and explicit. It is not that science uses its technical vocabulary in ways which fluctuate as knowledge increases, while the vocabulary of everyday speech is used in fixed senses; if anything the reverse is the case. Although we often say about words of everyday speech that '*X*s are *Y* by definition', there is no academy imposing definitions on everyday usage. If I regularly find myself as energetic after moussaka in August as I would be after a salad, I shall probably revise my usage of the term **heavy meal** to exclude moussaka.

This is how natural languages differ from the kind of artificially perfect 'languages' constructed by logicians such as Carnap: the natural languages are not so much 'woolly' or 'imperfect' as *creative*. This is awkward for the logician; but it is questionable whether we as users of natural languages should regard their creativity as a disadvantage. It is surely only because of our ability constantly to apply old words in new ways that we can continue to use our languages to get to grips with a world which refuses to be predictable.

Does the creativity of language use entail that semantic description is wholly impossible? I would argue not. Complete semantic description is impossible; but there is a lesser goal which is attainable and is worth attaining.

We may draw a distinction in the vocabulary of a natural language between *lexical* and *grammatical* items – between 'full' and 'empty' words, in traditional Chinese terminology. Lexical items are members of the large open syntactic classes (nouns, verbs, adjectives, and so on), which intuitively seem to carry most of the substance of our communication. Grammatical items are formatives, belonging to small syntactic classes or perhaps unique in their syntactic distribution, such as **of, -ing, the, -ed**, and so on, which seem intuitively to function more as markers of the structure of sentences containing them than as bearers of meaning in themselves. Now the various inference-pairs valid (or apparently valid) in a natural language such as English fall into two classes: those whose validity depends at least in part on the meanings of individual lexical items, and those whose validity depends exclusively on the structure of and grammatical items occurring in the sentences. The inference of, say, **Evelyn is female** from **Evelyn is John's mother** is an inference of the former kind (a *lexical inference*, let us say), since it depends on the meaning of **female** and **mother**. On the other hand, the inference of, say, **The watch was dropped** from **John dropped the watch** is a purely *grammatical inference*: it is independent of the meanings of individual lexical items. (The inference would be equally valid if we substituted, e.g., **butter** for **watch** and **melt** for **drop**.) Similarly, we may distinguish *lexically-analytic* sentences (e.g. **Mothers are female**) from *grammatically-analytic* sentences (e.g. **Either John won or not**).

Sentences whose analyticity is in doubt (e.g. **Chairs have legs**) seem always to be sentences which, if analytic at all, are lexically analytic. The growth of knowledge does not affect the rules of grammatical inference, only those of lexical inference. It appears that the distinction between grammatically-analytic sentences and others may be a quite sharp, determinate distinction, even if the 'others' cannot be clearly divided into lexically-analytic and synthetic. Quine, in his objections to the notion of analyticity, specifically exempts grammatical analyticity (which he calls, somewhat question-beggingly, 'logical truth'). Admittedly, the distinction depends on the existence of a clear division of the vocabulary into lexical and grammatical items, and this is not as obvious as it might be. Michael Halliday has argued that the lexical-item/grammatical-item distinction is itself a gradient one: on which side should, e.g., the modal verbs (**may, can, will**, etc.) come? If there is no sharp distinction between grammar and lexis, then perhaps we must abandon any attempt at semantic description. But I shall assume that we can find some way of demarcating grammar sharply from lexis.

Now, if it is legitimate to treat the systems constructed by logicians as partial semantic descriptions of natural languages, it is noticeable that they have invariably dealt with words such as **if, not, all, must**, etc., which at least arguably fall on the 'grammar' side of the grammar/lexis divide. Let us define the notion *restricted semantic description* as a specification of just the

157

grammatical inference-pairs of a language. For instance, in a restricted semantic description of English, the semantic representation of **Either John won or not** must be a theorem, but the semantic representation of **Mothers are female** will *not* be a theorem. Now there is no reason why we should not produce a complete *restricted* semantic description of a natural language; and, although this is a much smaller-scale project than semantically-minded linguists have commonly hoped to undertake, it is surely worth while in itself. To attempt a complete *unrestricted* semantic description of a natural language, by contrast, is merely to chase a rainbow.

Assuming that we are now clear about what it is to describe the semantics of a natural language (at least in the restricted sense), an obvious question is whether the apparatus involved in semantic description is related in any particular way to the complex apparatus which turned out in chapter 5 to be needed for *syntactic* description. In fact we have already noticed that the rules of inference seem to be rules of the same formal type as syntactic transformation rules. However, the two kinds of description turn out to be related even more closely than this.

Consider again the sentence **They want to win**; we suggested that the semantic representation of this sentence will have the structure **they want [they win]**. However, the *deep syntactic structure* of this sentence will also be **they want [they win]**. The derivation of the sentence involves a syntactic transformation known as 'Equi-Noun-Phrase Deletion', which may be symbolized as follows:

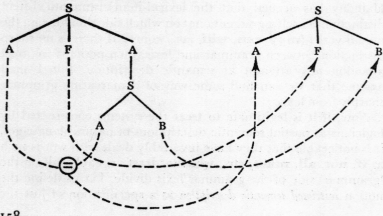

In other words, the subject of a subordinate clause is deleted when it is identical to that of the main clause. (I omit for simplicity the further apparatus needed to account for the use of **to** and the verb inflection **-s**.) Equi-NP Deletion is justified on the same kinds of ground as other syntactic transformation. Thus, **they win** occurs as an independent sentence while **win** does not;* it is easier to specify that any sentence may occur as object of **want** and to derive the exceptions by means of the transformation, than to have one special auxiliary symbol in the base for clauses which can occur after **they want** (including **you win** and **Mary win** but not **they win**), a separate symbol for clauses occurring after **you want**, etc.

This leads to a remarkable notion: perhaps the syntactic deep structures of sentences are in general identical to their (restricted) semantic representations! (We have already seen another piece of evidence for this: **John ate fish and meat** is derived syntactically from the pair of sentences **John ate fish** and **John ate meat**, and is synonymous with the conjunction of these two sentences.) This idea has become known as the *generative-semantics hypothesis*. If this hypothesis were true, the bewildering complexity which linguistics has revealed lurking below the surface of language would begin to make more sense. The correlation rules needed in semantic description, which logicians have failed to discuss, would simply be the same transformational rules that linguists need anyway for *syntactic* description, independently of semantics. The only extra component we would need to add to a grammar in order to turn it into a semantic description would be a set of rules of inference; and these will perhaps be the relatively simple rules which logicians have analysed in great detail.

Since the generative-semantics hypothesis is such an interesting and attractive idea, we must make sure to be clear what we mean by it; in particular, we must guard against turning it into a trivial matter of definition. If it is to be worth hypothesizing that the deep structures of sentences are identical to their semantic representations, then the definition of 'deep structure' must be independent of meaning, and the definition

---

* It is true that in English **Win** can occur alone as an imperative; the argument would be clearer in the case of a language which distinguished infinitives and imperatives morphologically.

of 'semantic representation' must be independent of syntax.

Linguists have not always been careful about this. Thus, when Chomsky argued in *Syntactic Structures* that the grammar of English should incorporate a Passivizing transformation, he justified it partly on the grounds that it provided a relatively simple way of defining the set of strings which occur as sentences of English; but he added that the Passivizing transformation had the advantage of explicitly formalizing a relationship which English-speakers intuitively feel to hold between sentences such as **John hit Bill** and **Bill was hit by John**. What we intuit is presumably the relationship of synonymy. If we allow semantic facts, such as synonymy, to count as evidence for syntactic transformations and hence for the deep structures of sentences, we can hardly be surprised if the deep structures we posit turn out to reflect the semantic properties of the sentences!

Chomsky himself has shown little interest in the generative-semantics hypothesis, so he cannot be reproached for using arguments which render the hypothesis vacuous. Presumably the younger linguists who enthusiastically advocate the hypothesis ought to be the most careful to preserve its empirical status. Remarkably enough, the 'generative semanticists' are the worst offenders with respect to confusing syntactic and semantic data. (By and large the generative semanticists are the same group of scholars whose methodology was criticized at several points in chapter 4.) To take a single example, in a recent article Robin Lakoff makes the point that we should 'try to reserve the term "ungrammatical" ... for anomalies that arise out of violations of syntactic rules alone: **John and Bill is here**' (my punctuation). In other words, since linguists use asterisks to mark strings which are to be forbidden by a grammar, asterisks should never appear with sentences which are odd for purely semantic reasons. Quite correct. Yet the very *first* string Mrs Lakoff asterisks is **John is a strict vegetarian and he eats lots of meat**, which is clearly odd *only* because it is contradictory; as a sentence of English it is perfectly good. This first example is quite typical both of Mrs Lakoff's article and of the writings of the generative semanticists as a whole.

The generative semanticists' confusion is even worse confounded by an ambiguity in their use of the term 'deep structure'. These scholars are among those who believe in the possibility of unrestricted semantic description; for instance, they hold that a semantic description of English should predict that **Bill dies** follows from **John kills Bill**. In this connection they suggest that the latter sentence should have a semantic representation in terms of 'primitive semantic markers', e.g. **John** CAUSE **[Bill** DIE].* If semantic representations are constructed out of these semantic markers, then the rules relating semantic representations to natural sentences must contain *lexical transformations* which convert groups of markers (e.g. CAUSE and DIE) into lexical items (e.g. **kill**), as well as the ordinary transformations, such as Equi-NP Deletion or Passivizing, which reorder or delete grammatical and lexical items. In standard versions of Chomskyan linguistics, transformations have to be ordered with respect to one another; if we posit a special class of lexical transformations, we may ask whether all lexical transformations precede all other transformations, and, if so, we may adopt some name for the structures occurring at that point in a derivation after all lexical transformations have applied but before any other transformations have applied. Since, in the history of Chomskyan linguistics, the term 'deep structure' has been used for the structures defined by the constituency base of a grammar, it might seem appropriate to choose some other term for the unrelated notion discussed here. However, the generative semanticists have chosen to convert the term 'deep structure' to this new use; after all, since they believe the output of the base consists of semantic representations, they already have the term 'semantic representation' available for 'deep structure' in its earlier sense! They then argue that in fact some lexical transformations follow some non-lexical transformations, i.e. there are no 'deep structures' (in the new sense); if there are no deep structures, then deep structures are not distinct from semantic representations, which is what the generative-semantics hypothesis asserts.

---

* We may note that this kind of analysis does not follow even granted the generative semanticists' premises; we can perfectly well express the lexical inferability of sentences about dying from sentences about killing by means of a rule of inference, say 'A₁ **kill** A₂ ⟹ A₂ **die**', without breaking **kill** down semantically or syntactically into 'components' CAUSE and DIE. But the writers in question do not appreciate the role of rules of inference in semantic description.

In other words, the generative semanticists reduce their hypothesis to a series of terminological quibbles; which does not prevent them hailing it as a discovery of the first magnitude.

But the generative-semantics hypothesis is too important to be left to the generative semanticists. The hypothesis can, if we wish it, be a purely empirical one. Provided we are careful to exclude semantic facts from the evidence for syntactic analysis, there is absolutely no *a priori* reason why the inferences made by speakers of English should relate more closely to the underlying structures revealed by that syntactic analysis than to the overt forms of the respective sentences. Yet, over and over again, transformations which can be justified on purely syntactic grounds do have the property of deriving sentences from underlying structures for which relatively simple rules of inference are available. There is clearly something correct about the generative-semantics hypothesis.

It is also clear, however, that the hypothesis is not the whole truth: there are counter-examples to it. Consider the sentence **No one can serve God and Mammon**. Any reasonable syntactic analysis derives this by Co-ordination Reduction from the same deep structure (in the standard sense) that gives rise to **No one can serve God and no one can serve Mammon**. If deep structures are identical to semantic representations, then these two sentences have the same semantic representation, which is to say that they are synonymous. But they are clearly not.

The known counter-examples to the generative-semantics hypothesis are not simply a random assortment: they all involve certain categories of formative, including *quantifiers* (words like **all, some, no**) and negative particles. (Thus, if we replace the quantifier **no one** by the non-quantifier **John** in the sentences cited, the two sentences become synonymous and the problem disappears.) Chomsky has outlined what seems to be the true situation: semantic representations of natural sentences are identical neither to deep structures nor to surface structures, but are some simple function of the two − deep structures display the participants in the process described by each clause (e.g. **John wants to win** is about John winning rather than about winning in general), while surface structures contribute information about the 'scope' of the quantifiers and negative particles.

This proposal, if it can be made precise, seems even more intuitively appealing than the original generative-semantics hypothesis, since it provides a role for syntactic transformations. The idea that deep structures were semantic representations explained why our sentences have deep structures, but it failed to explain why they also have *surface* structures: it would seem simplest just to utter untransformed deep structures. Several suggestions have been put forward. Thus, Putnam points out that many transformations have an abbreviatory effect. Also, surface structures might represent a compromise between the many-tiered semantic trees typical of our messages and the linear structure imposed on speech by the sound medium: many transformations have the property of 'flattening out' the trees to which they apply, replacing hierarchical structure by ordering of grammatical formatives. Neither of these suggestions seem wholly adequate as they stand, though. If both deep and surface structures are needed to represent adequately the content of our messages, then the complexity of natural syntax becomes much more comprehensible.

We introduced the topic of semantics at the end of chapter 6 by promising to show that the syntactic universals on which Chomsky bases his linguistic nativism are in no way an automatic consequence of the fact that sentences in natural languages are bearers of meaning. It has taken us most of this chapter to explain what it means to call sentences 'meaningful'. It is now time to redeem the promise made in the previous chapter.

In the first place, the syntactic universals of natural language are clearly related closely to the semantic properties of those languages. The logical systems which underlie natural languages, as we have seen in the case of the sentential calculus, are systems whose formation rules are constituency rules and whose rules of inference are 'transformational rules' in the technical sense defined within Chomskyan theory – rules which convert trees into other trees in ways which depend solely on that part of the structure of the trees lying nearest to the root.*

* Within formal logic, the term 'transformation rule' is used simply as a synonym

The rule of *modus ponens*, for instance, says that we may infer S_2 from a pair of formulae S_1 and $S_1 \supset S_2$; and the term '$S_1 \supset S_2$' here applies not to *any* formula containing an instance of $\supset$, but only to those in which $\supset$ is immediately dominated by the root. Perhaps it does not follow inevitably that any spoken language used to give overt expression to such a logic must have a syntax based on constituency rules and transformations, but this would at least seem to be a very natural way to do the job.

The question we must ask, then, is the following: are there any *a priori* reasons why a logical system must use constituency formation rules and transformational rules of inference?

Chomsky himself, surprisingly, suggests that logic, by its very nature, involves hierarchical structure (and, presumably, hierarchy-modifying rules) akin to syntactic constituency structure and transformational rules:

> 'It is difficult to imagine any coherent characterization of semantic content [Chomsky writes] that cannot be translated into some "canonical notation" modeled on familiar logics, which can in turn be represented with properly bracketed expressions where the brackets are labeled [i.e. constituency trees].'

If this were so, Chomsky's arguments for linguistic nativism would collapse: Toulmin would be quite right to claim that

---

for 'rule of inference'. It is only in the special linguistic sense of 'transformation' that one can meaningfully ask whether rules of inference must necessarily be transformational in form. (Cf. the use of 'derivation' in linguistics and logic, see pp. 104: 146.) The logician may object that most of the rules of inference of a given logic, such as the sentential calculus, may be replaced by axiom-schemata, such as $S_1 \supset [S_2 \supset S_1]$. (An *axiom-schema* is a limiting case of rules of inference: while a rule such as *modus ponens* defines an infinitely large set of cases in which a formula may be immediately inferred from two previous formulae in a derivation, and a rule such as the negative-elimination rule $\sim \sim S \Rightarrow S$ defines an infinitely large set of cases in which a formula may be immediately inferred from one previous formula, an axiom-schema defines an infinitely large set of cases in which a formula called an axiom, e.g. $p \supset [q \supset p]$, may be immediately inferred from no previous formulae.) But the schemata of axiomatic versions of the sentential calculus are just as 'transformational' as the ordinary rules of inference: $S_1 \supset [S_2 \supset S_1]$ defines as an axiom any formula whose constituency tree has this structure at the root. There will undoubtedly be a number of alternative, equally simple semantic descriptions for a natural language; the empirical statements made in this section about natural-language semantics are claimed to apply to all reasonable descriptions.

natural languages simply contain the appropriate structure to carry out their tasks. But we shall see that Chomsky's view of logic is unjustified: his nativist arguments are better than he knows.

It is true that the artificial logical systems which have been constructed by logicians over the last hundred years, from the *Begriffsschrift* of Gottlob Frege (the father of modern logic) onwards, have overwhelmingly been hierarchically-structured systems. But that is not surprising. Whether they admitted it or not, even the most formalist of logicians have in practice chosen to study systems having a relatively direct relationship with natural languages. If natural languages are all 'transformational', then it is hardly remarkable that extant artificial logics are 'transformational' too.

In the case of syntax, in order to ask whether the transformational property of natural languages was predictable *a priori*, we had to define a class of entities which had those properties we feel a 'language' must have to be worthy of the name, without incorporating a requirement of transformational structure in the definition. The notion of 'stringset' – i.e. any (infinitely large, though definable) class of sequences of words – fitted this bill; and we then found that many stringsets did indeed lack the properties defined by transformational theory, for instance the prime-number language is not a transformational language.

What we need now is an analogous definition of a class of entities possessing the characteristics which something must have to be worthy of the name 'logical system', which does not incorporate transformational structure as part of the definition. Logicians have not concerned themselves with the boundaries of the concept 'logical system', since they have avoided considering the psychological question whether the nature of our reasoning processes is determined in part genetically. However, it is possible to formulate a suitable definition. This involves a number of technicalities which it would be inappropriate to go into here; but, essentially, whereas we define a language as an (infinitely large) set of sentences, we define a logic as an (infinitely large) set of immediate inference-pairs of sentences.

It is then clear that logics whose infinitely-numerous immediate inference-pairs can be specified by a finite set of transformational rules of inference (and whose formulae must therefore be defined by a constituency grammar) are a minority among the range of 'possible logics' allowed by the definition. As an example of an 'unnatural' logic, consider the logic whose set of formulae are the sentences of the prime-number language – the set of prime-length strings of words of Chinese – and whose only rule of inference runs as follows: from a set of premisses whose lengths are respectively a, b, c, . . . one may infer any formula whose length is the next prime number above $a + b + c + \ldots$, and which uses the same words in the same order (repeating if necessary). Thus, the lowest prime above $3 + 7$ is 11, so from, e.g., **Wo ai ni** and **Ta ta ta chi chi chi ta** one may infer, e.g., **Wo ai ni ta ta ta chi chi chi ta wo.**

This *prime-number logic* seems intuitively quite absurd. Yet it has well-formed formulae and inferences, just like familiar logics. How can we know that, say, the inhabitants of Mars do not operate with this logic, rather than with a transformational one? The world we live in does not seem to consist of prime numbers and sums of primes; but then, when we look at the world, we do not see labelled constituency trees either. One might argue that there would be no possible systematic way of translating the Martians' arguments into English, preserving validity. This is no doubt true; but the Martians might find the notion of a language like English absurd for the exactly symmetrical reason.*

The logic of human thought is transformational logic. The semantic representations of our sentences are defined by constituency grammars, the fixed rules of grammatical inference are transformational rules, and even the rules which we create spontaneously in order to draw lexical inferences seem always to be transformational (certainly the examples we have men-

---

* Readers with logical training may object that interesting logics have the properties of *consistency* and *completeness*; conceivably it might be that the only logics having both these properties are transformational ones, and that we use transformational logics for this reason. But certainly non-transformational logics can be consistent (i.e. may contain formulae which are not theorems): *no* formula of the prime-number logic is a theorem, for instance. As for completeness, this is defined in various ways, but all definitions known to me presuppose that logical systems are based on hierarchical constituency structure. In other words, to require logics to be complete is to treat 'logic' as synonymous with 'transformational logic' *by definition*, which is not interesting.

tioned have all been so). Hierarchical structure pervades our thought-processes, even where these are least predictable. And this structural invariance in human speech and argument is a purely empirical finding; our languages and logics might, without contradiction, be other than they are. Widening our scope to deal with semantics as well as syntax does not destroy the arguments for linguistic nativism; it makes them all the more compelling.

8

People as Computers

According to the nativist view for which we have been arguing in this book, a consideration of linguistic structure tells us something about how we are built. The existence of arbitrary bounds on the diversity of human languages is interpreted as following from some innately-determined aspects of our mental structure. The obvious question to ask at this point is 'How are we built, then?' What model of human mental structure emerges from the findings of linguistics?

Here Chomsky and other linguists fall silent. Linguists have not so far concerned themselves with explaining the linguistic universals by constructing models of psychological machinery. This has been sensible enough: Chomskyan linguistics is a young subject, and it has seemed more fruitful to concentrate on constructing an accurate theory of language, before going on to produce a higher-level hypothesis about mental structure in order to explain the theory of language. By now, though, although very many details of the theory of language are in dispute, the broad outlines of the theory seem solid enough for it to be worth while to move on to the next step.

In this final chapter, accordingly, I shall outline a theory of the mechanics of the human mind based on Chomsky's theory of language. The reader should be warned, though, that this material is very much more speculative than what has gone before. Indeed, the model to be presented here has a number of obvious flaws which I do not at present know how to remedy. However, I believe it is high time that linguists considered the kinds of question discussed here; perhaps the shortcomings of my own work will spur others to improve on it.

The strategy we adopt is to compare Man with another type of organism which uses complex languages, namely the digital computer. A computer uses a language, or 'machine code', with fixed rules; since computers are designed by men, we know all about the internal workings of computers, and in particular we know the relationship between the internal structure of the machine and the language with which the machine operates. Therefore we may think of ourselves as facing a proportion to be solved: what is to human language as the internal mechanisms of a computer are to the computer's language? Or, to put it another way: what kind of computer would use languages of the kind we have identified as natural languages?

The relations between computers and their languages are the subject of a branch of mathematics called *automata theory*. The term *automaton* denotes an abstract entity which is related to a computer in the way that, say, a mathematical function is related to the line on the graph paper used to represent that function: that is, a computer is a physical realization of the kind of mathematical system called an 'automaton'. A graph may be smudged, though we would not talk of a function being smudged; similarly, a computer may break down, but we would not talk of an automaton breaking down. Another difference is that 'automaton' is a much more general concept than 'computer': only automata of very particular kinds are realized physically as computers, depending on available technology, uses to which the computer will be put, and so on. For all these reasons it will be simpler and will involve fewer assumptions to talk about 'automata' rather than 'computers', though we shall sometimes use 'computers' to mean 'automata of the class to which real computers correspond'.

An automaton is an object that can be in any one of a (finite or infinite) number of *states*. In an ordinary digital computer, for instance, different states are realized as different distributions of electrical charge over a network of ferrite 'cores'; but when we talk of abstract automata we are not interested at all in how the states may be physically realized. An automaton has a set of possible inputs and a set of possible outputs: often these will be sentences of a language (though the input language will not necessarily be the same as the output language). The internal states, inputs and outputs are related by sets of rules. The *input rules* are statements of the form 'If the automaton is in state x and receives input p, then

169

it moves to state y'. The *output rules* are statements of the form 'If the automaton enters state x, then it produces output q'. In addition to the input and output rules there are a set of *computing rules* – statements of the form 'If the automaton is in state x and nothing is input then it moves to one of the states $y_1, y_2, \ldots,$ or y_n'. An ordinary digital computer is *deterministic*, which is to say that none of its computing rules provides more than one possible *successor state* y for any given state x. (Obviously the behaviour of a computer must be predictable, if it is to be useful in practice.) But in general we may allow automata to be *non-deterministic*, i.e. we may allow some states to have alternative successor states.

Some states may have no successor states at all: if the automaton reaches such a state, it *halts*. In general we may envisage the biography of an automaton as consisting of a series of stretches, each of which begins when the automaton shifts into a new state in response to input, after which it runs through a series of different states in accordance with the computing rules (possibly generating output at certain points), until either it reaches a halting state or a fresh input shifts it into a new state. Nothing guarantees that either of these eventualities need occur: a given state may lead to an endless series of successor states which happen never to be interrupted by further input. (In practice, computer systems are arranged so that they always do halt before too long; and a new input is submitted to a computer only when it has halted.)

An automaton is fully defined by specifying its sets of states, inputs, and outputs, together with the input rules taking certain pairings of state and input into new states, the output rules associating certain states with certain outputs, and the computing rules controlling the moves of the automaton from state to state when not receiving input.

In the case of an actual computer, the range of possible inputs are called *programs*. The task facing the programmer who wants to use the computer to solve a given problem is to find a program that shifts the computer into a state which initiates a series of successor states, such that outputs generated by some of the successor states constitute a solution to the programmer's problem, while the series reaches a halting state as quickly as is consonant with generating these outputs (since the cost of using a computer is proportional to the length of the series of states it passes through).

We may illustrate our definition of 'automaton' by describing, in terms of our definition, a very simple digital computer of the kind in everyday use. Such a machine comprises three parts: a *store*, a *counter*, and a *working register*. Each of these elements may be thought of as a container for numbers: to specify the state the machine is in at a given time, we have to say what numbers are in its store, counter, and working register. For technical reasons, practical computers represent numbers in 'binary' rather than the familiar 'decimal' notation (so that the only digits are 0 and 1, and the columns represent units, twos, fours, eights, . . ., rather than units, tens, hundreds, thousands, . . .). But, to keep things simple, we shall describe an imaginary computer that uses decimal notation. At any given time, the store of this machine will contain a series of one thousand five-digit numbers: thus, it might have 23970 in the first position, 84887 in the second position, 00021 in the third position, and so on up to the thousandth position. The counter always contains a single three-digit number, representing one of the positions in the store: thus 002 would represent the second position, which in the case above is occupied by the number 84887. (The number 000 represents the thousandth position in store.) Finally, the working register always contains a single five-digit number.

Taking store, counter and working register together, we see that the automaton has 5008 places each of which can be occupied by any one of the ten digits 0, 1, 2, . . ., or 9. Therefore the number of different states available to the automaton is 10^{5008} (i.e. '1' followed by 5008 zeros). To call this number 'astronomical' would be a gross understatement. Suppose we thought of the different states as tiny particles distributed evenly throughout the entire physical universe, including not only our own galaxy, but the countless other galaxies together with the vast reaches of empty space between them; then, on a standard estimate of the radius of the universe, each cubic millimetre of this colossal volume would contain as its share something like 2×10^{4918} ('2' followed by 4918 zeros) of the particles – a number whose vastness comes no nearer to being humanly graspable than did the total number of states. Yet the automaton we are describing is very simple as real-life computers go. The machine which prepares your bank statements has a state-set compared with which 10^{5008} is a trivially small number.

Any sequence of not more than one thousand five-digit numbers is a valid input to our automaton. The number of possible inputs is thus comparable in hugeness to the automaton's range of possible states.

The rules controlling the working of the automaton are quite simple, however. There is just one input rule and one computing rule. The input rule says that, whenever a sequence of n five-digit numbers is input, these numbers are placed in the first n positions of store, replacing whatever numbers were there before, and the counter is set to 001. The working register is unaffected, as are the later positions in store when n is less than 1000.

The computing rule depends on a code whereby a five-digit number can be interpreted as an instruction, with the first two digits indicating the operation to be performed and the last three digits indicating a position in store containing the number to be used in the operation. Thus, suppose 27 is the code for 'add to the working register': then 27002 means 'add the number in position 002 (in the case quoted, this number is 84887) to the number in the working register'. (Addition is always possible, because any digit that would have to be carried into a non-existent sixth column is simply dropped: 99999 + 00001 = 00000.) A score or so of two-digit combinations are defined as representing different elementary operations: 'add to the working register', 'multiply into the working register', 'copy the number in the working register into the specified position in store', 'add one to the counter if the specified number is even', and so on. The single computing rule runs as follows: if the number in the counter is c, execute the instruction coded by the five-digit number in position c of store, and then add 1 to the counter. Thus, after receiving input, the automaton will execute the instructions in positions 001, 002, 003, and so on, until one of these instructions interrupts the sequence by changing the number in the counter.

If the first two digits of the number in position c are a pair for which no operation is defined, the machine halts.

One of the digit-pairs, say 35, will code the instruction 'output the number in the specified position in store'. Thus, if the number in position c is 35001, the automaton will print out the contents of position 001 : in this case, '23370'. And this is the only output rule: so the range of possible outputs is the set of five-digit numbers.

There is virtually no limit to the range of problems an automaton of this kind can be used to solve; although the automaton can perform only simple operations on numbers, provided a problem is clearly enough defined it is always possible to represent the range of possible solutions numerically and to break down the instructions for solving the problem into a long sequence of the very elementary numerical operations which the automaton can perform. For instance, our problem might be to work out when and for how long to fire the rockets of a spacecraft in order to land safely on the moon, given information about position and speed of the spacecraft provided by the instruments on board. Suppose this latter information – the *data* for the problem – can always be represented by means of ten five-digit numbers. Then we may be able to find some sequence of, say 400 five-digit numbers which translate into appropriate instructions for manipulating the data. On an occasion when the problem arises, we input to the computer a 410-number program consisting of the 400 instructions followed by the ten data numbers taken from the instruments; the computer then outputs a sequence of numbers which represent firing times for the rockets, according to a code chosen in advance by the programmer.*

Even if our problem is concerned with words rather than with numerically-measurable quantities, as for instance when computer techniques are used in stylistic analysis of texts whose authorship is disputed, we can represent letters, punctuation, etc. by arbitrary numerical codes and use the same machine to solve the problem. In practice we shall arrange

* The practising programmer may object that data and program are separated in practice in a way not reflected in my account. This is one of the complications about computers which is of great importance in real computing situations, but which for our purposes is irrelevant and better ignored.

for the coding and decoding between letters and their internal, numerical representation in the computer to be carried out automatically – in other words, we shall use a more complex machine than I have described, which allows letters as well as numbers to occur in input and output – but again this refinement does not concern us here.

This, then, gives us a picture of what we mean by the notion *automaton*. But what has all this to do with human mental mechanisms?

We have seen that an automaton is a device defined by input rules which specify how an input sentence moves it from one state to another, computing rules which specify how it passes through different states spontaneously (i.e. when not receiving input), and output rules which specify that entry to certain states causes it to produce output. From the example, we can see how the nature of the input language for an automaton is closely related to the nature of the internal states available to that automaton. In the case described, an automaton-state consisted largely of a sequence of five-digit numbers, and the programs acceptable to the automaton also consisted of sequences of five-digit numbers.

It is attractive to think of a human mind as an automaton whose different states will correspond to different structures of knowledge or belief. The input rules for this automaton will specify how one's pattern of beliefs is modified by what one hears; and the computing rules will describe the activity known as *thinking*, by which we infer or hypothesize new beliefs on the basis of what we already know or believe to be the case – i.e. how we move from one internal state to another independently of input. (Unlike the computer we have described, a human 'mental automaton' will presumably be non-deterministic – we do not feel that our thinking processes flow along rigidly determined paths. This is no problem: it is as easy to describe non-deterministic as deterministic automata.)

We should stress immediately that we do not intend the states of the automata we shall describe to be simply equated with 'states of mind' in the everyday sense. There are many factors which contribute to a person's 'state of mind' – whether he is happy or sad, weary or fresh, even whether he is awake or asleep – which will be ignored in our discussion. The automata we describe will represent only those small subparts of people's minds that deal with explicit propositional knowledge or belief; we shall not attempt to consider how a person's beliefs modify or are modified by his emotions, his state of attentiveness, and so forth.

To treat a human mind, or part of it, as a kind of (non-deterministic) automaton, and to view the act of saying a sentence to a person as a case of programming an automaton, is a very attractive idea. Since we now have a fairly rich theory about the structure of human language, this notion opens up the possibility of a more substantive theory than has previously been available of the mechanics of human thought.

One might suppose that it is foolhardy for linguists to speculate about the machinery of thinking, since this might seem to be the province of neurophysiology. However, the neurophysiologist is in the position of someone who takes the casing off a very complex computer and inspects the tangled mass of wiring inside: it is relatively easy for him to make discoveries about the nature of the individual components out of which the circuitry is constructed, but much harder to work out the over-all logic of the whole system. If we did not know how digital computers were organized, it is arguable that we would be much likelier to find out by experimenting with input and output than by taking the casing off and looking at the wiring – particularly if experiments of the latter kind were subject to the ethical constraints that limit research on human brains. One may compare the problem of discovering how humans think to the construction of a tunnel through a mountain, which neurophysiologists are attacking from one side and less biologically-minded researchers, such as linguists, from the other. Some parts of the problem can clearly be solved only by neurophysiologists; but at present it looks quite possible that the most central discoveries may fall to the linguists rather than the biologists.

Although the analogy between minds and automata is *a priori* appealing, the kinds of automaton which computer manufacturers have translated into physical reality do not seem promising as sources for a concrete theory of the machinery of mind. The machine language of the automaton we defined above, for instance, is not at all reminiscent of human languages. The latter contain infinitely many sentences, only the simplest of which are used in practice; the computer language contains a vast but finite set of programs, and those programs which are useful in practice are not typically 'simple' in any obvious sense. Furthermore, the machine language contains nothing resembling the constituency structure which we have found to characterize human languages.

Fortunately, as mentioned briefly in chapter 6, computers' machine languages are not the only programming languages in current use. Most programs are composed in 'high-level' programming languages, and computers are equipped with 'compiler programs' which convert high-level programs into machine-language programs in order to spare human programmers the need to write in machine language directly. Now, given an automaton A whose machine language is L_A, and a compiler program P, written in L_A, which translates some high-level language L_P into L_A, then we may think of the *system* composed of automaton A together with compiler P as jointly constituting a new automaton, say A', whose input language is L_P. No automaton with the properties of A' actually exists as a physical computer of metal and plastic, but this is for purely technical reasons: the automaton A' can be described just as precisely as the automaton A which does physically exist. A programmer programming the system made up of A and P will typically think of the machine he is interacting with as having the properties of A'; he may be quite ignorant about the very different properties of A.

Now, high-level programming languages typically do display structural characteristics similar to those of natural languages: high-level programming languages are commonly constituency languages defined by recursive rules, for instance. So high-level languages, and the automata whose input languages they are, may offer a much more fruitful source of hypotheses about the human mind than do concrete computers and their machine languages.

Let me begin by sketching an example of a high-level language and its associated automaton. The example I describe is based on the language APL: however, I shall simplify APL drastically for ease of exposition. Since the resulting system is fairly different from the model on which it is based, I shall defer to the sensibilities of readers who may be familiar with 'genuine' APL by giving my system an arbitrary name of its own: 'Z'.

To define the system Z, we first define the set of possible states of a Z-speaking (or, better, 'Z-comprehending') automaton. Any Z-state is a set of Z-objects, where a 'Z-object' is a pairing of a Z-identifier with a Z-property. A Z-identifier is simply any sequence of capital letters (e.g. **DIANA**), and acts as the *name* of the Z-object bearing it. A Z-property can be a number (e.g. 27 or −5·6), a sequence of numbers (e.g. 27 −5·6 594), a sequence of sequences of numbers (we treat, e.g., the 2-by-3 matrix:

$$\begin{array}{ccc} 27 & 3 & 0\cdot2 \\ 5 & -1 & 27 \end{array}$$

as a sequence of two sequences each of three numbers), and so on. Any finite set of Z-objects is a legitimate Z-state, provided no two of them have the same identifier (it is perfectly in order for a Z-state to contain objects with different identifiers but the same property). Thus, for instance:

$$\{(\textbf{DIANA}, 27), (\textbf{BILL}, 27\ -5\cdot6\ 594), (\textbf{JOHN}, 27)\}$$

is a Z-state containing three objects. Obviously there are infinitely many possible Z-states.

We now define the language L_Z of possible programs which may be input to the Z-comprehending automaton. We can achieve this with the following constituency grammar:

$$S \rightarrow I \leftarrow D$$

$$D \rightarrow \left\{ \begin{array}{l} I \\ P \\ T \\ MF\ D \\ D\ DF\ D \\ S \end{array} \right\}$$

(Notice that the second, left-pointing arrow in the first rule is a formative of L_Z – unlike the right-pointing arrow which is the usual instruction to rewrite 'S' as 'I← D'. The braces indicate that 'D' may be rewritten either as 'I' or as 'P' or . . . .)

The symbol 'I' may be rewritten as any Z-identifier, and 'P' as any Z-property. 'T' is rewritten as one of a small range of special terminal symbols which name different Z-properties depending on the occasion on which the program is input to the automaton: for instance, **today** is a T formative which names the Z-property 12 4 1974 if it occurs in a program input on 12 April 1974. Finally, 'MF' and 'DF' can be rewritten as any of a range of symbols which represent what a mathematician would call monadic and dyadic (*partial*) *functions* from Z-properties into Z-properties. For instance, + represents the dyadic function of *addition* which takes e.g. the Z-property 4 and the Z-property 6 into the Z-property 10 (or the sequences 4 2 and 6 7 into the sequence 10 9). The symbol **sub** represents the **indexing** function, which takes the sequence 27 $-5·6$ 594 and the number 2 into the number $-5·6$, because this is the second element of the sequence. (Indexing is a 'partial' function because, e.g., '27 $-5·6$ 594 **sub** 5' has no meaning: the sequence has no fifth member.) Examples of monadic functions are ! for *factorial*, which takes, e.g., 5 into 120 (i.e. $5 \times 4 \times 3 \times 2 \times 1$), or **dimension**, which would take, e.g., the matrix displayed on p. 177 into the sequence 2 3, because it is a 2-by-3 matrix.

Both 'S' and 'D' occur on the right-hand side as well as the left-hand side of the rules defining L_Z, so clearly there are infinitely many well-formed L_Z programs.

In order to describe the input rules which specify how a Z-program moves the automaton from one Z-state to another, let us consider an example of a Z-state and the effect of a particular Z-program on it. The example will be an utterly trivial one: unfortunately, any sensible example would be too complicated to serve our purposes. Consider the Z-state {(**DIANA**, 2), (**DOZEN**, 12)} – i.e. a state containing two objects, one called **DIANA** and having the property 2, the other called **DOZEN** and having the property 12. We shall present a program which changes this state into a new state containing two further objects in addition to **DIANA** and **DOZEN**: one called **MONTH**, whose property will be the number of the month in which the program is input (e.g. 7 if the program is input in July), and another called **OYSTERS** whose property will be 12 if the program is input in a month with an 'r' in it, otherwise o.

The program can be written linearly, for convenience, as:

OYSTERS←DOZEN × ((**MONTH** > **8**) **or** (**5** > **MONTH**
← (**today sub DIANA**)))

It has the following constituency structure (in which the 'D' and 'S' nodes are given numerical subscripts to simplify the following discussion):

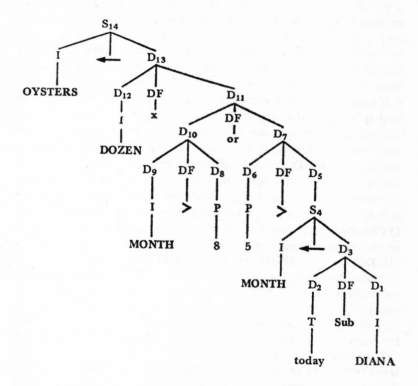

We 'evaluate' the program (i.e. spell out the effect it has on the state to which it is input) by beginning at the lowest nodes of its constituency tree and working upwards, selecting a particular Z-property to be associated with each D node, and creating a new Z-object for each S node encountered.

179

In the first place, D_1 dominates **DIANA** which identifies an object with the property 2, so D_1 refers to 2. If the program is input on 12 April 1974, then D_2 refers to the Z-property 12 4 1974. As we have seen (12 4 1974) **sub** 2 is 4, so D_3 refers to 4. Now S_4 creates a new Z-object with the identifier **MONTH** and the property 4: this object (**MONTH**, 4) is added to the Z-state, and D_5 automatically refers to the property, 4, of the object created by the S which it dominates. The dyadic function > takes two numbers x, y into the number 1 if x is greater than y and into the number 0 if x is less than or equal to y (think of 1 and 0 as standing for 'true' and 'false', respectively): D_6 represents 5 and 5 is greater than 4, so D_7 represents 1. By similar logic, D_{10} represents 0 (4 is less than 8). The dyadic function **or** is defined only for 0 and 1 as arguments: the function gives 1 if at least one of the arguments is 1, 0 if both are 0. (A sentence **p or q** is true if at least one of **p** and **q** is true, false if **p** and **q** are both false.) Accordingly, in this case, D_{11} represents 1. (If the program were input in an r-less month, say July, it is easy to verify that D_7 and D_{10}, and hence also D_{11}, would all represent 0.) D_{12} represents the property of the Z-object named **DOZEN**, i.e. 12, so D_{13} represents 12×1, that is 12, in an r-ful month and 12×0, that is 0, in an r-less month; finally, S_{14} creates a new object named **OYSTERS** and with the property 12 or 0. Thus, if the act of programming occurs in April, the new state is {(**DIANA**, 2), (**DOZEN**, 12), (**MONTH**, 4), (**OYSTERS**, 12)}.

This illustrates the input rules of Z. Z has no computing rules: every Z-state is a halting state. (When one programs a computer in a high-level language, rather than breaking a task down into a long series of simple steps, one uses individual function-names to stand for arbitrarily complex relations between arguments; accordingly, there is no need for a high-level system to include computing as well as input rules.) As for output, the one output rule specifies a particular identifier, **OUTPUT**, such that every time a new Z-object is created having that identifier, the property of the object is printed out: thus, if the identifier **OYSTERS** had been replaced by **OUTPUT** in the above program, '12' (or '0') would have been printed out.

Having seen something of the workings of the automaton A_Z corresponding to the high-level computer programming language Z, let us now consider the nature of the automaton A_{Eng} which represents the range of belief-structures and thought-processes available to an English-speaking human. Just as a Z-state contains a set of Z-objects with properties drawn from a fixed class of Z-properties, so a state of A_{Eng} will contain a set of objects I shall call *referents*. The referents in a person's A_{Eng}-state correspond to the entities he knows of. Suppose some person P knows of the existence of a red car C; then P's A_{Eng}-state will include a referent c corresponding to C. Each lexical item of English will correspond to a possible property for referents in A_{Eng}-states. Following the logician Peter Geach, I shall use the notation '§( )' to turn lexical items into names of referent-properties: if P knows that C is a red car, then c will have the properties §(**red**) and §(**car**). (An element of a mental state cannot be red, but it can be §(**red**).)

P's A_{Eng}-state will include not only referents representing physical objects, but referents for any individual entities of which P is aware and which he can take definite descriptions to denote: there will be referents for characters in fiction, for abstractions like **the centre of this circle**, etc. etc. But, at any given time, P's A_{Eng}-state will contain only a finite number of referents. Given enough time, there is no limit to the number of objects whose existence P could deduce or imagine; and I shall suggest that for P to deduce or imagine the existence of some entity B is for P's A_{Eng}-state to acquire a new referent representing B. But deduction and imagination take time: in a finite amount of time P's A_{Eng}-state will have acquired only finitely many referents. The referents in P's A_{Eng}-state will not necessarily be in a one-to-one relationship with the individuals which they represent in the outside world: thus, if P is investigating a murder, his A_{Eng}-state may include a §(**murderer**) referent possessing '§' properties corresponding to all the characteristics P infers the murderer to possess, and a separate §(**butler**) referent with properties corresponding to what P knows about the butler, while unbeknownst to P the butler is in fact the murderer.

Consider sentences (i) and (ii) addressed to P (and let us simplify things initially by supposing that P does not previously know of any red cars – we shall consider the more general case shortly):

(i) **I bought a red car yesterday.**
(ii) **I sold the red car today.**

The phrase **a red car** in (i) will create a referent with the properties §(**red**) and §(**car**) in P's A_{Eng}-state. On the other hand, when P hears (ii) the phrase **the red car** will pick out the referent which **a red car** has previously created (in order to act on it in ways which will be discussed later). In other words, the distinction between **the red car** and **a red car** is quite parallel to the distinction between D and S nodes, respectively, in the system $\mathcal{Z}$: the former selects an entity from the current state, the latter adds an entity to the current state.

Of course, in a real-life situation it is quite likely that P will know of more than one red car; most definite descriptions are not in practice complete enough to specify unambiguously a unique individual among all the entities of which the hearer is aware. P will take **the red car** to refer to one among the various red cars of which he is aware which is in some way closer than the others to the focus of his attention (whether because it has recently been spoken of, or for other reasons). This will translate into our theory as the notion that the referents in an A_{Eng}-state are arrayed in some kind of space, one point of which constitutes the current focus. In due course we shall consider the nature of this space, and the factors which determine the position in it of the referents and focus of attention; for the moment, let us simply assume that the notion can be made precise. Then we can say that any phrase consisting of the word **the** followed by a series $w_1, w_2, \ldots w_n$ of adjectives and noun will pick out the nearest referent to the hearer's focus of attention having all the properties §(w_1), §(w_2), ..., and §(w_n). Thus, **the car** will pick out the nearest §(**car**) referent, while **the red car** will select the nearest referent which is both §(**red**) and §(**car**). It ought to follow that the nearest referent of all to the focus should be referred to as **the**; in English, a rule of syntax replaces **the** as a complete referring expression by **he, she** or **it**.

$\mathcal{Z}$-objects can be referred to by their identifiers. The obvious candidates as natural-language equivalents of identifiers are proper names. However, although some logicians have discussed proper names, under the label *singular terms*, as if they are the equivalent of Z-identifiers, English proper names in fact do not behave in this way. A Z-state in which two distinct objects bear the same identifier is simply not a well-formed state; if an S node creates a Z-object with an identifier which is already in use, the old object is automatically destroyed. In English, on the other hand, locutions like:

Do you mean my Charles or your Charles?
The London in England is bigger than the London
in Ontario.

are normal enough. Many proper names apply to only one referent in an average A_{Eng}-state, but many apply to more than one referent. We shall take it that proper names correspond to properties for referents in just the same way as common nouns: **London** selects the nearest §(**London**) referent to the hearer's focus, as **the car** selects the nearest §(**car**) referent. (There is good evidence that a sentence such as **London is large** starts off as **The London is large** in deep structure: the syntactic distinction between proper and common nouns is a superficial one introduced by a transformation in English. I am presupposing that, when deep and surface structures differ, it is the deep structure of a sentence which correlates more directly with the effect the sentence has on its hearer's A_{Eng}-state.)

We have yet to explain how phrases such as **your Charles**, or genitive constructions in general, select particular referents. The 'basic' sense of the genitive is commonly taken to be possession, as in **John's car**; however, the genitive often represents other relationships, as in **your Charles** just mentioned,* or **John's father**, **John's country**, **the origin of the problem**, **the density of the liquid**, etc. etc. Even a phrase like **John's car**, though often paraphrasable as **the car which John owns**, will also frequently be used in situations where the most appropriate paraphrase would be **the car we saw narrowly miss running John down, the car which John keeps saying he'd like to buy if he only had**

---

* Grammarians do not usually use the term 'genitive' in connection with possessive pronouns such as **your**; but I take it that the rule which substitutes **your** for **you's** or **of you** is a superficial phenomenon in English.

the money, or other expressions of purely idiosyncratic and ephemeral relationships between the objects denoted by the two halves of a genitive construction.

The notion that referents in an A_{Eng}-state are arranged at different distances from one another permits a neat account of this situation. In a phrase of the form A's B, or **the B of A,** the A part of the phrase will as usual select the nearest referent to the hearer's focus (say r_A) having properties corresponding to the lexical items of A, while the phrase as a whole will select the *nearest referent to r_A* having properties corresponding to the lexical items of B. Thus, in the case of **John's car, John** selects the nearest §(**John**) referent to the focus, and **John's car** selects the nearest §(**car**) referent to the referent selected by **John.** As we shall see when we discuss the organization of the referent-space, ownership is only one of the factors that may cause a §(**man**) referent to be close to a particular §(**car**) referent in an A_{Eng}-state.

Certain English words, known as *deictics* or *token-reflexives*, correspond to the formatives categorized as 'T' in the language Z; these include **I, you, today, here,** and so on. Deictics, like definite descriptions, select referents; but their referents depend on features of the speech-act in which they are used, and are independent of the position of focus and referents in the hearer's A_{Eng}-state. This is why a deictic never occurs as head of a genitive construction — we do not say **the greengrocer's you** (with the genitive **'s**), because **you** always refers to the referent representing the addressee of the current speech-act, so that it would be pointless to modify **you** with a genitive phrase.

So far we have discussed only referents corresponding to nominal phrases in syntax, and representing individuals in the outside world. But some referents will represent what would more normally be called 'facts' or 'events' than 'individuals'. Consider a sentence such as **Mary discovered that John bought the car**: here the subject, **Mary,** selects an individual referent, but the object, namely the clause **that John bought the car,** selects what we shall call a *propositional referent* representing the fact that John bought the car. We may suppose that the referents in an A_{Eng}-state are linked in a graph structure in which propositional referents dominate sequences of (propositional or individual) referents.* Thus, suppose P knows that John bought a car; then his A_{Eng}-state will include a structure of the following form:

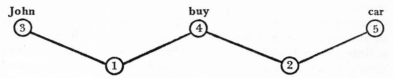

Here, the unlabelled referents r_1 and r_2 are individual referents representing John and the car respectively, while the labelled nodes are propositional referents: r_4 represents the fact that the denotatum† of r_1 brought the denotatum of r_2, r_5 represents the fact that the denotatum of r_2 is a car, and r_3 represents the fact that the denotatum of r_1 is a John ('is called John', as we usually say). To say that a referent, e.g. r_2, has the property §(**car**), is to say that there exists a propositional referent, in this case r_5, labelled **car** and dominating r_2.

We have seen that an 'indefinite' nominal phrase, e.g. **a car**, creates a new individual referent; similarly, a sentence creates a new propositional referent. Thus, suppose P's A_{Eng}-state contains the structure presented above, together with a §(**Mary**) referent, and P subsequently hears the sentence **Mary discovered that John bought the car**; then P's A_{Eng}-state will acquire a new propositional referent labelled **discover** and dominating the §(**Mary**) referent together with r_4. In the following figure, broken lines show the material added by this sentence:

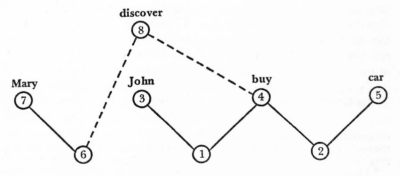

* A 'graph', in the sense used here, is the mathematical term for a structure

185

Notice that propositional referents, like individual referents, may be referred to by pronouns: if r_4 is close enough to P's focus of attention, the sentence **Mary discovered it** will suffice.

(I assume that some individual referents denote points of time, and that propositional referents will normally dominate a time referent among others. Where, as here, a verb in the preterite occurs with no phrase overtly indicating a point of time, I take it that the nearest time referent to the hearer's current focus of attention is dominated by the new propositional referent: one does not normally say e.g. **John bought the car** unless the hearer can be expected to know what occasion one is speaking about. In other words, preterite tense selects the nearest §(**time**) referent, as **he** selects the nearest §(**male**) referent. There is independent, syntactic evidence that preterite tense and pronouns share a common origin in the deep structure of English. To avoid clutter, I omit time referents in diagrams.)

The indefinite/definite article distinction makes it clear whether a nominal phrase is to create a new individual referent or select a pre-existing referent. **That** clauses, on the other hand, may either create new propositional referents or pick out old ones. Thus, in the example given above, if P's A_{Eng}-state already contains r_4, then the object clause in **Mary discovered that John bought the car** will select it to be dominated by r_8; but if there is no such referent, the clause will first create a **buy** referent dominating r_1 and r_2, and then move on to create the **discover** referent dominating r_6 and this new referent. The absence of syntactic distinction between clauses creating new propositional referents and clauses reidentifying old propositional referents is not surprising. Either John bought the car at the time in question or he did not; there will never be two referents both labelled **buy** and dominating the same sequence of three individual referents (including the time referent), so, if one's A_{Eng}-state includes r_4 and one hears the phrase **that John bought the car**, then one knows this phrase must refer

---

composed of a set of nodes linked by lines branching upwards and downwards; the nodes may or may not be labelled. Thus a constituency tree is a special case of a graph in which all branching is in one direction away from a single 'root' node.

† I use the term 'denotatum' for the real entity in the outside world corresponding to a 'referent' in an A_{Eng}-state.

to r_4 rather than calling for the creation of a new propositional referent. If there were no distinction between **the car** and **a car,** on the other hand, then one would have no way of knowing, on hearing the description **car,** whether r_2 or some new $\S(\textbf{car})$ referent was intended.

The graph structure into which an individual referent enters can be used to pick out that referent by means of relative clauses. Thus, if **the car** selects r_2, then the phrase **the man who bought the car** will select the nearest referent to the hearer's focus having the property $\S(\textbf{man})$ and such that some referent labelled **buy** dominates a pair of referents comprising it and r_2. If the hearer knows that John is a man (i.e. if his $A_{\textbf{Eng}}$-state includes, in addition to the structure diagrammed on p. 185, a referent labelled **man** and dominating r_1), then **the man who bought the car** will select r_1.

However, notice the difference between *restrictive* and *non-restrictive* relative clauses, as in **The man who bought the car is old** *v.* **The man, who bought the car, is old.** In the first case, the relative clause is part of the definite description: it specifies a property of the target referent. In the latter sentence, on the other hand, **the man** acts as a complete definite description and picks out the nearest $\S(\textbf{man})$ referent to the focus; the relative clause creates a new **buy** referent dominating the $\S(\textbf{man})$ and $\S(\textbf{car})$ referents, before the main clause creates an **old** referent dominating the $\S(\textbf{man})$ referent. The function of non-restrictive relative clauses in English is quite comparable to that of embedded S nodes in the language $\mathcal{Z}$.

The principle that each sentence received by a hearer creates a new referent in the hearer's $A_{\textbf{Eng}}$-state suggests a natural way of capturing within the theory the notion of a 'focus of attention', which varies with the topics being discussed: we may define the focus of attention as the most recently-created referent at any given time. The graph structure associated with propositional referents offers a way of formalizing the notion of 'distance' between referents: we can define the distance between any two referents as the minimum number of lines of the graph that have to be traversed to get from one referent to the other. Thus, consider the sequence of sentences:

(iii) **John bought a car.**

(iv) **The car hit a man.**
(v) **He called the police.**

Assume the hearer's A_{Eng}-state already contains a referent (say, r_1) with the properties §(**John**) and §(**man**). After hearing (iii) and (iv) but before (v), his A_{Eng}-state will include the following structure, with the focus at r_8 (the referent created by (iv)):

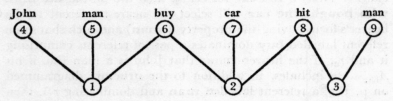

This structure contains two referents to which **he** could refer, namely r_1 and r_3; r_3 is one line away from the focus and r_1 is three lines away. Therefore the theory predicts that **he** in (v) will be taken to refer to r_3 rather than to r_1, and this prediction seems correct: **he** in (v) will be taken to denote the man who has been hit, rather than John. (Notice that this cannot be predicted from the *situation* described: when a driver hits a pedestrian, the driver is as likely as the pedestrian to call the police.)

I am suggesting that the possible states of the automaton representing the belief-structure of an English-speaker will be a range of labelled graphs conforming to certain constraints related to the semantics of the English vocabulary (a node labelled with a noun must dominate a single node, a node labelled with a transitive verb must dominate a sequence of nodes representing subject, object, time, etc.). There will be no limit to the number of nodes in an A_{Eng}-state, so the number of possible states will be infinite. We have already examined the input rules which determine what change a given sentence will produce in a given A_{Eng}-state.* The computing rules will correlate with the rules of inference of English. Thus, if the

---

*Sometimes, a grammatical English sentence will fail to produce any change in a given A_{Eng}-state – e.g. a sentence using **the red car** input to a state containing no §(**red**) §(**car**) referent. Similarly, in Z a program which incorporates an identifier corresponding to none of the current Z-objects will fail to change the current Z-state. We describe such a case in natural language as an instance of *failure of presupposition*.

latter rules permit us to derive x **owns** y from x **buys** y – i.e. if it is part of the meaning of **buy** and **own** that one who buys something owns it – then an A_{Eng}-state as diagrammed on p. 188 will be liable at any time to acquire a new node labelled **own** and dominating r_1 and r_2.* Clearly, A_{Eng} will be non-deterministic: the average A_{Eng}-state, and the rules of inference of English, will both be quite complex, so that at any given time there will be very many possible next states available to the automaton.

What of output rules? In the case of Z, whenever a Z-state acquired an object named **OUTPUT**, the property of that object was printed out on a sheet of paper. We may imagine that action is linked to thought in this way also in the human case. Suppose some referent r_0 in an A_{Eng}-state represents the 'owner' of the automaton; then we may suppose that, whenever the automaton acquires a referent labelled **assert** and dominating r_0 in subject position and some propositional referent r_1 in object position, the owner of the automaton utters a sentence which asserts the proposition represented by r_1. And, supposing r_2 represents some person Q, if a **hit** referent is created dominating the pair (r_0, r_2) then the automaton-owner hits Q.†

The foregoing is only the merest sketch of the kind of automaton that would appropriately be programmed in a natural language such as English. There are many central aspects of English semantics with which we have not attempted to deal. These include, for instance, negation (note that one can follow a sentence such as **John bought a car** by speaking of **the car that John bought**, but one cannot follow **John did not buy a car** by speaking of **the car that John did not buy**); truth-functional connectives (**if, or,** etc.); quantification (**all, some, no**) and plurals in general; the distinction between 'opaque' and 'transparent' reference (**Holmes said that the murderer**

---

* I assume that an A_{Eng}-state will include some device for indicating ordering between referents representing points of time, and that the inference-rule relating **buy** and **own** will specify that the time referent dominated by the new **own** node must follow that dominated by the **buy** node.

† These remarks may sound as if I am treating humans as mindless robots – 'automata' in the pejorative, deterministic sense – but quite the reverse: remember that the referents whose creation correlates with the automaton-owner's actions are brought into being by the process we have identified with thinking. There is nothing disrespectful to our species in suggesting that our actions are controlled by our thought.

was bald may mean that Holmes said **'The murderer is bald'**, or it may mean that Holmes said **'The butler is bald'**, and we, though not Holmes, know that the butler is the murderer); and many other features of natural language familiar to logicians. However, let us suppose that by elaborating our theory further we shall be able to make room for these various phenomena (though I should stress that, at present, this counts as a pious hope rather than a well-founded anticipation). Let me at this point introduce two problems connected with the theory as presented so far with which I *can* deal.

The first is that I have made no allowance for the fact that speakers may not be believed. If P hears John, the denotatum of r_2, say **I bought a car yesterday**, then, according to the rules I have sketched, P's automaton must acquire a §(**car**) referent representing John's new car. But in practice P may obviously choose to disbelieve John: what happens to this automaton in that case?

The second problem is that it is simply untrue that a person acquires beliefs about the existence of entities or the truth of propositions only by being told about them. P may come to believe that John bought a red car either because John (or someone else) tells him so, or because P watched the transaction take place. The car may subsequently be denoted by the phrase **the red car**, and the proposition about it by the clause **that John bought the red car**, irrespective of whether the referents denoting the car and the proposition were created in response to speech or observation.

The answers to these two problems are related. I suggest that the sight of John buying a car is the kind of input to a person that has the effect on his A_{Eng}-state which I have so far attributed to the hearing of the sentence **John bought a car**: this sight creates a **buy** node dominating nodes representing John and the car. On the other hand, hearing John say **I bought a car** (or hearing, e.g., Mary say **John bought a car**) has a more complex effect: as well as the **buy** node, it creates an **assert** node dominating the node representing John (or Mary) together with the new **buy** node.* Notice that, if John tells

---

* J. R. Ross has given syntactic evidence that the deep structure of an apparently simple sentence such as **John bought the car** is something like **I assert that [John bought the car]** – which, if true, makes my account all the more plausible.

you he has bought a car, you may doubt that he has in fact bought a car but you are not free in the same way to doubt that John has *asserted* that he has bought a car. You may, of course, doubt the latter also – 'Did he really say the words I thought he said?', 'Can I be sure it was John speaking?' – but this is to doubt the accuracy of one's observations, as one may doubt whether John bought a car after watching him buy it, rather than doubting the truth of what is said to one.

Clearly, there are enormous problems about how observations via the senses of a complex and continuous environment result in state-changes corresponding to the input of a discrete sentence: why did my view of John handing over a cheque on the car-dealer's forecourt change my A_{Eng}-state in the way which corresponds to the sentence **John bought a car**, rather than any of the (surely) infinitely many other propositions which could be corroborated on the evidence of my current sense-inputs? However, these problems are in no sense created by the theory presented in this chapter: these are already familiar problems in psychology and in the philosophy of science.

Once we agree to treat simple declarative sentences as creating propositional referents labelled **assert,** there is no special difficulty in handling sentences which perform other 'speech-acts'; e.g. **Shut the door!** will establish a referent labelled **command** and dominating referents representing speaker, hearer, and the proposition that the hearer will shut the door. Presumably the rules of inference will permit referents representing propositions about the world to be created on the basis of referents representing assertions, together with referents representing beliefs about the truthfulness of those making the assertions (often, though not always, we believe what we are told). Similarly, one can imagine that there might be rules of inference which will change an A_{Eng}-state created by reception of the sentence **Shut the door!** to a state which causes its owner to shut the door. Like many of the other rules of inference of English, those involved here will presumably be probabilistic rather than yes-or-no; one way in which the theory needs to be extended is to allow propositional referents to be associated with different strengths of belief.

Assuming that solutions can eventually be found to the many difficulties which currently beset this theory (and I must re-emphasize the gravity of some of these difficulties), then we see that the theory provides us, at last, with an answer to the question why humans should spend their time exchanging the peculiar objects called 'sentences'. Just as the computer which we discussed at the beginning of this chapter contained a 'store' of information possessing a certain structure, namely a 5-by-1000 matrix of digits, and the programs acceptable to the computer displayed a structure related to that of the internal information store, so (according to the present theory) a human contains a store of information organized in a particular way, and the structure universal to human languages reflects the organization of human information storage. We speak in hierarchical constituency structures, not because the world imposes constituency structure on us, but because our psychological machinery happens to impose constituency structure on the world. To talk to someone is to add something to his internal 'model' of the world: since a person's world-model controls his actions, if we speak the truth to him we help him to act relatively rationally. At any given time, a person's world-model is quite finite and in principle describable; and, although the particular elements making up a person's world-model depend solely on what he happens to have experienced and what people happen to have said to him, the general principles constraining the over-all form of the model (the fact that it contains hierarchical graph structure rather than, for instance, a matrix of digits) are determined by the fact that he was born human.

In chapter 7, we argued that intuition was an unsatisfactory guide to the construction of a semantic description of English. We now see how it can in principle be dispensed with. The intuitions we used in chapter 7 were intuitions about which sentences follow from which others: in terms of the automaton A_{Eng}, this corresponds to which particular states are liable to succeed other states by virtue of the computing rules. The internal states of A_{Eng} are not directly observable. But we can observe the inputs to and outputs from English-speaking automata: the inputs are what a person sees and is told, the outputs are what he does and says. The problem which we have begun an inadequate first attempt to solve here is that of positing machinery which, given the inputs available to a person, produces outputs which correspond to what that person in fact does and says: the computing rules incorporated in such a hypothesis will represent the semantics of the person's language, but the hypothesis as a whole will be tested against perfectly objective data. We may of course use intutions about the semantics of the language as a short cut to the construction of a hypothesis, but (as in the case of syntax), though intuition may be useful in practice, observation is the ultimate test of the theory in principle. Our account implies that the task of semantic description cannot in principle be separated from the problem of explaining human rationality – that is, of stating the laws which determine how a person will act in given circumstances; although this conclusion may seem inconvenient I do not believe it is incorrect.

Since we have agreed that a human is not a *deterministic* automaton, we clearly cannot expect to be able to predict his actions or utterances with certainty. This is not in itself a difficulty for the programme we have outlined. We may envisage a theory of human rationality offering a range of alternative possibilities for any given circumstances: the theory will be refuted if the person concerned acts in none of the predicted ways, while the principle of maximum refutability requires the theory to offer as few alternatives as possible. The remarks made in chapter 7 about the creativity of lexical inference, though, may seem to lead to greater problems of principle. It is clear that, if we are going to account for the links between a man's experiences and his actions in terms of computing rules corresponding to the rules of inference of his language, then even the simplest situation – say, a heard command which is followed immediately by action in obedience to the command* – is likely to involve some computing rules corresponding to lexical rules of inference; and we have argued that no fixed set of such rules can be stated for a natural language. Therefore, one may conclude, it is in principle impossible to define even a non-deterministic English-com-

---

* Most human actions are presumably determined at least in part by inputs much remoter in time than in this case; we educate children in order to enable them to act rationally years hence.

prehending automaton; if the only empirical controls on the semantic description of a language are observations of the inputs and outputs of an automaton which uses that language, it follows that there can be no empirical description even of the grammatical aspect of natural-language semantics.

The conclusion may be correct. Perhaps the semantics of natural languages are in principle inaccessible to scientific inquiry. But it is not quite clear that this is so, even granting what we said in chapter 7 about the creativity of lexical inference. We argued there that, even though the *particular* rules of lexical inference in a language cannot be specified, one can draw rigid bounds round the range of *possible* rules: for instance, these will always be structure-dependent rules, even though one could in principle conceive of non-structure-dependent rules of inference. The translation of that notion into the terms of this chapter will be that A_{Eng}, rather than being an automaton whose computing rules are fixed once and for all, is liable to change its computing rules (as well as its state) from time to time; but there will nevertheless be rigid constraints on what is a possible computing rule for A_{Eng} – not just any rule for going from one A_{Eng}-state to another will do. This limitation on A_{Eng} is possibly enough to render our hypotheses about A_{Eng} testable in principle. In practice, clearly, the tasks of showing that a hypothesis about A_{Eng} is testable, and of testing it, will be very difficult; but then, no one supposes that natural-language semantics and human rationality are simple subjects to study.

The theory we have unfolded in these last pages, if some version of it can eventually be made to survive criticism, suggests that the digital computer is a machine enjoying a rather special relationship with our species. It is in fact widely recognized that the computer has a special place among the various machines that Man has invented: it is often distinguished as a 'general purpose' machine, while all our other inventions are seen as fulfilling particular, restricted functions. Looking at a digital computer, though, it is hard to understand what gives it this universality which it clearly does possess: a computer, as a complicated system of metal, plastic, etc., is what it is just as definitely and inflexibly as a car or a spinning-wheel are what they are.

Just as we have treated computers as special cases of the abstract notion of 'automaton', so we may, if we wish, analyse other machines – cars, for instance – in terms of automata theory. The different possible states a car can be in are determined by whether the engine is running, the gear it is in, the quantity of petrol in the tank, and so on. The inputs consist of petrol, the key in the ignition, pressure on the pedals, movement of the steering wheel, etc. Possible outputs consist of motion at various speeds and in different directions. Just as we can think of the store of a computer as a stylized model of the world, or at least of those aspects of the world about which it receives information, so we might choose to think of the internal state of a car as a representation of those aspects of the world concerning which the car receives information. The metaphor is much less appealing in the case of the car than in the case of the computer, however. Why is this? May it not be, at least in part, because the structure which a car imposes on its internal state is very different from the structure of human belief-systems, while computers' internal states have structures much closer to those of our own minds?

Neither a car nor a computer can see the world as it is 'in itself': they can only form a model of the world based on the limited data provided by their respective 'sense organs', and constrained by the inherent organization of their respective internal machinery. But then, according to Kant, mankind is in much the same position; it is only that, standing outside cars and computers, we can directly *see* the difference between immanent and transcendent reality in their case – we can only suppose that there may be such a difference in our own case. If computers appear to be relatively 'general purpose' machines, perhaps this is because they see the world through roughly the same Kantian spectacles as ourselves.

In building computers – more particularly, in designing the abstract computing 'systems' formed by adding a compiler for a high-level language to a physical computer – Man has perhaps, for the first time, come close to creating machines *in his own image*. If so, then no wonder that computers seem to us 'special' by contrast to all our other machines.

And, if the study of grammar promises to lead to deeper

understanding of the machines who invented the spinning-wheel, the car, and the computer, then no wonder we grammarians are happy in our work!

Notes

These notes are intended mainly to guide the reader to literature bearing on points discussed in the text, and to state the sources of quotations; they do not pretend to be an exhaustive bibliography of linguistics. Where a topic is the subject of continuing controversy, apart from one or two standard works I sometimes list a relatively recent article, so that the reader who wishes to pursue the topic further can discover what has been written by working back from the references there. Whenever possible I list articles which have been reprinted in easily accessible anthologies.

The works referred to are listed by author's surname in the bibliography following these notes, except for Chomsky's works, to which I refer by short titles (e.g. *Aspects* for *Aspects of the Theory of Syntax*, 1965), and my own, to which I refer by three-letter abbreviations (e.g. *ITO* for 'The Irrelevance of Transformational Omnipotence', 1973): Chomsky's and my works are listed separately from the main bibliography.

The quotation from the Confucian *Analects* which appears on p. ix might be freely translated, in this context: 'I am only passing these ideas on, I cannot claim any originality; and, although I believe in them, I retain a sneaking affection for the old days.' Those who, like myself, first became involved with linguistics in pre-revolutionary days will recognize the sentiment!

Chapter 1: Introduction

Robins (1967) gives a lucid account of the development of linguistics from its earliest beginnings; for nineteenth-century historical linguistics, see Pedersen (1931). De Saussure's lectures were edited and published posthumously by his students under the title *Cours de Linguistique Générale* (1916). Boas's Introduction to the 1911 *Handbook of American Indian Languages* represents the beginnings of synchronic linguistics in America; it has now been reprinted separately (Boas 1968). Readers of Bloomfield's *Language* (1933) are warned that the British edition replaces Bloomfield's transcription of his own

197

pronunciation of English with English pronunciation and thereby makes it impossible to discover Bloomfield's view on phonology.

Chomsky has published a number of books since *Syntactic Structures* (1957), of which the most important are *Aspects of the Theory of Syntax* (1965), his longest but most confused and unsatisfactory work, and *Language and Mind* (1968). The clearest brief account Chomsky has given of his views on language is perhaps that contained in the first half of his *Problems of Knowledge and Freedom* (1972); the second half of this book expounds Chomsky's idiosyncratic political and social theories.

The Joos quotation is taken from p. 96 of *Readings in Linguistics I* (Joos 1957), an excellent anthology of articles in the American tradition of descriptive or 'structural' linguistics. For 'structuralism' in the French sense, see, e.g., Boudon (1968), Runciman (1969).

Chapter 2: The Implications of Linguistics

Apart from Chomsky's various writings, E. H. Lenneberg's *Biological Foundations of Language* (1967) is particularly relevant to much of the material in this chapter; cf. also Lenneberg (1969). On teleological explanations in science, see, e.g. chapter 12 of Ernest Nagel's *Structure of Science* (1961); cf., recently, Hirschmann (1973). The Martian parable is quoted in n. 15, p. 812 of Stich (1972). For objections to Chomsky's claim about 'degenerateness', see the contributions by M. D. S. Braine and by S. Ervin-Tripp to Slobin (1971), or p. 109 of Labov (1972a).

Abercrombie's remark is quoted from p. 20 of his *Elements of General Phonetics* (1967). Philip Lieberman's articles are collected in *The Speech of Primates* (Lieberman 1972); cf. Dart (1959). (Reisman 1973 is sceptical about Lieberman's claim that the Neanderthaler was inarticulate.) For Alvin Liberman's work on speech-specific hearing mechanisms, see, e.g., Liberman et al. (1967), Mattingly & Liberman (1969). (For other aspects of language processing by the human brain, see, e.g., Geschwind 1964, Kimura 1973, and also T. Nagel 1971, who outlines the fascinating results of recent 'split-brain' experiments.)

Chomsky's review of Skinner's *Verbal Behavior* (1957) appeared in *Language* in 1959.

On ethology, see Tinbergen (1951) and Schiller (1957); the latter includes a partial English translation of Konrad Lorenz's classic 1935 article 'Companionship in Bird Life'. For a survey covering the dancing 'language' of bees and the communication systems of other non-human species, see Wilson (1972). Hubel and Wiesel's discovery is concisely explained on p. 24 of R. L. Gregory's *The Intelligent Eye* (1970).

Psychology in Europe was never as dogmatically empiricist as in America; for instance, Jean Piaget's work on invariant aspects of the order in which children acquire abstract concepts, such as the conservation of quantity, is strongly nativist in tone. (For accounts of Piaget's work, see Ginsburg & Opper 1969, Pulaski 1971.) One relatively early American representative of newer trends in psychology is K. S. Lashley (1951). Chomsky refers to Lorenz's and to Lashley's work in his review of Skinner, but appears to feel that psychologists have not taken their lessons sufficiently to heart. (I should stress, though, that Chomsky is much better informed about recent developments in psychology than are many of his followers within linguistics; the latter sometimes write as if psychology was a monolithically Skinnerian subject until Chomsky published *Syntactic Structures* and began putting it to rights!) In connection with Broadbent (1973), cf. my *NBD*.

Descriptivism, realism, and other views on the status of scientific theories are discussed in chapter 6 of E. Nagel (1961). The terms 'God's-truth' and 'hocus-pocus' were coined by F. W. Householder (1952).

Chomsky's *Cartesian Linguistics* appeared in 1966; various linguistics journals have reviewed it unfavourably, and see also Aarsleff (1970), Cooper (1972), Percival (1972). Chomsky is defended by Harry Bracken (1970); cf. Chomsky's 'Problems and Mysteries'.

Apart from the notions of nativism and mentalism defined in the text, a third doctrine often confused with these is Descartes's doctrine of *dualism*, according to which the 'physical' and the 'mental' are fundamentally distinct 'substances'. Chomsky quite correctly treats dualism as a purely philosophical issue to which his work has no relevance (*Aspects*, p. 193).

S. Körner's *Kant* (1955) is a lucid introduction to that philosopher. The contrast between Descartes's and Kant's versions of rationalism is brought out clearly in the first pages of R. Blanché's *Contemporary Science and Rationalism* (1967).

On emergentism see, e.g., E. Nagel (1961, pp. 366–80), and Lambert & Brittan (1970, p. 100 *et seq.*). Chomsky has voiced his criticism of Darwinism mainly in unpublished lectures, but see pp. 59–62 and 82–3 of *Language and Mind*. K. R. Popper draws the analogy between biological evolution and the progress of science in various papers reprinted in his *Objective Knowledge* (1972): see, e.g., 'Of Clouds and Clocks'. My allusion to Scriven refers to 'Explanation and Prediction in Evolutionary Theory' (1959); cf., recently, Kochanski (1973). Darwin discusses the problems posed for his theory by the human eye, and by the honeycomb-building behaviour of bees, in chapters 6 and 7 of *The Origin of Species* (1859). For Wallace see, e.g., Wallace (1870), Eiseley (1958, ch. 11).

Chapter 3: *The Scope of Linguistic Descriptions*

The question of how to classify the various kinds of speech found in the world into individual 'languages' and 'dialects' of those languages – or whether, indeed, any such classification can be justified – is dealt with by the branch of linguistics called *sociolinguistics*. See for instance the introduction to Pride & Holmes (1972), together with various papers included there (particularly Haugen 1966, Labov 1970); numerous other papers by William Labov (see his collection *Sociolinguistic Patterns*, 1972c); Bailey & Shuy (1973).

Problems about the scientific status of the 'social sciences' are well discussed by Rudner (1966), and see various articles in Ryan (1973). Popper states his principle of refutability in *The Logic of Scientific Discovery* (1934), and, more concisely, in the title essay in his *Conjectures and Refutations* (1963). Magee (1973) offers a clear introduction to Popper's thought.

Hockett states his objections to the identification of languages with stringsets in *The State of the Art* (1968), and cf. Wilks (1972). On the gradience issue, see also Bolinger (1961), Ross (1972), G. Lakoff (1973). Chomsky discusses the treatment of strings which are not clearly either grammatical or ungrammatical on p. 14 of *Syntactic Structures*. (Notice that the all-or-nothing assumption about grammaticality is not affected by proposals for distinguishing various degrees of ungrammaticality, cf. Chomsky, 'Methodological Remarks', Katz 1964c: Chomsky and Katz maintain a sharp distinction between strings which are fully grammatical and those which are ungrammatical to a greater or lesser degree.) Chomsky stresses the fact that 'Every time an adult reads a newspaper, he ... comes upon countless new sentences' in his review of Skinner (p. 563 of the reprint in Fodor & Katz 1964); his emphasis on the notion of 'creativity' comes somewhat later – see, e.g., 'Current Issues in Linguistic Theory' (1964) or the preface to *Aspects*.

For Sapir's views on linguistic creativity, see various articles collected in Sapir (1949), particularly 'The Status of Linguistics as a Science' (1929), or the brief 1931 note reprinted in Hymes (1964). For Whorf's ideas, see the articles collected in Whorf (1956), e.g. 'Science and Linguistics' (1940) or 'The Relation of Habitual Thought and Behaviour to Language' (1941). Wittgenstein's belief in linguistic creativity was a feature of the philosophy he adopted in the later part of his life, as represented by *Philosophical Investiga-*

tions (1953); on the lack of defined boundaries for the applicability of 'game', see §§ 3, 66ff. of *Philosophical Investigations*. (The newcomer to Wittgenstein should be alerted to a source of potential misunderstanding: Wittgenstein chooses to use the word 'game', which he has selected to illustrate the undefinability of words of everyday language, also as a technical term in his account of how language works. Peter Strawson (1954) characterizes this double use of 'game' as 'ingenious', but I find it unnecessarily confusing.)

Peter Winch attacks the notion of 'social science' in *The Idea of a Social Science* (1958); his views are discussed, e.g., by Ryan (1970).

It should be mentioned that, apart from the syntactic universals of language with which the body of this book deals, Chomsky and other contemporary linguists also believe in a theory of phonological universals, i.e. of constraints on the ways in which natural languages exploit the phonetic possibilities physically available to Man. This theory stems from Roman Jakobson (1942); its current state is represented by Chomsky & Halle's *Sound Pattern of English* (1968). However, the theory of phonological universals seems to be vacuous (i.e. unfalsifiable) as usually interpreted, and false under any interpretation which renders it falsifiable (*UPA, OFN*); so it will not be considered further here.

Chapter 4: The Evidence for Linguistic Theories

This chapter deals with linguistic *methodology*; we ask how well the theories which linguistics have adopted stand up, when examined in the light of the various general principles for theory-choice with which the philosophy of science is concerned. An excellent introduction to the philosophy of science is Hempel's *Philosophy of Natural Science* (1966), and see works by Popper and E. Nagel already cited. Methodology has been a neglected area in Chomskyan linguistics, although see Botha (1968, 1973), Labov (e.g. 1971, 1972a), Derwing (1973), Dougherty (1973, forthcoming).

The philosophy of science is itself a subject in which old orthodoxies have recently been challenged by iconoclastic views. Notably, T. S. Kuhn's *Structure of Scientific Revolutions* (1962) advances the idea that, when an established scientific theory is replaced by a 'better' one, there can be no rational criteria for choosing between the two, and the contest is decided exclusively on the basis of criteria such as the personal charisma of their respective proponents; cf. also Feyerabend (1970), and papers by Kuhn and others in Lakatos & Musgrave (1970). (Kuhn would deny that the preceding is a fair summary of his views, but his denials are unconvincing.) On Kuhn's account, it is difficult to see why anyone would bother to pursue science; although individual scientists' judgements often are swayed by irrational considerations, it is normally felt that the whole point of science is that scientific method enables the community to rise above the irrationality of its members. Kuhn's view of scientific method has had great appeal for linguists and other social scientists, a phenomenon which Williams (1970) explains adequately by referring to the proverb about the drowning man and the straw. Fortunately, Kuhn's view is in a sense self-falsifying: since the present author happens to be impervious to Kuhn's charisma, either what Kuhn says is false or he gives me no reason to believe it true. The most satisfying attempts to revise the 'classical' philosophy of science in order to meet genuine difficulties have been made by Imre Lakatos, whose death while this book was being written was a tragic loss to the philosophical world: see Lakatos (1970, 1971). Lambert & Brittan (1970) give a lucid account of the current state of play in the philosophy of science; see also Scheffler (1967, 1972).

The remark by Chomsky on p. 60 is quoted from Hill (1962, p. 158); cf. also Chomsky's 'Methodological Remarks'. In my account of why introspective data are inappropriate for science I follow N. R. Hanson's *Patterns of Discovery* (1958). (For the 'swamp' metaphor, see p. 111 of Popper's *Logic of Scientific Discovery*, 1934.) To justify the amount of space I devote to the question about intuitions, I should perhaps stress that Chomsky's statement that the data for linguistics are speakers' intuitions is far from an isolated aberration: it has become quite standard doctine in contemporary linguistics. J. R. Ross, for instance, remarks (1970) that, although intuitions 'may prove to be mistaken', linguistic theories nevertheless 'must' tally with them, since otherwise the linguist will feel 'dissatisfied'. (What would one say of a physicist who proposed abandoning Einstein's theory in favour of Newton's on the grounds that Newton's theory, although known to be false, was more intuitively satisfying than relativity?) Botha (1968, p. 70) and Labov (1971) give numerous references to passages in which Chomsky and other linguists claim that speakers' intuitive knowledge is the data for linguistics, and discuss the nature of such data.

For the notion of 'simplicity' in science, see Goodman (1961), Hempel (1966, §4.4), Rudner (1966, §2.9). In some influential but extremely confusing remarks on p. 38 *et seq.* of *Aspects*, Chomsky claims that this notion has no relevance for linguistics. Where more than one grammar is compatible with the data about a given language, according to Chomsky the choice between them will be made by an 'evaluation measure' which can be established empirically as part of the general theory of language, so that there is no room for an *a priori* simplicity criterion to operate (although Chomsky, following

Willard Quine, explicitly stated the opposite in *Syntactic Structures*, p. 14). With respect to the further question (whether an *a priori* simplicity criterion is needed to choose between alternative empirically-adequate general theories of language), Chomsky appears to hold, on p. 39 of *Aspects*, that the principle of maximum refutability will suffice to eliminate all but one such theory, so that again the *a priori* criterion has no place. (However, p. 38 and p. 39 of *Aspects* contradict each other on the question whether an *a priori* simplicity criterion applicable to theories of language is even available, let alone needed; subsequent remarks by Chomsky have not made his views any clearer.) There is in reality little doubt that the principle of maximum refutability will be insufficient, either to select a unique theory of language, or to select unique grammars of attested languages given a well-supported theory of language; so that *a priori* judgements of relative simplicity will be needed at both levels of theorizing. The question is discussed in detail in *SLT*; cf. also S. Peters (1972a), Stich (1972), Chomsky & Katz, 'What the Linguist is Talking About'.

Chomsky's discussion in *Aspects* involves the distinction he draws between *observational, descriptive*, and *explanatory adequacy* of linguistic theories (cf. 'Current Issues'). In my terms, an 'observationally adequate theory' is an unrefuted grammar, a 'descriptively adequate theory' is a grammar which is not only unrefuted but also maximally strong and simple, and an 'explanatorily adequate theory' is an unrefuted and maximally strong and simple general theory of language. However, Chomsky's belief that speakers' intuitions are part of the data for linguistics makes it difficult to compare his terminology with mine.

Another pair of terms which Chomsky uses in connection with the ideas discussed in this chapter are *competence* and *performance* (see, e.g., *Aspects*, p. 4). Thus Chomsky would describe my diagram on p. 68 by saying that circle X represents the speaker's 'competence' or 'knowledge of his language', while Y represents his 'performance', i.e. 'actual use of language in concrete situations', which is determined only in part by his grammar and partly by non-linguistic factors. However, Chomsky uses the terms 'competence' and 'performance' ambiguously to cover a number of different distinctions, and some of his arguments about linguistic methodology are invalid because they equivocate on these terms. Fodor & Garrett (1966) point out one such equivocation, although they are far from doing full justice to the multiple ambiguities of Chomsky's usage; cf. also Moravcsik (1969). Other scholars have extended Chomsky's terms still further (Campbell & Wales 1970, Hymes 1971). By now the terms 'competence' and 'performance' are a hindrance rather than a help to clear thought about language, and I prefer to avoid using them.

My suggestion that the grammar of English should ignore occasional slips that people make with respect, e.g., to the subject-verb agreement rule may seem to contradict my earlier remark that English with split infinitives is as appropriate a language for the linguist to describe as English without them. One of the first things the student is told about linguistics is that it is a 'descriptive' rather than 'prescriptive' discipline: we describe the languages people actually speak, not the ones they believe they ought to speak. However, I am assuming that there is a clear difference between rules such as the one forbidding split infinitives and rules such as the subject-verb agreement rule in English, in that the former are artificial creations of pedagogues (no English speaker avoids split infinitives unless he has been explicitly taught to do so), while the latter are an integral part of the living language (although the existence of the subject-verb agreement rule may be brought to one's attention at school, one obeys it – except for occasional slips – before one is explicitly taught the rule). If so, then it is sensible for the linguist to describe the version of English which splits infinitives, since this is clearly a 'natural' language, while the version of English which avoids splitting infinitives is a relatively artificial construct, and accordingly less appropriate as a basis for an investigation of human nature; the same argument would not apply in the case of rules of the second kind. (It may be that I am mistaken about the status, for some English speakers, of the two particular rules cited, but the general distinction between rules which one has to be explicitly taught and rules which one learns to obey by imitating the behaviour of others is surely clear enough.)

The unreliability of speakers' intuitions about which strings are grammatical for them is emphasized by Labov in various articles already cited, and by Fillmore (1972), Householder (1973). Moravcsik (1969) suggests that one must know what is grammatical in order to speak grammatically, but this is simply false.

My reference to Charles Fries is to his *Structure of English* (1952).

Ryle distinguishes 'knowing how' from 'knowing that' in *The Concept of Mind* (1949). Hockett discusses Chomsky's confusion of the two notions on pp. 62–3 of *The State of the Art* (1968), and Harman in 'Psychological Aspects of the Theory of Syntax' (1967) and 'Linguistic Competence and Empiricism' (1969). For Chomsky's replies, see 'Linguistics and Philosophy', together with his comment on Harman's paper, in Hook (1969), and more recently 'Knowledge of Language'. The Stich quotation is taken from 'What Every Speaker Knows' (Stich 1971); cf. Graves, Katz, *et al.* (1973).

Katz equivocates on 'mentalism' in 'Mentalism in Linguistics' (1964b). Chomsky discusses Twaddell on pp. 193–4 of *Aspects*. For Chomsky's treatment of self-embedding, see pp. 286–7 of Chomsky & Miller, 'Introduction to the Formal Analysis of Natural Languages' (1963); Miller (1964); *Aspects*, p. 14. Reich puts forward his alternative theory in 'The Finiteness of Natural Language' (1969); I discuss the pros and cons of Reich's theory towards the end of my *RLD*.

Bar-Hillel (1971b) makes the point that it is not for linguistics to declare ungrammatical strings which are ruled out for 'pragmatic' reasons. For Montague's work, see Montague (1973) and earlier articles cited there, together with Thomason (forthcoming) and my *TRM*. (I have slightly modified the example sentence I quote from Thomason in order to make my point clearer.) Postal voices his defeatist views in 'The Best Theory' (1972); George Lakoff advocates 'global rules' in his 1970 article under that title.

Chapter 5: Rules and Languages

Constituency notation, together with unrestricted-rewrite and finite-state notations, are defined in *Syntactic Structures*. The branch of linguistics that investigates which classes of stringsets can be defined by various classes of rule is known as *mathematical linguistics*. The classical articles in this field are those by Chomsky and George Miller in Luce, Bush, & Galanter (1963); more recently, see e.g. Hopcroft & Ullman (1969). Gross (1972) offers an introductory textbook.

For philosophical discussions of speech as 'rule-governed behaviour', see e.g. D. S. Shwayder's *Stratification of Behaviour* (1965), J. R. Searle's *Speech Acts* (1969). I discuss difficulties that arise between philosophers' and linguists' use of the term 'rule' in *RGZ*.

Transformational grammar, although of course discussed by Chomsky in *Syntactic Structures* and many subsequent works, is more satisfactorily explained in recent textbooks such as Grinder & Elgin (1973), Kimball (1973). Marina Burt's *From Deep to Surface Structure* (1971) is probably the most accessible statement of a reasonably plausible and complete transformational grammar of English, although the book contains a number of inconsistencies.

The standard argument that attested languages cannot in general be defined with constituency notation is by Paul Postal (1964a; 1964b, ch. 7), and refers to the American Indian language Mohawk. However, Floyd Lounsbury, under whom Postal studied Mohawk, has pointed out that Postal's data are incorrect (cf. Reich 1969). Postal also mentions the claim that the use of the word **respectively** makes English a non-constituency language: thus, since verbs agree with subjects in English, one might claim that there are overlapping dependencies in sentences like **My brother, my parents, and my wife sails, watch television, and cooks respectively** (my example). But I do not believe the subject-verb agreement rule works like this: the sentence quoted would sound more natural to me if *all* the verbs were plural, agreeing with the co-ordinated subject phrase as a whole – in which case there are no overlapping syntactic dependencies after all.

Postal also has a number of arguments to the effect that constituency notation is not *strongly adequate* to define English and other attested languages, even if it is *weakly adequate*. By this he means that, even if it defines the correct stringset, a constituency grammar will assign the wrong tree structures to grammatical strings. This notion of 'strong adequacy' presupposes that the data against which our grammars are tested include intuitions about the structures of our sentences; since they do not, only 'weak adequacy' is relevant.

It should be added that the arguments for incorporating transformations in our grammars become much less forceful once we realize that grammars are to be tested only against observations of behaviour, not against introspections about structure. Thus Michael Brame maintains, in forthcoming work, that very many, although not all, of the transformations found in standard transformational grammars of English should be rejected in favour of a constituency base which produces the structures in question directly. Thus, rather than deriving **The boy is kicked by a girl** via an optional Passivizing transformation from an underlying structure that would otherwise give **A girl kicks the boy** we should perhaps treat it as syntactically parallel to, say, **The boy is fearful of the outcome** – i.e. we should analyse **kicked by a girl** as an adjectival phrase. It will be clear from my discussion that an argument against transformations is far from being an argument against linguistic nativism (although it might be an argument against the 'generative-semantics hypothesis': see chapter 7).

Katz compares Chomsky with Democritus in *The Underlying Reality of Language* (1971).

The fact that all stringsets can be defined transformationally has been proved for various versions of transformational theory by Stanley Peters & R. W. Ritchie and other writers: for accessible references see e.g. S. Peters & Ritchie (1969), Bach (1971b), Wall (1971). I give further references in my account of how an 'omnipotent' theory of language may nevertheless make refutable claims (*ITO*). On the universal-base hypothesis, see, e.g., the articles by Charles Fillmore and by Emmon Bach in Bach & Harms (1968), and G. Lakoff (1970a). Chomsky discusses the universality of syntactic categories on p. 28 of *Aspects*. (Note, incidentally, that, since a claim about universality of syntactic categories seems comprehensible only as an assertion about the *form* of grammars, the distinction Chomsky draws there between 'formal' and 'substantive' universals does not stand up – the syntactic categories are the only example Chomsky gives of 'substantive' syntactic universals.) For hypotheses about constraints on possible transformations, see Bach (1965, 1971a).

S. Peters & Ritchie (1973) prove that not all 'context-sensitive' stringsets can be defined by transformational grammars with 'context-free' constituency bases and without the use of 'filtering'. For Hamburger & Wexler's findings, see their two joint papers in Hintikka, Moravcsik, & Suppes (1973), and cf. my discussion in *TRM*. For empirical evidence about what data are used by a child learning his first language, see Brown, Cazden, & Bellugi (1969), Brown & Hanlon (1970); the former paper concludes that:

> 'it seems . . . to be truth value rather than syntactic well-formedness that chiefly governs explicit verbal reinforcement by parents – which renders mildly paradoxical the fact that the usual product of such a training schedule is an adult whose speech is highly grammatical but not notably truthful.'

Chapter 6: Objections to Linguistic Nativism

For Chomsky's 'agnosticism' about the origins of language, cf. Toulmin (1971); articles by G. W. Hewes and others in *Current Anthropology*, vol. 14 (1973), give a fair picture of our ignorance at present about this problem. For Putnam's 'what else' objection, see Putnam (1967), and cf. Black (1970).

The quotation by Jane van Lawick-Goodall is taken from p. 225 of her *In the Shadow of Man* (1971). Both the Gardners' and the Premacks' experiments are described in separate articles in Schrier & Stollnitz (1971), and cf. Ploog & Melnechuk (1971), Jane Hill (1974). For the Washoe experiment, see also R. & B. Gardner (1969), Brown (1970a). (The use of sign language *between* chimpanzees is reported in *Newsweek*, 1 October 1973.) On American Sign Language, see Stokoe (1972); the 'syntaxlessness' of sign language is discussed by Tervoort (1968), Schlesinger (1971). For the Sarah experiment, see D. Premack (1970a, 1971), A. & D. Premack (1972).

The notion that hierarchical structure in syntax may be related to hierarchical mechanisms in perception is argued (not altogether convincingly) by Lenneberg (1967, chapter 7). For the link between

H

decision trees and linguistic constituency trees, see Cohen (1973), and cf. Miller, Galanter & Pribram (1960). I am not sure how seriously C. Peters intends his suggestion (1972) that the sexual activity of rhesus monkeys involves constituency structure, but, if the claim is true, one may surely make the same point that I make in the body of the text with respect to the possibility of constituency structure in visual perception or biochemistry: it is not *logically necessary* that sexual activity should show constituency patterning, and no one noticed that it did before Chomsky pointed out the prevalence of this kind of patterning in speech.

I discuss the objections of Derwing (1973) to Chomsky's nativism in my *RDG*.

As Putnam (1967) deduces the set of syntactic categories *a priori*, so Thomas Bever (e.g. 1970, 1971) argues that many of the individual transformations of English, far from being arbitrary, have straightforward psychological motivation. However, just as Putnam deduces the particular syntactic categories of natural language only on the assumption that language possesses constituency structure, so Bever explains individual transformations only given the assumption that natural languages use structure-dependent transformations rather than any other kind of rules for reordering sentences; so an attack on Chomsky's nativism based on Bever's arguments would miss its mark in the same way as Putnam's attack.

For Toulmin's suggestion that universals of language structure may be explained by reference to the functions of language, see Toulmin, 'Brain and Language' (1971), and p. 465 *et seq.* of *Human Understanding*, vol. 1 (1972a); I have replied in *CLF*. Toulmin refers to Karl Bühler's *Sprachtheorie* (1934). Rhees (1959) points out how far Wittgenstein's 'block/slab' language is (cf. *Philosophical Investigations*, §2) from attested natural languages. Albert Weiss (1925) claims that the function of language is to promote the division of labour. For modern discussions of the functions of human language, see e.g. Robinson (1972), Halliday (1973) – neither of whom, however, give reasons why languages using constituency bases and structure-dependent transformations should be particularly appropriate for fulfilling the functions they discuss.

Toulmin has responded to my *CLF*: see Toulmin (1972b). Toulmin's argument against me rests essentially on a failure to appreciate that the syntactic universals attributed by Chomskyan linguistic theory to human languages constitute an empirical, refutable scientific claim. Toulmin's note includes a couple of relatively *ad hominem* remarks to which I may perhaps reply here. In the first place, Toulmin charges me with 'naïve' misunderstanding of Chomsky's thought, quoting, as evidence for his own interpretation of Chomsky, some remarks made in informal discussion after unpublished lectures Chomsky gave at Oxford in 1969: Toulmin prefaces his report of these remarks with the words 'as Sampson will recall'. Since I lived in Connecticut at the time, I have no way of knowing what Chomsky said at Oxford. However, as I base my account of Chomsky's ideas primarily on his extensive published works, while Toulmin appears to rely heavily on one series of unpublished lectures, I see little reason to revise my interpretation of Chomsky. (I might add that the point seems scarcely crucial: what we want to discover is the nature of language, not the nature of Chomsky's views about language.) Secondly, Toulmin marks 'sic' the phrase 'another species of organisms', quoted from CLF. I am not clear whether Toulmin means to take exception to the grammatical solecism of pluralizing 'organism' here, which he introduced by misquoting my article, or to the use of 'organism' to refer to an inanimate computer, in which case I must appeal to the authority of the English dictionary.

Chapter 7: Syntax and Meaning

An earlier version of much of the material in this chapter is in my CSR. The notion of language linking two independently-describable 'planes' of reality has been widespread in linguistics since de Saussure's Course and Hjelmslev's Prolegomena to a Theory of Language (1943); the latter is criticized accordingly by Lyons (1962). Chomsky makes explicit his agreement with the notion, e.g. at the beginning of his 'Deep Structure, Surface Structure, and Semantic Interpretation'.

There is a wealth of introductory textbooks on logic; Hugues Leblanc's Techniques of Deductive Inference (1966) is one that can be recommended, and see also G. Hunter's Metalogic (1971). Quine's Philosophy of Logic (1970) contains a clear account of the relationship between formal logic and natural language.

The footnote on p. 145 refers to my SMC.

Katz & Fodor's article 'The Structure of a Semantic Theory' (1963) is trenchantly criticized by Yehoshua Bar-Hillel (1967, 1969a).

Carnap's approach to language is exemplified by his Logical Syntax of Language (1934).

For arguments against the existence of a sharp analytic/synthetic distinction in natural language, see White (1950), Quine (1951). The possibility of establishing such a distinction by empirical tests has been debated between Katz and Quine: cf. Katz (1964a, 1967); Quine (1967); Cohen (1967); Katz (1968), and p. 250 et seq. of

Katz's *Semantic Theory* (1972). For experimental work, see the references to the work of Næss, Apostel, and others, in n. 6, p. 67 of Quine's *Word and Object* (1960); and cf., recently, Stemmer (1972). The earliest suggestion known to me that natural-language semantics involves probabilistic rules was made by Bar-Hillel (1969b); cf. Zadeh (1971), G. Lakoff (1972), Labov (1973). Wilks (1972) outlines a natural-language semantic description which modifies its own rules by interacting with texts.

The Wittgenstein quotation on p. 155 is taken from §79 of *Philosophical Investigations*. My reference to Halliday is to p. 267 of his 'Categories of the Theory of Grammar' (1961).

On the generative-semantics hypothesis, see, e.g., McCawley (1968), Postal (1970, §5), G. Lakoff (1970c), Chomsky, 'Deep Structure, Surface Structure, and Semantic Interpretation', Partee (1971), Postal (1972). The quotation from Robin Lakoff is taken from n. 1, p. 115 of R. Lakoff (1971). On the notion of 'lexical transformation', see, e.g., Chomsky's 'Remarks on Nominalization' and 'Some Empirical Issues', Fodor (1970), Watt (1973), my *TRM* and *RCT*.

The Chomsky quotation on p. 164 is taken from 'Some Empirical Issues'. For Frege's work on logic, see, e.g., Geach & Black (1952). The ideas I discuss in the last pages of the chapter are more fully developed in a forthcoming article, *EHN*.

Chapter 8: People as Computers

The material of this chapter is presented more fully and formally in my *NLS*. Apostel (1971) discusses the question 'What type of automata would produce and use structures such as natural languages [possess]?' My own tentative answer may be compared with the exciting work of Terry Winograd (*Understanding Natural Language*, 1972). (The principal differences between Winograd's and my approaches are that Winograd is interested more in the practical problems of programming an automaton to respond to idiomatic, 'surface-structure' English, and less in distinguishing universal features of syntax from features which are specific to English – and which must therefore be part of the English-speaker's 'software' rather than 'hardware', in computing terms.) Minsky (1968) presents a collection of earlier articles on related problems.

For the automaton/computer distinction, see, e.g., Putnam (1960). Automata theory is scarcely a distinct subject from mathematical linguistics, and the works mentioned in the latter connection on p. 205 will introduce the reader to automata theory. Hollingdale & Tootill (1965) provide a good introduction to the digital computer; on high-level languages, see Higman (1967). The language APL was defined by Iverson (1962); Pakin (1968) offers a practical textbook.

Geach defines his '§' notation in *Mental Acts* (1957). For a summary of various logicians' opinions about proper names, see Cheng (1968). Sloat (1969) analyses the syntax of proper names. McCawley (1971) links tense and pronouns in English syntax.

On 'failure of presupposition', see Strawson (1950). Strawson maintains, as against Russell (1905), that a declarative sentence including a definite description which is not instantiated fails to make an assertion (rather than making a false assertion). On my theory, Strawson is right, with respect to natural language; to succeed in making an assertion is to succeed in creating an **assert** node in the hearer's automaton-state, and whether or not one's utterance achieves this depends not merely on its syntactic form but on the hearer's prior automaton-state. I have shown elsewhere (*NPL*) that my theory offers a satisfying solution to the paradox of the Liar ('What I am now saying is false' – true or false?).

Ross (1970) discusses the syntax of declarative sentences; however, his arguments are attacked by Fraser (1970), Anderson (1970), Matthews (1972). For philosophical and psychological discussions of the problem of how we derive propositional beliefs from observation of the non-linguistic environment, see respectively Hanson (1958) and Gregory (1970).

I use the term 'model' to indicate the relationship between a person's automaton-state and the world he lives in. 'Model' is a key term for another current school of thought about how to explicate the semantics of natural languages: many logicians and linguists have recently suggested that this should be done in terms of the branch of logic called *model theory* (see, e.g., Lewis 1970, papers by Hintikka and others in Hintikka, Moravcsik, & Suppes 1973). However, although model theory may have its uses, it cannot replace the kind of account of natural language which I offer in this chapter. For one thing, the theoretical entities with which model theory deals are infinitely complex, and therefore can have nothing to do with the psychological machinery of human beings; secondly, although one can explicate the distinction between true and false sentences in model-theoretic terms, model theory does not attempt to explain what *use* it is to hear true sentences. Cf. *RBH, TRM,* N. & C. J. Jardine (1973), Potts (1973).

Willard Quine, in his *Word and Object* (1960; cf. Quine 1968a, Davidson & Hintikka 1969) advances a view – the 'thesis of the indeterminacy of radical translation' – which may seem to contradict my claim that a semantic description of English rests ultimately on empirically-testable observation. Quine's thesis, briefly, says that between any two languages there may always be alternative 'translation manuals' which are incompatible (in the sense that different translation manuals convert sentence S of L_1 into S' and into S" respectively of L_2, although S' and S" are not synonymous in L_2), while the alternative translation manuals are equally well supported by all empirical evidence; and consequently we have no right to associate sentences of our own language with absolute meanings, since translation from English into English can be viewed as a special case of translation from L_1 into L_2 – I have no right to *presuppose* that **cats like milk** in your mouth is synonymous with my **cats like milk**. In so far as Quine is arguing that 'meanings' are not 'things' that sentences have alongside pronunciations, I agree (cf. chapter 7). If he means further to claim that an empirically-based semantic theory of a natural language is in principle impossible, I do not see that he makes his case. It is logically possible that there might be some theory of, say, chemistry, which is quite incompatible with the standard theory, but which turns out to be supported just as well (and no better) by the evidence as is the standard theory; it would surely be unreasonable for chemists to cease theorizing because of this logical possibility. (Cf. Quine, 1968b.) Quine's thesis is discussed further in a special number of Synthese (vol. 27, nos. 3/4, 1974) edited by J. G. Troyer & S. C. Wheeler.

On the problem of explaining human rationality, see, e.g., Miller, Galanter & Pribram (1960), Watkins (1970). My behaviourist approach to semantic analysis may be compared with chapter 2 of Bloomfield's *Language*.

Bibliography

1 Works by Avram Noam Chomsky

Syntactic Structures (Mouton 1957).

Review of Skinner's *Verbal Behavior*, *Language*, 35 (1959), pp. 26–58 (reprinted in Fodor & Katz 1964, Jakobovits & Miron 1967).

'Some Methodological Remarks on Generative Grammar', *Word*, 17 (1961), pp. 219–39.

(*with G. A. Miller*) 'Introduction to the Formal Analysis of Natural Languages', in Luce, Bush, & Galanter 1963.

'Current Issues in Linguistic Theory', in Fodor & Katz 1964 (reprinted separately by Mouton 1964).

Aspects of the Theory of Syntax (MIT Press 1965).

Cartesian Linguistics (Harper & Row 1966).

Language and Mind (Harcourt, Brace, & World 1968; enlarged edn published by Harcourt Brace Jovanovich 1972).

(*with M. Halle*) *The Sound Pattern of English* (Harper & Row 1968).

'Linguistics and Philosophy', in Hook 1969 (reprinted in *Language and Mind*, enlarged edn).

'Comments on Harman's Reply', in Hook 1969.

'Deep Structure, Surface Structure, and Semantic Interpretation', in *Studies in General and Oriental Linguistics Presented to Shirō Hattori*, eds R. Jakobson & S. Kawamoto (TEC Co. (Tokyo) 1970; reprinted in Steinberg & Jakobovits 1971 and in *Studies on Semantics*).

'Remarks on Nominalization', in Jacobs & Rosenbaum 1970 (reprinted in *Studies on Semantics*).

Problems of Knowledge and Freedom (Fontana 1972).

'Some Empirical Issues in the Theory of Transformational Grammar', in Peters 1972b (reprinted in *Studies on Semantics*).

Studies on Semantics in Generative Grammar (Mouton 1972).

'Knowledge of Language', in *Minnesota Studies in Philosophy of Science*, eds K. Gunderson & G. Maxwell, vol. 6 (forthcoming); excerpts in *Times Lit. Supp.*, 15 May 1969.

(*with J. J. Katz*) 'What the Linguist is Talking About', *J. of Philos.*, 71 (1974), pp. 347–67.

'Problems and Mysteries in the Study of Human Language' (forthcoming).

213

2 Works by the author

CLF 'Can Language Be Explained Functionally?', *Synthese*, 23 (1972), pp. 477–86.

NPL 'Natural Language and the Paradox of the Liar', *Semiotica*, 5 (1972), pp. 305–23.

CSR 'The Concept "Semantic Representation" ', *Semiotica*, 7 (1973), pp. 97–134.

RGZ Review of J. S. Ganz, *Rules*, *Lingua*, 32 (1973), pp. 160–4.

ITO 'The Irrelevance of Transformational Omnipotence', *J. of Ling.*, 9 (1973), pp. 299–302.

TRM 'Thoughts on the Recent Marriage of Philosophy and Linguistics', *York Papers in Ling.*, 4 (1974), pp. 195–219; revised version to appear in *Foundations of Lg.*

UPA 'Is There a Universal Phonetic Alphabet?', *Lg*, 50 (1974), pp. 236–59.

NBD 'A Note on Broadbent's Defence of Empirical Psychology', *Brit. J. Psych.*, 65 (1974), pp. 471–4.

SMC 'The Single Mother Condition', *York Papers in Ling.*, 4 (1974), pp. 27–40; revised version in *J. of Ling.*, 11 (1975).

RLD Review of D. G. Lockwood, *Introduction to Stratificational Linguistics*, *Lingua*, 34 (1974), pp. 235–51.

RDG Review of Derwing 1973, *J. of Literary Semantics*, 4 (1975).

RCT Review of Chomsky, *Studies on Semantics*, *J. of Literary Semantics*, 4 (1975).

RBH Review of Bar-Hillel 1971a, *Philosophia*, 4 (1974), pp. 385–92.

OFN 'One Fact Needs One Explanation' *Lingua*, (forthcoming).

NLS 'Natural Language as a Special Case of Programming Languages' (forthcoming).

EHN 'An Empirical Hypothesis about Natural Semantics' (forthcoming).

SLT (*with Margaret Gilbert*) 'The Simplicity of Linguistic Theories' (forthcoming).

3 Other works

Aarsleff, H., 'The History of Linguistics and Professor Chomsky', *Lg.*, 46 (1970), pp. 570–85.

Abercrombie, D., *Elements of General Phonetics* (Edinburgh Univ. Press 1967).

Adams, P., ed., *Language in Thinking* (Penguin 1972).

Anderson, S. R., 'On the Linguistic Status of the Performative/ Constative Distinction', in *Mathematical Linguistics and Auto-*

matic Translation, Report NSF-26 (the Computation Laboratory of Harvard University 1970).

Apostel, L., 'Further Remarks on the Pragmatics of Natural Languages' (1971), in Bar-Hillel 1971a.

Bach, E. W., 'On some Recurrent Types of Transformations', in *16th Annual Round Table Meeting on Linguistics and Language Studies, Monograph Series on Languages and Linguistics*, ed. C. W. Kreidler (Georgetown Univ. School of Languages and Linguistics, 1965; reprinted in O'Brien 1968).

Bach, E. W., 'Questions', *Ling. Inquiry*, 2 (1971a), pp. 153–66.

Bach, E. W., 'Syntax since *Aspects*', in *22nd Annual Round Table Meeting, Monograph Series on Languages and Linguistics*, ed. R. J. O'Brien (Georgetown Univ. School of Languages and Linguistics 1971b).

Bach, E. W. & R. T. Harms, eds, *Universals in Linguistic Theory* (Holt-Rinehart-Winston 1968).

Bailey, C.-J. & R. W. Shuy, eds, *New Ways of Analyzing Variation in English* (Georgetown Univ. Press 1973).

Bar-Adon, A. & W. F. Leopold, eds, *Child Language* (Prentice-Hall 1971).

Bar-Hillel, Y., Review of Fodor & Katz 1964, *Lg.*, 43 (1967), pp. 526–60 (reprinted in Bar-Hillel 1970).

Bar-Hillel, Y., 'Universal Semantics and the Philosophy of Language', in *Substance and Structure of Language*, ed. J. Puhvel (Univ. of California Press 1969a; reprinted in Bar-Hillel 1970).

Bar-Hillel, Y., 'Argumentation in Natural Languages', in *Akten des XIV. Internationalen Kongresses für Philosophie*, vol. 2 (Verlag Herder (Vienna 1969b); reprinted in Bar-Hillel 1970).

Bar-Hillel, Y., *Aspects of Language* (North-Holland 1970).

Bar-Hillel, Y., ed., *Pragmatics of Natural Languages* (Reidel 1971a).

Bar-Hillel, Y., 'Out of the Pragmatic Wastebasket', *Ling. Inquiry*, 2 (1971b), pp. 401–7.

Bever, T. G., 'The Cognitive Basis for Linguistic Structures', in Hayes 1970.

Bever, T. G., 'The Integrated Study of Language Behaviour', in Morton 1971.

Black, M. 'Comment on Chomsky's "Problems of Explanation in Linguistics" ', in Borger & Cioffi 1970.

Blanché, R., *Contemporary Science and Rationalism* (1967; English transl., Oliver & Boyd 1968).

Bloomfield, L., *Language* (Holt 1933; British (revised) edn, Allen & Unwin 1935).

Boas, F., *Introduction to the 'Handbook of American Indian Languages'* (Ge orgetown Univ. Press 1968).

BIBLIOGRAPHY

Bolinger, D. L., *Generality, Gradience, and the All-or-None* (Mouton 1961).

Borger, R. & F. Cioffi, eds, *Explanation in the Behavioural Sciences* (Cambridge Univ. Press 1970).

Botha, R. P., *The Function of the Lexicon in Transformational Generative Grammar* (Mouton 1968).

Botha, R. P., *The Justification of Linguistic Hypotheses* (Mouton 1973).

Boudon, R., *The Uses of Structuralism* (1968; English trans. Heinemann 1971).

Bracken, H. M., 'Chomsky's Variations on a Theme by Descartes', *J. of the Hist. of Philos.*, 8 (1970), pp. 180–92.

Broadbent, D. E., *In Defence of Empirical Psychology* (Methuen 1973).

Brown, R., 'The First Sentences of Child and Chimpanzee' (1970a), in Brown 1970b (reprinted in Ferguson & Slobin 1973).

Brown, R., *Psycholinguistics* (Free Press 1970b).

Brown, R., C. B. Cazden, & U. Bellugi, 'The Child's Grammar from I to III', in *Minnesota Symposia on Child Development*, vol. 2, ed. J. P. Hill (Univ. of Minnesota Press 1969; reprinted in Bar-Adon & Leopold 1971, Brown 1970b [omitting the section from which my quotation is drawn], and Ferguson & Slobin 1973).

Brown, R. & C. Hanlon, 'Derivational Complexity and Order of Acquisition in Child Speech', in Hayes 1970 (reprinted in Brown 1970b).

Bühler, K., *Sprachtheorie: die Darstellungsfunktion der Sprache* (Fischer (Jena) 1934).

Burt, M. K., *From Deep to Surface Structure* (Harper & Row 1971).

Campbell, R. & R. J. Wales, 'The Study of Language Acquisition', in *New Horizons in Linguistics*, ed. J. Lyons (Penguin 1970).

Carnap, R., *The Logical Syntax of Language* (1934; English trans. K. Paul, Trench, Trubner 1937).

Cheng Chung-ying, 'Eliminability of Singular Terms Reconsidered', *Foundations of Lg.*, 4 (1968), pp. 282–95.

Chomsky, A. N. – for Chomsky's works, see section 1.

Cohen, L. J., Review of J. J. Katz, *The Philosophy of Language*, *J. of Ling.*, 3 (1967), pp. 163–5.

Cohen, L. J., 'Is Contemporary Linguistics Value-Free?', *Soc. Science Info.*, 12, no. 3 (1973), pp. 53–64.

Cooper, D. E., 'Innateness: Old and New', *Philos. Review*, 81 (1972), pp. 465–83.

Copi, I. M. & J. A. Gould, eds, *Contemporary Readings in Logical Theory* (Macmillan 1967).

Dart, R. A., 'On the Evolution of Language and Articulate Speech', *Homo*, 10 (1959), pp. 154–65.

Darwin, C., *The Origin of Species* (1859; reprinted by Penguin 1968).
Davidson, D. & G. Harman, eds, *Semantics of Natural Language* (Reidel 1972, also in *Synthese*, 21 nos. 3/4 & 22 nos. 1/2, 1970).
Davidson, D. & K. J. J. Hintikka, eds, *Words and Objections* (Reidel 1969, also in *Synthese*, vol. 19 nos 1/2, 1968).
Derwing, B. L., *Transformational Grammar as a Theory of Language Acquisition* (Cambridge Univ. Press 1973).
Dingwall, W. O., ed, *A Survey of Linguistic Science* (Linguistics Programme, University of Maryland 1971).
Dougherty, R. C., 'A Survey of Linguistic Methods and Arguments', *Foundations of Lg.*, 10 (1973), pp. 423–90.
Dougherty, R. C., *Methodology and Argumentation in Linguistic Research* (forthcoming).
Eiseley, L., *Darwin's Century* (Doubleday 1958).
Ferguson, C. A. & D. I. Slobin, eds, *Studies of Child Language Development* (Holt-Rinehart-Winston 1973).
Feyerabend, P. K., 'Against Method: Outline of an Anarchistic Theory of Knowledge', in *Minnesota Studies in the Philosophy of Science*, vol. 4, eds M. Radner & S. Winokur (Univ. of Minnesota Press 1970).
Fillmore, C. J., 'On Generativity' (1972), in S. Peters 1972b.
Fillmore, C. J. & D. T. Langendoen, eds, *Studies in Linguistic Semantics* (Holt-Rinehart-Winston 1971).
Fodor, J. A., 'Three Reasons for not Deriving "Kill" from "Cause to Die" ', *Ling. Inquiry*, 1 (1970), pp. 429–38.
Fodor, J. A. & M. Garrett, 'Some Reflections on Competence and Performance', in *Psycholinguistics Papers*, eds J. Lyons & R. J. Wales (Edinburgh Univ. Press 1966).
Fodor, J. A. & J. J. Katz, eds, *The Structure of Language* (Prentice-Hall 1964).
Fraser, B., 'A Reply to "On Declarative Sentences" ', in *Mathematical Linguistics and Automatic Translation, Report NSF-24* (the Computation Laboratory of Harvard University 1970).
Fries, C. C., *The Structure of English* (Harcourt, Brace 1952).
Gardner, R. A. & B. T., 'Teaching Sign Language to a Chimpanzee', *Science*, 165 (1969), pp. 664–72 (reprinted in Adams 1972).
Geach, P., *Mental Acts* (Routledge & Kegan Paul 1957).
Geach, P. & M. Black, eds, *Translations from the Philosophical Writings of Gottlob Frege* (1952; 2nd, revised, edn Blackwell 1960).
Geschwind, N., 'The Development of the Brain and the Evolution of Language', in *17th Annual Round Table Meeting on Linguistics and Language Studies, Monograph Series on Languages and Lin-*

guistics, ed. C. I. J. M. Stuart (Georgetown Univ. School of Languages and Linguistics 1964; reprinted in O'Brien 1968).

Ginsburg, H. & S. Opper, *Piaget's Theory of Intellectual Development* (Prentice-Hall 1969).

Goodman, N., 'Safety, Strength, Simplicity', *Philos. of Science,* 28 (1961), pp. 150–1 (reprinted in *The Philosophy of Science,* ed. P. H. Nidditch, Oxford Univ. Press 1968).

Graves, C., J. J. Katz, *et al.*, 'Tacit Knowledge', *J. of Philos.*, 70 (1973), pp. 318–30.

Gregory, R. L., *The Intelligent Eye* (Weidenfeld & Nicolson 1970).

Grinder, J. T. & S. H. Elgin, *Guide to Transformational Grammar* (Holt-Rinehart-Winston 1973).

Gross, M., *Mathematical Models in Linguistics* (Prentice-Hall 1972).

Halliday, M. A. K., 'Categories of the Theory of Grammar', *Word,* 17 (1961), pp. 241–92.

Halliday, M. A. K., *Explorations in the Functions of Language* (Edward Arnold 1973).

Hanson, N. R., *Patterns of Discovery* (Cambridge Univ. Press 1958).

Harman, G., 'Psychological Aspects of the Theory of Syntax', *J. of Philos.,* 64 (1967), pp. 75–87.

Harman, G., 'Linguistic Competence and Empiricism', in Hook 1969.

Haugen, E., 'Dialect, Language, Nation', *American Anthropologist,* 68 (1966), pp. 922–35 (reprinted in Pride & Holmes 1972).

Hayes, J. R., ed., *Cognition and the Development of Language* (Wiley 1970).

Hempel, C. G., 'Primate Communication and the Gestural Origin of Language', *Current Anthropology,* 14 (1973), pp. 5–12.

Hewes, G. W., 'Primate Communication and the Gestural Origin of Language', *Current Anthropology,* 14 (1973), pp. 5–12.

Higman, B., *A Comparative Study of Programming Languages* (Macdonald 1967).

Hill, A. A., ed., *Third Texas Conference on Problems of Linguistic Analysis in English* (Univ. of Texas Press 1962).

Hill, Jane, 'Possible Continuity Theories of Language', *Lg.,* 50 (1974), pp. 134–50.

Hintikka, K. J. J., J. M. E. Moravcsik & P. Suppes, eds., *Approaches to Natural Language* (Reidel 1973).

Hirschmann, D., 'Function and Explanation', *Aristot. Soc. Suppl. Vol.,* 47 (1973), pp. 19–38.

Hjelmslev, L., *Prolegomena to a Theory of Language* (1943; revised English trans. Univ. of Wisconsin Press 1961).

Hockett, C. F., *The State of the Art* (Mouton 1968).

Hollingdale, S. H. & G. C. Toothill, *Electronic Computers* (1965; Penguin revised edn 1970).

Hook, S., ed., *Language and Philosophy* (New York Univ. Press 1969).

Hopcroft, J. E. & J. D. Ullman, *Formal Languages and their Relation to Automata* (Addison-Wesley 1969).

Householder, F. W., Review of Z. S. Harris, *Methods in Structural Linguistics, International J. of American Ling.*, 18 (1952), pp. 260–8.

Householder, F. W., ed., *Syntactic Theory I* (Penguin 1972).

Householder, F. W., 'On Arguments from Asterisks', *Foundations of Lg.*, 10 (1973), pp. 365–76.

Hunter, G., *Metalogic* (Macmillan 1971).

Hymes, D. H., ed., *Language Culture and Society* (Harper & Row 1964).

Hymes, D. H., *On Communicative Competence* (Univ. of Pennsylvania Press 1971; excerpts reprinted in Pride & Holmes 1972).

Iverson, K. E., *A Programming Language* (Wiley 1962).

Jacobs, R. A. & P. S. Rosenbaum, eds, *Readings in English Transformational Grammar* (Ginn 1970).

Jakobovits, L. A. & M. S. Miron, eds, *Readings in the Psychology of Language* (Prentice-Hall 1967).

Jakobson, R., *Child Language, Aphasia, and Phonological Universals* (1942; English trans. Mouton 1968).

Jardine, N. & C. J., 'Model-theoretic Semantics and Natural Language' (1973), in Keenan (forthcoming).

Joos, M., ed., *Readings in Linguistics I* (1957; 4th ed. Univ. of Chicago Press 1966).

Katz, J. J., 'Analyticity and Contradiction in Natural Language' (1964a), in Fodor & Katz 1964 (reprinted in Olshewsky 1969).

Katz, J. J., 'Mentalism in Linguistics', *Lg.*, 40 (1946b), pp. 124–37 (reprinted in Jakobovits & Miron 1967).

Katz, J. J., 'Semi-sentences' (1964c), in Fodor & Katz 1964.

Katz, J. J., 'Some Remarks on Quine on Analyticity', *J. of Philos.*, 64 (1967), pp. 36–52.

Katz, J. J., 'Unpalatable Recipes for Buttering Parsnips', *J. of Philos.*, 65 (1968), pp. 38–40.

Katz, J. J., *The Underlying Reality of Language and its Philosophical Import* (Harper & Row 1971; published in Britain under the title *Linguistic Philosophy* by Allen & Unwin 1972).

Katz, J. J., *Semantic Theory* (Harper & Row 1972).

Katz, J. J. & J. A. Fodor, 'The Structure of a Semantic Theory', *Lg.*, 39 (1963), pp. 170–210 (reprinted in Fodor & Katz 1964, Jakobovits & Miron 1967).

Keenan, E., ed., *Proceedings of the 1973 Cambridge Colloquium on Formal Semantics of Natural Languages* (forthcoming).

Kimball, J. P., *The Formal Theory of Grammar* (Prentice-Hall, 1973).

Kimura, D., 'The Asymmetry of the Human Brain', *Scientific American*, 228, no. 3 (March 1973), pp. 70–8.

219

Kochanski, Z., 'Conditions and Limitations of Prediction-Making in Biology', *Philos. of Science,* 40 (1973), pp. 29–51.

Körner, S., *Kant* (Penguin 1955).

Kuhn, T. S., *The Structure of Scientific Revolutions* (Univ. of Chicago Press 1962; 2nd, enlarged, edn 1970).

Labov, W., 'The Study of Language in its Social Context', *Studium Generale,* 23 (1970), pp. 30–87 (reprinted in *Advances in the Sociology of Language,* vol. 1, ed. J. A. Fishman, Mouton 1971; excerpts reprinted in *Language and Social Context,* ed. P. P. Giglioli, Penguin 1972, and in Pride & Holmes 1972).

Labov, W., 'Methodology', in Dingwall 1971.

Labov, W., 'Some Principles of Linguistic Methodology', *Language and Society,* 1 (1972a), pp. 97–120.

Labov, W., 'Where Do Grammars Stop?', in *23rd Annual Round Table Meeting, Monograph Series on Languages and Linguistics,* ed. R. W. Shuy (Georgetown Univ. School of Languages and Linguistics 1972b).

Labov, W., *Sociolinguistic Patterns* (Univ. of Penn. Press 1972c).

Labov, W. 'The Boundaries of Words and their Meanings', in Bailey and Shuy (1973).

Lakatos, I., 'Falsification and the Methodology of Scientific Research Programmes', in Lakatos & Musgrave 1970.

Lakatos, I., 'History of Science and its Rational Reconstructions', in *Boston Studies in the Philosophy of Science,* vol. 8, eds R. Buck & R. S. Cohen (Reidel 1971).

Lakatos, I. & A. Musgrave, eds, *Criticism and the Growth of Knowledge* (Cambridge Univ. Press 1970).

Lakoff, G., *Irregularity in Syntax* (Holt-Rinehart-Winston 1970a).

Lakoff, G., 'Global Rules', *Lg.,* 46 (1970b), pp. 627–39.

Lakoff, G., 'Linguistics and Natural Logic', *Synthese,* 22 (1970c), pp. 151–271 (this vol. republished as Davidson & Harman 1972).

Lakoff, G., 'Hedges: a Study in Meaning Criteria and the Logic of Fuzzy Concepts', in *Papers from the 8th Regional Meeting, Chicago Linguistic Society* (University of Chicago 1972).

Lakoff, G., 'Fuzzy Grammar and the Performance/Competence Terminology Game', in *Papers from the 9th Regional Meeting, Chicago Linguistic Society* (University of Chicago 1973).

Lakoff, R., 'If's, And's, and But's about Conjunction', in Fillmore & Langendoen 1971.

Lambert, K. & G. G. Brittan, *An Introduction to the Philosophy of Science* (Prentice-Hall 1970).

Lashley, K. S., 'The Problem of Serial Ordering in Behaviour', in *Cerebral Mechanisms in Behaviour,* ed. L. A. Jeffress (Wiley 1951; reprinted in Saporta 1961).

van Lawick-Goodall, J., *In the Shadow of Man* (Collins 1971).
Leblanc, H., *Techniques of Deductive Inference* (Prentice-Hall 1966).
Lenneberg, E. H., *Biological Foundations of Language* (Wiley 1967).
Lenneberg, E. H., 'On Explaining Language', *Science*, 164 (1969), pp. 635–43.
Lewis, D., 'General Semantics', *Synthese*, 22 (1970), pp. 18–67 (this vol. republished as Davidson & Harman 1972).
Liberman, A. M., *et al.*, 'Perception of the Speech Code', *Psych. Review*, 74 (1967), pp. 431–61.
Lieberman, P., *The Speech of Primates* (Mouton 1972).
Luce, R. D., R. R. Bush & E. Galanter, eds., *Handbook of Mathematical Psychology*, vol. 2 (Wiley 1963).
Lyons, J., Review of *Trends in European and American Linguistics*, ed. C. Mohrmann, *American Anthropologist*, 64 (1962), pp. 1117–24.
McCawley, J. D., 'The Role of Semantics in a Grammar', in Bach & Harms 1968.
McCawley, J. D., 'Tense and Time Reference in English', in Fillmore & Langendoen 1971.
Magee, B., *Popper* (Fontana 1973).
Matthews, P. H., Review of Jacobs & Rosenbaum 1970, *J. of Ling.*, 8 (1972), pp. 125–36.
Mattingly, I. M. & A. M. Liberman, 'The Speech Code and the Physiology of Language', in *Information Processing and the Nervous System*, ed. K. N. Leibovic (Springer 1969).
Miller, G. A., 'The Psycholinguists', *Encounter*, 23 (1964), pp. 29–37 (reprinted in Miller, *The Psychology of Communication*, Penguin 1968).
Miller, G. A., E. Galanter & K. H. Pribram, *Plans and the Structure of Behaviour* (Holt-Rinehart-Winston 1960).
Minsky, M., ed., *Semantic Information Processing* (MIT Press 1968).
Montague, R., 'The Proper Treatment of Quantification in Ordinary English', in Hintikka, Moravcsik & Suppes 1973.
Moravcsik, J. M. E., 'Competence, Creativity, and Innateness', *Philosophy Forum*, 1 (1969), pp. 407–37.
Morton, J., ed., *Biological and Social Factors in Psycholinguistics* (Logos 1971).
Nagel, E., *The Structure of Science* (Routledge & Kegan Paul 1961).
Nagel, T., 'Brain Bisection and the Unity of Consciousness', *Synthese*, 22 (1971), pp. 396–413.
O'Brien, R. J., ed., *Georgetown University Round Table Selected Papers on Linguistics 1961–1965* (Georgetown Univ. Press 1968).
Olshewsky, T. M., ed., *Problems in the Philosophy of Language* (Holt-Rinehart-Winston 1969).

Pakin, S., *APL\360 Reference Manual* (Science Research Associates 1968).

Partee, B. H., 'On the Requirement that Transformations Preserve Meaning', in Fillmore & Langendoen 1971.

Pedersen, H., *The Discovery of Language* (1931; English trans. Indiana Univ. Press 1962).

Percival, W. K., 'On the Non-existence of Cartesian Linguistics', in *Cartesian Studies*, ed. R. J. Butler (Blackwell 1972).

Peters, C. R., 'Evolution of the Capacity for Language', *Man*, n.s. 7 (1972), pp. 33–49.

Peters, S., 'The Projection Problem' (1972a), in S. Peters 1972b.

Peters, S., ed., *Goals of Linguistic Theory* (Prentice-Hall 1972b).

Peters, S. & R. W. Ritchie, 'A Note on the Universal Base Hypothesis', *J. of Ling.*, 5 (1969), pp. 150–2.

Peters, S. & R. W. Ritchie, 'Nonfiltering and Local-filtering Transformational Grammars', in Hintikka, Moravcsik & Suppes 1973.

Ploog, D. & T. Melnechuk, 'Are Apes Capable of Language?' *Neurosciences Research Programme Bull.*, 9 (1971), pp. 599–700.

Popper, K. R., *The Logic of Scientific Discovery* (1934; English trans. Hutchinson 1968).

Popper, K. R., *Conjectures and Refutations* (Routledge & Kegan Paul 1963).

Popper, K. R., *Objective Knowledge* (Clarendon Press 1972).

Postal, P. M., 'Limitations of Phrase Structure Grammars' (1964a), in Fodor & Katz 1964.

Postal, P. M., *Constituency Structure*, International *J. of American Ling.*, 30 no. 1 (1964b), pt 2 (reprinted by Mouton 1967).

Postal, P. M., 'On the surface verb "remind" ', *Ling. Inquiry*, 1 (1970), pp. 37–120 (reprinted in Fillmore & Langendoen 1971).

Postal, P. M., 'The Best Theory' (1972), in S. Peters 1972b.

Potts, T. C., 'Model Theory and Linguistics' (1973), in Keenan (forthcoming).

Premack, A. J. & D. A., 'Teaching Language to a Chimpanzee', *Scientific American*, 227 no. 4 (Oct. 1972), pp. 92–9.

Premack, D. A., 'The Education of Sarah', *Psychology Today* (Sept. 1970a), pp. 55–8.

Premack, D. A., 'A Functional Analysis of Language', *J. of the Experimental Analysis of Behav.*, 14 (1970b), pp. 107–25 (reprinted under new title in Schrier & Stollnitz 1971).

Premack, D. A., 'Language in Chimpanzee?', *Science*, 172 (1971), pp. 808–22.

Pride, J. B. & J. Holmes, eds., *Sociolinguistics* (Penguin 1972).

Pulaski, M. A. S., *Understanding Piaget* (Harper & Row 1971).
Putnam, H., 'Minds and Machines', in *Dimensions of Mind,* ed. S. Hook (New York Univ. Press 1960).
Putnam, H., 'The "Innateness Hypothesis" and Explanatory Models in Linguistics', *Synthese,* 17 (1967), pp. 12–22 (reprinted in *Boston Studies in the Philosophy of Science,* vol. 3 (1968), and in Searle 1971).
Quine, W. van O., 'Two Dogmas of Empiricism', *Philos. Review,* 60 (1951), pp. 20–43 (reprinted in Quine, *From a Logical Point of View,* 2nd, revised, edn, Harvard Univ. Press 1961, and in Olshewsky 1969).
Quine, W. van O., *Word and Object* (MIT Press 1960).
Quine, W. van O., 'On a Suggestion of Katz', *J. of Philos.,* 64 (1967), pp. 52–4.
Quine, W. van O., 'Ontological Relativity', *J. of Philos.,* 65 (1968a), pp. 185–212 (reprinted in Quine, *Ontological Relativity and Other Essays,* Columbia Univ. Press 1969; partially reprinted under the title 'The Inscrutability of Reference' in Steinberg & Jakobovits 1971).
Quine, W. van O., 'Reply to Chomsky', *Synthese,* 19 (1968), pp. 274–83 (this vol. reprinted as Davidson & Hintikka 1969).
Quine, W. van O., *Philosophy of Logic* (Prentice-Hall 1970).
Reich, P. A., 'The Finiteness of Natural Language', *Lg.,* 45 (1969), pp. 831–43 (revised version in Householder 1972. [NB readers consulting the reprint are warned that Figs 6 and 8 are printed in place of each other.])
Reisman, K., 'Neanderthal Man Speaks?', *Ling. Inquiry,* 4 (1973), pp. 562–4.
Rhees, R., 'Wittgenstein's Builders', *Proc. Aristot. Soc.,* 60 (1959), pp. 171–86 (reprinted in Rhees, *Discussions of Wittgenstein,* Routledge & Kegan Paul 1970).
Robins, R. H., *A Short History of Linguistics* (Longman 1967).
Robinson, W. P., *Language and Social Behaviour* (Penguin 1972).
Ross, J. R., 'On Declarative Sentences', in Jacobs & Rosenbaum 1970.
Ross, J. R., 'The Category Squish', in *Papers from the 8th Regional Meeting, Chicago Linguistic Society* (Univ. of Chicago 1972).
Rudner, R. S., *Philosophy of Social Science* (Prentice-Hall 1966).
Runciman, W. G., 'What Is Structuralism?', *Brit. J. of Sociology,* 20 (1969), pp. 253–65 (reprinted in Runciman, *Sociology in its Place and Other Essays,* Cambridge Univ. Press 1970, and in Ryan 1973).
Russell, B., 'On Denoting', *Mind,* 14 (1905), pp. 479–93 (reprinted in *Readings in Philosophical Analysis,* eds H. Feigl & W. Sellars,

Appleton-Century-Crofts 1949, and in Copi & Gould 1967, Olshewsky 1969).

Ryan, A., *The Philosophy of the Social Sciences* (Macmillan 1970).

Ryan, A., ed., *The Philosophy of Social Explanation* (Oxford Univ. Press 1973).

Ryle, G., *The Concept of Mind* (Hutchinson 1949).

Sampson, G. R. – for the author's works, see section 2.

Sapir, E., 'The Status of Linguistics as a Science', *Lg.*, 5 (1929), pp. 207–14 (reprinted in Sapir 1949, Hymes 1964).

Sapir, E., 'Conceptual Categories in Primitive Languages', *Science*, 74 (1931), p. 578 (reprinted in Hymes 1964).

Sapir, E., *Selected Writings of Edward Sapir in Language, Culture, and Personality*, ed. D. G. Mandelbaum (Univ. of California Press 1949).

Saporta, S., ed., *Psycholinguistics* (Holt-Rinehart-Winston 1961).

de Saussure, F., *Course in General Linguistics* (1916; English trans. McGraw-Hill 1966).

Scheffler, I., *Science and Subjectivity* (Bobbs-Merrill 1967).

Scheffler, I., 'Vision and Revolution: a Postscript on Kuhn', *Philos. of Science*, 39 (1972), pp. 366–74.

Schiller, C. H., ed., *Instinctive Behaviour* (International Universities Press 1957).

Schlesinger, I. M., 'The Grammar of Sign Language and the Problems of Language Universals', in Morton 1971.

Schrier, A. M. & F. Stollnitz, eds., *Behavior of Nonhuman Primates*, vol. 4 (Academic Press 1971).

Scriven, M., 'Explanation and Prediction in Evolutionary Theory', *Science*, 130 (1959), pp. 477–82.

Searle, J. R., *Speech Acts* (Cambridge Univ. Press 1969).

Searle, J. R., ed., *The Philosophy of Language* (Oxford Univ. Press 1971).

Shwayder, D. S., *The Stratification of Behaviour* (Routledge & Kegan Paul 1965).

Skinner, B. F., *Verbal Behavior* (Appleton-Century-Crofts 1957; extracts reprinted in Saporta 1961, Jakobovits & Miron 1967).

Sloat, C., 'Proper Nouns in English', *Lg.*, 45 (1969), pp. 26–30.

Slobin, D. I., ed., *The Ontogenesis of Grammar* (Academic Press 1971).

Steinberg, D. D. & L. A. Jakobovits, eds., *Semantics* (Cambridge Univ. Press 1971).

Stemmer, N., 'Steinberg on Analyticity', *Lg. Sciences*, 22 (1972), p. 24.

Stich, S. P., 'What Every Speaker Knows', *Philos. Review*, 80 (1971), pp. 476–96.

Stich, S. P., 'Grammar, Psychology, and Indeterminacy', *J. of Philos.*, 69 (1972), pp. 799–818.

Stokoe, W. C., *Semiotics and Human Sign Languages* (Mouton 1972).

Strawson, P. F., 'On Referring', *Mind*, 59 (1950), pp. 320–44 (reprinted in Copi & Gould 1967; *The Theory of Meaning*, ed. G. H. R. Parkinson, Oxford Univ. Press 1968; Olshewsky 1969).

Strawson, P. F., Review of Wittgenstein 1953, *Mind*, 63 (1954), pp. 70–99 (reprinted in *Wittgenstein: the Philosophical Investigations*, ed. G. Pitcher, Doubleday 1966).

Tervoort, B. T., 'You Me Downtown Movie Fun?', *Lingua*, 21 (1968), pp. 455–65 (reprinted in Householder 1972).

Thomason, R. H., 'Some Extensions of Montague Grammar' (forthcoming).

Tinbergen, N., *The Study of Instinct* (Clarendon Press 1951; enlarged edn 1969).

Toulmin, S. E., 'Brain and Language: a Commentary', *Synthese*, 22 (1971), pp. 369–95.

Toulmin, S. E., *Human Understanding*, vol. 1 (Clarendon Press 1972a).

Toulmin, S. E., Reply to *CLF*, *Synthese*, 23 (1972b), pp. 487–90.

Wall, R. E., 'Mathematical Linguistics', in Dingwall 1971.

Wallace, A. R. 'The Limits of Natural Selection as Applied to Man', in *Contributions to the Theory of Natural Selection* (Macmillan 1870)

Watkins, J. W. N., 'Imperfect Rationality', in Borger & Cioffi 1970.

Watt, W. C., 'Late Lexicalizations', in Hintikka, Moravcsik & Suppes 1973.

Weiss, A. P., 'Linguistics and Psychology', *Lg.*, 1 (1925), pp. 52–7.

White, M. G., 'The Analytic and the Synthetic: an Untenable Dualism', in *John Dewey: Philosopher of Science and Freedom* (Dial Press 1950; reprinted in *Semantics and the Philosophy of Language*, ed. L. Linsky, Univ. of Illinois Press 1952).

Whorf, B. L., 'Science and Linguistics', *The Technology Review*, 42 (1940), pp. 229–31, 247–8 (reprinted in Whorf 1956, Saporta 1961).

Whorf, B. L., 'The Relation of Habitual Thought and Behavior to Language', in *Language Culture and Personality: Essays in Memory of Edward Sapir*, ed. L. Spier (Univ. of Utah Press 1941; reprinted in Whorf 1956, Adams 1972).

Whorf, B. L., *Language Thought and Reality: Selected Writings of Benjamin Lee Whorf*, ed. J. B. Carroll (Wiley 1956).

Wilks, Y. A., *Grammar, Meaning, and the Machine Analysis of Language* (Routledge & Kegan Paul 1972).

Williams, L. P., 'Normal Science, Scientific Revolutions, and the History of Science', in Lakatos & Musgrave 1970.

Wilson, E. O., 'Animal Communication', *Scientific American*, 227 no. 3 (Sept. 1972), pp. 53–60.

Winch, P., *The Idea of a Social Science and its Relation to Philosophy* (Routledge & Kegan Paul 1958).

Winograd, T., 'Understanding Natural Language', *Cognitive Psych.*, 3, no. 1 (1972; republished separately by Academic Press 1972).

Wittgenstein, L., *Tractatus Logico-Philosophicus* (1921; English trans. D. F. Pears & B. F. McGuinness, Routledge & Kegan Paul 1961).

Wittgenstein, L., *Philosophical Investigations* (1953; English trans. G. E. M. Anscombe, 2nd edn, Blackwell 1958).

Zadeh, L., 'Quantitative Fuzzy Semantics', *Info. Sciences*, 3 (1971), pp. 159–76.

Index

233